To Billy
From Aunt Ebby

Thought you would
enjoy this book
since you love football
and the Madden
football games.

Merry christmas,
Love aunt Ebby
&
uncle Bull

MADDEN

A Biography

MADDEN

A Biography

Bryan Burwell

TRIUMPH
BOOKS

Library of Congress Cataloging-in-Publication Data

Burwell, Bryan.
  Madden : a biography / Bryan Burwell.
    p. cm.
  ISBN 978-1-60078-379-1
  1. Madden, John, 1936– 2. Sportscasters—United States—Biography. 3. Football coaches—United States—Biography. I. Title.
  GV742.42.M33B87 2011
  070.449796092—dc22
  [B]

                              2011010519

This book is available in quantity at special discounts for your group or organization. For further information, contact:
  Triumph Books
  542 South Dearborn Street
  Suite 750
  Chicago, Illinois 60605
  (312) 939-3330
  Fax (312) 663-3557
  www.triumphbooks.com

Printed in U.S.A.
ISBN: 978-1-60078-379-1
Design by Patricia Frey
Photos courtesy of AP Images unless otherwise indicated

To Victoria, the actress. You know why this book is for you.

To my late parents, Harold and Ursula Burwell.
My father taught me to love sports, and Mom taught me
to appreciate the art of the English language. Both their
passions led to this book. I miss them both.

"And in Green Bay, Wisconsin, a man coaches a football team and wins...and wins...and suddenly he is not a coach at all. He is a Prussian drillmaster. He is Attila sweeping through Chalot. He is John Henry with a hammer in his hand, beating the rest of football to a pulp through brute strength, extra-sensory perception, and a diet of honey and wheat germ."

Author Jerry Izenberg, from a 1968 *Sport* magazine profile of Vince Lombardi (career coaching record: 96–34–6)

"Don't get me wrong, if he had to, John would get after your ass. But he didn't care about any of that dumb shit like how long your hair was, how you dressed, stuff like that. John was cool. All he cared about was, do your job and do it right."

Former Oakland Raiders safety George Atkinson on John Madden (career coaching record: 103–32–7)

CONTENTS

FOREWORD

"Why did it work? Because we listened to each other."

WHENEVER I THINK OF MY INCREDIBLE PARTNERSHIP WITH JOHN Madden, the first word that comes to mind is *respect*.

I'm not sure how football historians will ultimately look back on us, but if some consider us the best football broadcasting team ever, I take that as a great honor.

When we first got together on that makeshift broadcast platform high above old Tampa Stadium way back on November 25, 1979, I had no idea how long we would last or how wonderfully our personal and professional friendship would blossom. I never imagined that our presence in a stadium would one day signify the "Big Game" in the National Football League. All I knew was that I respected John and believed he respected me, too. I think part of it was because I had been a player before I became a broadcaster. John knew that I understood the game from the inside out. And I respected him because of the coach he had been and for his incredible knowledge of and passion for the game.

It didn't take long to discover that his knowledge and passion were contagious. It helped create a broadcasting partnership with me, producer Bob Stenner, and director Sandy Grossman that would last over two network stints at CBS and FOX. We looked at game film together like a coaching staff does. We prepared like coaches, which is how we knew why a player missed a block or made a great play. I remember John had us interview everyone on both teams before one Super Bowl broadcast. Seriously, we interviewed the *entire* teams, from the star quarterbacks to the last guys on special teams. Because of our preparation for the broadcast, we were never caught off guard by anything that happened during our three hours on TV. We were ready for any situation, and that's part of why America enjoyed watching and listening to John.

But the real essence of our broadcasting relationship was even simpler. Why did it work? Because we listened to each other.

In the following pages, I hope you too will listen and learn, because the John Madden you are about to discover is nothing at all like the person you think you know. I probably got to know him as closely as anyone. I know about his kids and his grandkids. I know about his wife, Virginia. He knows all about my family, too. And I can honestly say that the John Madden I know is totally different in person from the one you see on the air.

You might be surprised at just how different. He likes you to think he's this big ol' goofball, this lumbering guy who waves his hands a lot and gets excited when he talks and is completely immersed in football. Well, that surely is part of the John Madden I know. Regardless of how we started the evening—perhaps ordering dinner or sitting at a poker table—the conversation would always involve football. Before long, John would be moving salt and pepper shakers around to diagram a play.

But the John Madden I know is also a diverse and very intelligent man who loves reading everything he can get his hands on. He loves talking about politics, world affairs, and movies, and he has a strong opinion on just about everything.

When people ask me if there is one highlight from our time working together that stands out, I honestly can't choose just one. Why? Because to me, working with John Madden and being his friend has been 22 years of highlights.

—Pat Summerall

PROLOGUE

A Witness to America
September 8, 2010

THE HOTEL LOBBY IS QUIET—TOO QUIET, REALLY. THE BIG MAN sits unnoticed in the middle of the room, slouched in an overstuffed antique leather chair, quietly nursing a fresh cup of coffee. The bill of his blue cap obscures his famous face, which has entertained and enlightened generations of NFL fans and has excitedly sold us everything from beer to foot ointments with charming everyman sensibilities.

An old man in the far corner of this elegant hotel lobby did not bother to raise his eyes from his newspaper when John Madden came ambling into the room a few minutes ago wearing a disheveled khaki shirt and untied sneakers. And the twentysomethings in tuxedos who, no doubt, spent half the night upstairs in the bachelor's suite playing his eponymous video game seem oblivious to his presence as they assemble on the winding staircase for wedding photographs.

Perhaps they do not notice because the John Madden we think we know is so completely out of context in this place. The Madden we think we know—the Madison Avenue caricature of our recent memories—is a man who is always flailing his arms, bursting through our TV screen to sell us mufflers or cell phones, and peppering the air with a high-pitched burst of run-on football exuberance: *"SoEmmittSmithgetstheballandBOOM!! AndNateNewtongetshisBIG-O-BUTT goingandWHAP!!"*

The John Madden we think we know does not belong here. It is easier to imagine him at Tastee Freez or a diner or a truck stop somewhere on the highways of America, laughing and joking over grits and gravy in a Norman Rockwell–like tableau.

So who is the *real* John Madden? He is still a lot of that guy, but he is a little of this other guy, too. He has picked this place as a meeting spot. It is the charming Rose Hotel, located on a chic stretch of real estate in downtown Pleasanton, California. So why did he choose to meet here on a perfect autumn afternoon in the midst of antique tables, overstuffed French leather chairs, and so much cultured, raised-pinky, genteel ambience?

Well, mainly because he owns the place. It is part of the real-estate empire he has built with his two sons. If it makes you feel any better, he also owns a Holiday Inn and a Courtyard Marriott.

SO WHO IS THE *REAL* JOHN MADDEN?

"John Madden is totally different in person from what you see on the air," says one close friend. "A very private person, in many ways a lonely person with no habits other than football. A person who [is] very much a loner."

"John's complicated," says another longtime friend. "You'll find out soon enough that there's a lot more to him than that caricature you see on TV."

One writer once eloquently called him "a witness to America… the land, the people, the lifestyles, the thoughts, and the emotions that make up a society." Another described him as "a thinker whose thoughts do not compress easily." And there's this colorful take from one former AFC player who often felt the wrath of the coach's marching orders when facing Madden's notorious Oakland Raiders teams: "Fuck him. Fuck them. I still hate the Raiders."

Madden is also funny and engaging. He is tough and profane and slightly defensive and a whole lot smarter than you think. He is a charming celebrity who enjoys the company of strangers and also a fiercely private man who has a debilitating fear of flying. John Madden is arguably one of the two or three most unique men in the history of American professional football. Legendary coach. The greatest TV football color commentator ever and maybe the greatest *sports* commentator ever. And now, in his third professional incarnation, he is a marketing force and pop-culture icon. How many people can lay claim to having influenced generations of NFL fans in three separate but equally legendary careers?

Madden's story does not begin with him as a football coach, but you will see that his coaching career is the defining chapter of his life. You might need to be reminded of that now, because no one under the age of 45 can attest firsthand to the genius of Madden as a coach. Generation X only knows him as a video-game icon and Madison Avenue pitchman, and one must be older than 30 to have witnessed and fully appreciated the majority of his career as a sports-broadcasting giant.

But Madden is first and foremost a coach. He began his coaching career chomping nervously on a towel wrapped around his neck, berating officials with expletive-laced rants from the sideline. He was 33 years old, the youngest head coach in pro football, working for Al Davis' Oakland Raiders. He broke the mold of the traditional football coach not with an iron hand and a clenched jaw or an intractable regiment. Instead, he did it with a wink and a smile, charming his band of outrageous renegades.

It was the late 1960s, and pro football was different then. It was more primeval, less show business. It was Old Testament football, where players didn't wait for a commissioner to pass judgments on anyone who dared to break the written or unwritten rules of the game. They issued punishments in mean, violent, and unrepentant ways that made it clear justice would be served.

If the players were different then, so were the coaches. They were larger-than-life authoritarians like Vince Lombardi. NFL players lived a "my way or the highway" existence and had to answer to the stringent authority of coaches who had many rules—shirts and ties, curfews, and lots of other requirements that had nothing to do with winning games or collecting championships.

Men like Lombardi were the last bastions of conservatism in an ever-changing world. They drew their unwavering lines in the sand and forced every athlete to submit to their crew-cut, buttoned-down methods, even if it was clear that society's buttoned-down attitudes were on the way out.

Then along came John Madden, the antithesis of the conservative coaching ethos. He didn't believe in a lot of rules. He didn't care much about how a player dressed, what he did away from the field, how long his hair was, how late he stayed out at night, or any of the other things most head coaches of his time obsessed over.

He operated with the simplest rules that anyone in football—hell, anyone in all of American sports—had ever heard: "Be on time, pay attention, and play like hell when I tell you to."

His was a locker room full of reprobates and rascals who were partaking fully in the rich epicenter of American radicalism that was spawning all over the San Francisco Bay Area. Madden chose to lead—not harness, handle, or manage—these grown men in a way no one had dared to do before.

"I think he was [the first player's coach]," said Howie Long, the Hall of Fame defensive end who played for the Raiders just after Madden retired. "When I walked into that locker room, there were a lot of guys that John brought up and coached, and I can tell you, it sure as hell wasn't Villanova anymore. You couldn't find those guys at 'Nova. That was a tribute to John. He didn't care who you were, what you looked like, how you dressed or behaved. But the guys he had always showed up on Sundays, regardless of what they did on Wednesdays or Thursdays…and sometimes Fridays and Saturdays, too. They came and played, and that was all John ever cared about."

His professional accomplishments are legendary. His career record of 103–32–7 gives him the best regular-season winning percentage of any coach in NFL history (.750). He appeared in the postseason in eight of his 10 years as a head coach, won at least one playoff game seven times, and reached seven conference title games.

Then he suddenly left the sideline and improbably grew larger still. "Millions of football fans have come to know John as a media icon who redefined not only NFL broadcasting but sports broadcasting across the board," said Long. "John's presence at a game came to signify that the game had great meaning to both the viewing audience and, more importantly, to the players who were participating in the game. But then a new generation of younger football fans were exposed to the NFL because of John's video game. I can't tell you how many late nights I spent waiting for one of my three boys to get home at 1:00 AM because the newest *Madden* game was being released at midnight."

SO WHO IS THE *REAL* JOHN MADDEN?

On the table, there's a cup of coffee next to a pile of scattered newspapers. The sports page says Joe Torre is resigning as manager of the Los Angeles Dodgers at age 70. The 74-year-old Madden looks at the headline and laughs.

"Last week Joe was hanging out with Al [Davis] at practice, and Al asked me to come and spend some time with them, and that's when Joe told us…that he was going to resign," Madden says, chuckling. "I was thinking, *Oh boy, how am I going to keep this a secret? Geez, as much as I like to talk.* But I didn't think it was going to happen so soon."

Madden was only 42 when he got out of coaching, so I ask him if he could imagine coaching when he was 70 years old. "Oh, hell no," he laughs. "Never. But if the money was as good then as it is now—if somebody wanted to pay me $4 or $5 million a year to be their head coach—yeah, I could have hung around until my fifties. But that's it. No way I could have made it to 70 like Joe. No way."

The closest he gets to coaching now is the vicarious thrill provided by his two sons, Joe and Michael, who coach high school freshman football on Thursday nights, and the flag football games with Madden's grandsons on Saturday mornings.

On this particular Saturday, Madden has just come from watching his sons coach his grandsons. He still gets excited when he watches these games—probably too excited—but he's working on it. On Saturdays, he parks his big Ford pickup truck in the parking lot as close as he can get to the field. He won't get out of the truck and stand on the sideline because he knows that, even in retirement, he's still John Madden, and a random Madden sighting, even at an eight-year-old's flag football game, can draw a crowd and create a distraction.

On Thursday nights, though, he can find a spot in the stands at the high school field. He pulls his hat down tight, jacket collar snapped up, doing his best to blend into the background.

SO WHO IS THE *REAL* JOHN MADDEN?

Listen carefully, because maybe he really is exactly who you think he is.

"A while ago, I'm up in the stands and my son Joe was upstairs in the coaching box," Madden says.

His voice is starting to percolate up toward that familiar high pitch. His arms are swirling like giant windmills, and he begins to resemble the man you remember from those Miller Lite beer commercials.

"As the game is moving along, I'm looking as [my son's team] goes into a slot [formation] and no one's covering the [opponent in the] slot," Madden says. "Well, now I'm getting all fired up. The coach in me is coming out. I'm thinking, *Oh man! If they just run the outside guy....*"

As he talks, you can almost see the Xs and Os coming alive inside the old coach's head. I almost expect him to walk over to a giant flat-screen TV and start scribbling something on the Telestrator.

"OkayyouwannaMOVEthisguyRIGHTHERE…and then BAMit'sa TOUCHDOWN!!"

So the coach did what he always does in moments like this. He got all fired up. "I got up out of my seat and started to climb the bleachers to go tell Joe what I saw," Madden says.

But then he drops his head in mock shame.

"I swear to God, I got halfway there before I realized what I was doing," he says, his voice booming.

And then the coach remembered what time it really was.

Half past retirement.

"You big damned jerk," he recalls saying to himself. "Just go sit down!"

MADDEN

A Biography

1

CHASING THE AMERICAN DREAM

"When the virus of restlessness begins to take possession of a wayward man, and the road away from Here seems broad and straight and sweet, the victim must first find in himself a good and sufficient reason for going."

John Steinbeck, *Travels with Charley: In Search of America*

IT WAS A PART OF THE GREAT MYTHOLOGY OF 19TH-CENTURY America, spurred by the echoes of Horace Greeley's romantic, nationalistic rhapsody. *Go West, young man, go West and grow up with the country.* The bedrock concept of our great Western expansion was the quixotic promise that settlers were headed to the land of milk and honey on the plains and prairies. Greeley, the influential voice of Manifest Destiny from his perch as editor of the *New York Tribune*, believed a better life was out there for any hearty soul willing to exchange the poverty and rising unemployment in the industrial East for the agrarian life in the untamed American West.

Yet the cold reality confronting the first trickle of settlers who made their way into the heartland and beyond on covered wagons in the mid-1800s was that they were simply exchanging one hard road for another.

As tales of fertile farmlands and coal-rich hills just beyond the Mississippi River spread across the East Coast, a clan from the rugged Pennsylvania mining town of Wiconisco joined the westward flight. By the time John Madden's paternal great-grandfather, John F. Madden, arrived in Hardin County, Iowa, with his wife and two children in or about 1860, coal mining had expanded from the barren hills of southeastern Iowa to all portions of the territory. Like every other Midwestern state, Iowa was swept up in the craze of building railroads and expanding farther west as rapidly as possible. Wagon trains were being replaced by coal- and wood-burning locomotive trains that belched large gray plumes of ash and cinder. In 1836 Iowa's population was 10,531; by 1870 it had grown to nearly 1.2 million.

The Maddens were not fancy people. As best as can be traced, their roots as hardworking miners and farmers date back to the 18th century in Pennsylvania. They were never a part of the original American aristocracy. There was nothing highfalutin about them. They were poor folk with dirt under their fingernails. But they believed in the American Dream and chased it halfway across the continent, even if the so-called dream led them to grimy mining camps and parasitic company towns in the upper Iowa Valley outside of Clay and Eldora, where they dug coal, limestone, and clay out of the hard earth.

The Madden family's roots are no surprise to John Robinson. He is no social scientist. He's simply a retired football coach, and a damned good one. He won collegiate national championships at USC and NFL playoff games with the Los Angeles Rams. He also is one of John Madden's oldest childhood friends, and he has a theory about the everyman sensibilities that have long made Madden so popular with the masses. He believes they stem directly from those generations-deep, working-class family roots.

"I love great restaurants, he loves dives," Robinson says as he sits high above the football field at Denver's Invesco Field at Mile High Stadium. "I rode on his bus going across the country twice with him, and I swear, every day he picked the absolute worst restaurants in the world for us to eat at. Bad Mexican joints. Greasy-spoon diners. Grimy rib shacks. You know what I mean? All those places with red checkered tablecloths and jars for water glasses. I used to get mad [at] him and ask, 'Shit, can we ever go somewhere nice?'

"But those are John's kind of places because he genuinely likes people, ordinary people. And I think a lot of that is probably because John's dad was a mechanic. John's always been naturally attracted to the working stiff, the ordinary Joe. So I guarantee you if John would walk into this press box right now and had some free time on his hands, he's more likely to go over in a corner and talk to the electrician or the guy emptying the trash cans for an hour than sit around and talk to the play-by-play guy. He would just sit down and bullshit with that guy and be just as happy as ever."

More than 100 years after his ancestors made that first westward journey across the American plains, John Earl Madden routinely rolled across the same terrain in much higher style. As a broadcaster who had endured panic attacks while flying on airplanes, Madden hit the road and became a modern-day John Steinbeck in his own personal Rocinante, the tricked-out Greyhound bus named the Madden Cruiser. How many times did he make this cross-continental odyssey? One hundred? Two hundred? Six hundred? Is it possible that on many of his travels his bus followed the same path as his ancestors' strenuous pilgrimage in search of their American Dream?

In the wee hours of the morning on September 28, 1990, the 54-year-old Madden was in the back bedroom of the Cruiser. He was headed from his home outside of Oakland, California, to New York City to broadcast a football game. Over the first two days of the trip, Madden had indeed stopped in some of those salt-of-the-earth eateries that Robinson grumbled about—too many nameless truck stops, diners, dives, and convenience stores to mention. But all the while, the famous coach/broadcaster/huckster/video-game entrepreneur was mingling with America, doing what he has typically done on every one of these trips over the years: signing autographs at the gas station, shaking hands while woofing down his breakfast in the diner, and slicing off a piece of homemade rhubarb pie that someone brought him in the parking lot as he stood beside his famous bus.

He had eaten dinner at Grandpa's Steakhouse in Kearney, Nebraska, early in the evening. But now on the final day of this three-day cross-country trek, the bus would bring him within 40 miles of Clay and Eldora. With Madden asleep in the back, the Cruiser breezed right past the I-80/I-35 interchange near Des Moines without its passenger making even a simple acknowledgement of the moment. "I remember that we stopped for gas just outside Des Moines in the middle of the night," says *Sports Illustrated* football writer Peter King, who had hitched a ride with Madden to write an article about the journey. "But

I don't remember John ever mentioning a thing about his family being originally from Iowa. In fact, he had already fallen asleep by then, and I don't think he even woke up to look out the window when we stopped in Des Moines."

The landscape looked a lot different than it did the first time a member of the Madden clan set foot in Iowa in 1860. Long ribbons of asphalt and concrete extended in front of the Cruiser's glowing headlights. The sweeping prairies had been replaced by highway cloverleafs and suburban sprawl, which quickly give way to acres of fertile farmland the farther east they traveled.

When the coal-mining Maddens of Wiconsico County first settled in Iowa decades ago, the travel was far more arduous across the untamed plains and prairies. It would take more than a generation for a Madden man to emerge from underground and find work above it. By 1885 John F. Madden's family had swelled to six children—two girls (14-year-old Alice and eight-year-old Clara) and four boys (26-year-old Charles, 20-year-old John, 18-year-old George, and 16-year-old Will)—and the best way to travel was by the railways that were expanding all over the central part of the state. Coal and the railroads became so intertwined that captains of industry were creating companies that served both purposes. The Central Iowa Railway and the Eldora Railroad and Coal Company—which later became the Central Railroad of Iowa (1869–1878)—would become the chief source of employment for families like the Maddens.

Even at the height of the boom, mining at the Chaffin mines or, later, the Bennett and Blair mines was thankless and dangerous work. Drift mining was the standard method of drilling in Hardin County, with low-ceilinged tunnels dug horizontally into the mountain rather than in downward shafts deep into the earth. A single miner could roll down the inclined tunnel on a rail cart, pick into the vein, and wheel out between 85 to 125 bushels of coal per day, getting paid 4¢ per bushel. But it was a particularly dangerous operation, given to frequent tunnel collapses in the summer months when the earth was often too soft to be held up by the timber supports. It wasn't uncommon for horrifying mining disasters to either trap workers or bury them alive under tons of rubble.

Underground or above it, it was a harsh, unforgiving life. The towns and camps established by the railroad and mining company owners were full-service operations, including stores, saloons, and schools. If a man lived in the camp and worked in the mines, he leased the land, paid the rent, and shopped for food and supplies at the company store.

It was a rotten deal that ensured most working families were stuck in a crippling financial cycle. They worked for the mine, got paid by the mine, then spent that money on food and rent, returning all the money right back where it came from. And because drift mining tended to quickly exhaust the land of its precious ore, it wasn't unusual for a mine to close down within a year after opening.

In 1885 John F. Madden's three oldest boys, Charles, John, and George, all joined their father in the mines. Will, John Madden's grandfather, followed his siblings into the mines two years later. As railroad companies began buying coal from new mines sprouting up in Illinois and Kentucky at the turn of the century, the Maddens began to migrate from mining to farming as a way of life.

The first to escape the vicious cycle of mine work was Will. While he did spend most of his young adult life as a miner, by the time he was in his early thirties, he was ready to adopt a philosophy that seemed engrained in the Madden family ethos: never be afraid to pick up stakes if it means improving one's life.

THE 1900 U.S. CENSUS LISTS WILLIAM A. MADDEN as a 31-year-old recently married "teamster" with no children, still working in the drift tunnels in Eldora. But unlike his male siblings, his father, and his grandfather, Will Madden would not spend his entire life underground. Along with his wife, the former Louise Ketenber, he was raising two young sons—nine-year-old Lloyd and five-year-old Earl Russell—and operating a farm on the outskirts of Eldora.

The virus of restlessness would infect Will Madden, just as it had infected his grandfather 60 years earlier. In 1920 Will moved the family about 100 miles north, just over the state line, to Moscow, Minnesota, a small farming community populated with families of Norwegian, Austrian, German, and Danish descent.

In time, the next generation of Maddens would also feel the urge to wander. The 1930 census shows that Will's youngest son, Earl, moved away from home and left farming behind. He was 26 years old and living five miles away in nearby Austin. While Moscow's population was about 400 people, Austin was a bustling town of more than 12,000, most of them employed by the meat-packing company Hormel. Home to the headquarters of the famous processed-meat makers, Austin became known as Spam Town, USA.

But Earl did not find work in the factory. Instead, he was learning how to be an auto mechanic at a local service station. A few years later he married a deeply religious Irish Catholic woman named Mary Margaret Flaherty. They started a family quickly, their first child arriving on April 10, 1936—a full-faced, red-haired son they named John Earl Madden.

Before long, two daughters, Delores and Judy, joined the family. The Great Depression had started, and with automobile sales declining and many struggling families too impoverished to afford gasoline, it was becoming difficult to support a growing family on an auto mechanic's wages.

By the early 1940s, America was emerging from the Depression. Earl's older brother Lloyd had by then moved to California, and he told Earl that there was plenty of work for him in San Francisco. So nearly 90 years after the Maddens of Wiconsico County began the westward migration from the Pennsylvania coal mines to the great Western plains, the Maddens of Mower County, Minnesota, packed up their belongings and completed the transcontinental journey.

The Maddens found that Daly City, California, was indeed the land of milk and honey. Earl immediately found work at one of the largest auto dealerships in San Francisco, Les Vogel's Chevrolet. This was no cramped, single-stall garage like the mom-and-pop operation back in Austin. This was a state-of-the-art garage with an expansive service department for the popular local dealership, whose slogan in the 1940s was "Eye It, Try It, Buy It."

For an active six-year-old kid like John Madden, Daly City was a personal Shangri-la. He could smell the salt air of the Pacific Ocean every morning as he walked out the door of the family's modest bungalow at 213 Knowles Street. Even better for a boy who loved to play any sport he could find, he could simply walk 10 steps out his front door and find himself at a vacant lot turned playground. It was a stingy piece of earth, quite frankly, barely 20 yards wide and 40 yards deep. But to the boys in John Madden's neighborhood, it was their field of dreams.

"We used to play there all the time," Madden would recall years later. "We just called it Madden's Lot. So the game would be, 'Okay, we'll meet after school at Madden's Lot,' or 'We'll play the game at 2:00 at Madden's Lot.' And I assumed that it was my lot. And then one day they came in and started building a house there, and I think as a kid, that was probably the most disappointing day of my life. Here they built a house on Madden's Lot."

If that proved to be the greatest disappointment of his son's childhood, then Earl Madden's move across the country and all his hard work would have been worth it. While he did find steady employment at Les Vogel's, to Earl Madden it was always just work—grimy, tedious work under a hood or looking up at a raised chassis every day.

"My dad hated his job," says Madden. "That's why he probably never pushed me to get a job when I was a teenager. I remember as I got older and I started to want a little money in my pocket and to want the sort of things teenage boys want—cars, clothes, stuff like that—I told my dad that I wanted to work part time."

Earl Madden looked his son square in the eye and shook his head. "No, son," he said. "Don't start working until you have to. Once you start working, that's it."

"That's it," as in, end of your childhood, end of fun and games, grow up now. The Madden clan had been taking the hardest path in life for generations. It was always earnest work, but it was also a joyless existence. Go to the mines. Go to the field. Go to the garage. And somewhere along the way, Earl Russell Madden made a promise to himself that his son would have it better.

There would be a lifetime of work waiting for young John after he grew up. Earl just didn't see the point in rushing him. His father had gone into the Eldora mines by his 18th birthday, and as a kid Earl lived a strict farmer's life, held captive by the rigorous agrarian rhythms of the harvest. He understood that the fleeting joys of childhood should not be sullied punching a clock.

So young John Madden was allowed to do what his father could never do: keep playing games until he had to stop.

And when did he have to stop?

Just like every other kid—when the streetlights came on.

2
DALY CITY ROOTS

"For me, it was simple. I was always going to play. I was going to play forever. I think all players think that way, don't they? I was always going to play forever. You don't think that it is going to end. I was always thinking, Where am I going to play next?"

John Madden

IN THE SUMMER OF 1945, THE ORIGINAL CREW FROM MADDEN'S Lot was about to get a new running buddy. Johnny Robinson was born in Chicago but moved with his family to Provo, Utah, when he was six, then on to Daly City three years later. Call it happenstance, call it fate, call it incredibly great fortune, but when the Robinsons settled five blocks away from the Maddens, they set off a series of fortunate events that would ultimately shape two boys' lives forever.

Robinson and John Madden did not meet right away, and they did not meet in their Daly City neighborhood. Instead, their first encounter was, quite naturally, on a playing field. It was across the bay at Oaks Park, the ballpark of the now-defunct Pacific Coast League Oakland Oaks minor league team way out in Emeryville. "We went to this weekend baseball school when I first got [to California]," says Robinson. "John was a catcher, I was a catcher. And all the catchers were standing around before a drill. Now, you know how in situations like that when you have a bunch of guys at a camp or a tryout or something and you kind of survey the competition? Yeah, well, I looked around, and I saw John standing over there, and I thought to myself, *Hell, I know I'm better than him.*"

Funny thing was, Madden had been drawing a similar bead on Robinson. And wouldn't you know it? Madden had assessed the situation quite similarly.

Neither one of them could have known it then, but this would turn out to be the start of a lifetime of friendly competition between the two big Johns. Robinson and Madden were unmistakably kindred spirits. It was as if they had been separated at birth, two thick-boned youngsters with identical speech impediments (they both stuttered) and the same insatiable, audacious character.

Most of all, Robinson and Madden would be drawn together by their unmistakable love of sports. The two sparred constantly and found competition in even the smallest things they did together. Madden had two younger sisters but no brothers. Robinson did have a brother, but Jim was five years older, which meant nine-year-old John was more of a nuisance than a pal to his teenage sibling. Robinson and Madden were destined to become inseparable running buddies.

They competed at everything, even eating dessert. "If you bought an ice cream cone and a guy said 'Bites' before you said 'No bites,' you'd have to give him bites. So to prevent that, when a guy said 'Bites,' you'd spit on it," Madden remembered.

The way Robinson remembered it, the only person who ever actually spit on the ice cream cone was the cleverly repulsive young John Madden. "And [Robinson] still would eat the damned thing," says Madden.

"Oh yeah, that's how it was all the time," said Robinson. "If you listen to John, he makes it out like the reason I'd always do that is because I couldn't resist the food, like I was just greedy. But it was never about the food.... Well, okay, it was a *little* about the food. But mostly to me it was about the competition. It was always, 'You can't get an edge on me. You wanna spit on the ice cream cone? Fine, I'll still eat it! Screw you!'"

The brutal and endless verbal jabs would last a lifetime. Today, both men are in their seventies, and when discussing any variety of subjects, they sound like mature grandfathers and the dignified elder statesmen of the grand game of football. Yet let the conversation veer off to anything that has to do with their many experiences of youth, and everything changes. When talking about each other, their language is peppered with wicked barbs and hilarious vulgarities, and their adolescence seems to extend into infinity.

"He's full of shit," Robinson blurts out randomly.

"If that's what he said, that's bullshit," Madden jabs back.

They live to ride one another, and as long as the punch line is delivered at the other man's expense, life is good. Watch them talking, and you see them become two spry Peter Pans, never growing up, never growing old.

THESE FAST YOUNG FRIENDS WERE INSEPARABLE almost from the day they met. The magical bond was the games the young men played. "We were degenerately absorbed in sports, only sports," Robinson recalled. "Madden and I had it figured [out]. We'd play for the Yankees in the summer, the 49ers in the fall."

But before they figured out how to play for the Yankees and the 49ers, they had far more pressing business to attend to. The nine-year-old "brothers" had to figure out who was going to be the catcher for the Daly City Red Sox, their first Little League baseball team. Madden, Robinson, Ray Rosa, George Schrieber, Al Figone, and George McLeod all played for the Red Sox. The team was managed by Madden's father Earl, who found escape from the drudgery of tinkering with manifolds, carburetors, and transmissions by coaching nine- and 10-year-old boys.

On the first day of practice, both Robinson and Madden showed up with their catcher's mitts. "But that wasn't going to work," Madden remembered. "He was good. I thought I was better. My dad was manager of the team. I became the catcher."

It was a childhood anyone would have wanted, and it all revolved around sports. There was always a game, always a competition. When Madden's Lot was taken away from them, the boys were already growing too big for such a confined playing field anyway. So they moved down the street to Marchbank Park, a picturesque public facility that was set in a tree-shaded hollow.

Madden's first recollections of Marchbank Park sound very much like a young baseball romantic's first glimpse of the emerald grass upon entering a big-league ballpark for the first time. Young Madden knew this was a decided upgrade over the limited and poorly manicured Madden's Lot. It wasn't, of course, perfect. But to the boys in the neighborhood, Marchbank Park would be the launching point of every athletic fantasy they could imagine. This is where the city kids could play endless pickup games, the local Little Leagues could have organized ballgames, and lucky young players could serve as ball boys for the adult semipro teams that played there.

The summer was all about baseball. The boys looked forward to picking up the San Francisco paper every Friday morning, going to the back pages of the sports section, and finding their weekend schedules placed only a few pages away from the major league box scores. Madden loved being a ball boy for the Sarto A.C. semipro team. The biggest perk of his job wasn't the uniform or hanging out in the dugout and listening to grown men talk baseball. It was getting to scavenge through the scuffed-up baseballs and broken bats that were being discarded by the semipro teams.

It became Madden's job to keep the local boys stocked with equipment. If they had several rolls of tape and a hammer and nails, they could turn a splintered bat into a refurbished gem. They were from working-class families, and the boys knew this was the best and—on most occasions—*only* way to get good bats and balls. "We had a childhood with no money," said Robinson, "and because of that we played a lot of games where if you hit a ball over the fence and lost the ball, that was the game."

But not always. One day Robinson showed up lugging a brand-new bat. "He was the only guy ever to have a new bat," Madden recalled. "For $2.50—and where he got that I have no idea—he bought this bat. It was black. Neither of us had ever had a new one."

So where did the money come from? "John may not remember, but we were the big shits back then," says Robinson. "We went to Catholic grammar school together, Our Lady of Perpetual Help, and we were altar boys together, and we were pretty good at it, too. We got to do a lot of the weddings at the church. Every wedding you got tips, and that was usually about 10 bucks a shot right in our pockets. They let us do the high masses, too. Like I said, we were big-timers. Hell, at least we thought we were."

After getting paid and splitting the kitty, Robinson saved some of his share. Instead of just window-shopping the next time they went to the local Wilson's Sporting Goods store, Robinson remembers going down into owner Dick Wilson's basement, where the mother lode of baseball lumber was stored. Robinson was determined to discover and buy the most perfect bat that ever was carved out of a piece of northern white ash. The one Robinson chose was a perfect piece of black-stained wood that he called "Black Beauty."

"I was so in love with my bat," says Robinson. "And we had read somewhere that the best way to condition a bat so that it would never break was to get a big bone and rub the bat handle with it." So Robinson went to the butcher shop, got a big ham bone, and spent the next few weeks carrying around the bat and that big bone. "I boned that bat for a long time," Robinson says. "I wanted to get it just right."

"I remember he carried that bat everywhere we went, rubbing it with that damned bone," says Madden. "Shoot, he even took it to the movies one time, and I swear you could hear him in the dark just scraping away…. John wouldn't let you touch his bat. He didn't care if you picked up one of the old ones that had been taped up and nailed together. But he was protective of his new bat, so much so that he wouldn't even let you take [practice] swings with it."

One day, Robinson determined that Black Beauty was properly boned, hardened to last a lifetime. The boys went down the street to Marchbank Park for a pickup game. Now this is where it gets good. Robinson and Madden are notoriously entertaining storytellers, men who can weave a yarn with the best of them. They have been telling this story for so long to so many different audiences that the details are a bit fuzzy. There is the Madden version, the Robinson version, and somewhere in between is the truth.

Madden's version: "[Robinson] grabbed his perfectly boned bat, walk[ed] up to the plate, and on the first pitch, John swung, and connected, and—*BAM!* He split the Black Beauty in two!"

Robinson's version: "I'm in the outfield, and the first guy up is some guy I didn't even know. And I can see him from the outfield, and he picks up my bat." Before Robinson could make a move to avert disaster, this total stranger took a swing with Black Beauty. "He breaks it," says Robinson. "I could hear it from the outfield. You know how a bat sounds when it breaks."

More than 60 years later, Madden is transported back to that moment as if it happened yesterday. He is a giddy schoolboy again, still finding splendid satisfaction in the discomfort of his old pal. "Man, was he devastated," says Madden. "I can still see the look on his face. I thought it was the funniest thing."

As Robinson recalls his version of the story, he too is transported back in time, feeling the same stabbing pain to his gut: "Man, that was as close to suicide as I ever got. I wanted to cry. And of course everybody is laughing at me. I got no sympathy at all. It was nothing but jokes, and most of them were coming from my good pal John. But that's what happened. That's what it was like for us growing up in our little circle of friends. If you screwed up, you took shit from everyone."

They were goofy, rowdy adolescents doing what goofy, rowdy adolescents often did. In the 1940s, Madden, Robinson, and their friends could roam the streets of Daly City with great liberties. From the schoolyard to the playground, from ballparks to the movie theater, the boys led a perfect childhood that in hindsight could have been a slice out of one of those coming-of-age memoirs about growing up in the 1940s or '50s.

Life was always an adventure, particularly for Madden and Robinson. They would hop onto moving freight trains like hobos or jump on the back of a streetcar and travel 20 miles into San Francisco to watch a minor league baseball game or to see the 49ers play football. They would hitchhike to Stanford and Cal football games or slip under the fence at drive-in movie theaters, sit down in the gravel and dirt, turn on a speaker, and watch the show.

Occasionally, they would hitchhike to the 49ers' training camp at St. Mary's College across the bay in Moraga. "We were interested beyond just playing," Robinson remembered. "We had a lot of friends who went to games, but John and I were the only ones who went to practices.... We knew every 49er and where he played and tried the best we could to fathom what the coverages were. We'd talk, we'd wonder. We'd bounce things off each other for hours."

This, Robinson believes, was the breeding ground for their future ambitions as coaches. To hear Robinson tell it, by the time he and Madden started excelling in high school, they both were beginning to dream of a future where they were the great coaches they would eventually become. "Yeah, he always tells the story that we always knew we were going to be coaches," says Madden. "Bullshit. He might have always known, but not me. For me, it was simple. I was always going to play. I was going to play forever. I think all players think that way, don't they? I was always going to play forever. You don't think that it is going to end. I was always thinking, *Where am I going to play next?*"

"Well, he's full of shit," says Robinson, his booming laughter filling the room. "I would agree that we were no different than any other kids back then. We both dreamed of being great players. Like I've said before, we would play for the Yankees in the summer and the 49ers in the fall. But that was at age 10 when we wanted to be great players."

According to Robinson, by the time they reached high school, even as they were getting recognized for their athletic excellence, the horizon no longer seemed so infinite. "By the time we were age 17, we were just trying to get a [college] scholarship somewhere," Robinson says. "And by the time we got to college, we knew that pro stuff was out the window and were just trying to be coaches. Once we began to figure out that we weren't going to be those kind of players, then it became, 'Okay, let's be coaches.'"

AS HIGH SCHOOL BEGAN IN THE FALL OF 1950, the inseparable Madden and Robinson were about to be split up. They had spent the last few years together in Catholic grammar school at Our Lady of Perpetual Help, but now Madden would go to on to public high school at Jefferson Union, while Robinson continued his Catholic education at Junipero Serra High School in nearby San Mateo. They would still hang out at the pool hall together on the weekends and hitchhike or jump onto the freight trains and streetcars in the summer. But in the autumn and winter months, they were establishing their individual identities.

Madden was playing football, basketball, and baseball at Jefferson but did not take his studies seriously at all. He spent a bit too much time hanging out on the street corners and in the neighborhood pool hall or cruising around town in the 1940 Cadillac his father bought him. It was big and black and looked like a hearse. The fellas called Madden's monstrosity of an automobile "the Tank." "It actually really pissed him off when [they called] it 'the Tank,'" says Robinson. But no one complained when they were being hauled around town by Madden, particularly since it only cost each of them 50 cents to help fill up the gas tank.

Madden tried hard to follow his father's advice about not getting a job until he had to. But that didn't mean he wasn't interested in a little easy money. He began caddying at golf courses in the area, getting $1.50 a bag for an 18-hole loop around the course at Lake Merced Country Club on Sunday mornings. It was there he met one of the club's most famous members, Lefty O'Doul, the manager of the Pacific Coast League San Francisco Seals and a former major league player and two-time National League batting champion with a lifetime .349 career batting average. O'Doul would play there in the mornings, then take a carload of the caddies to the Seals game in his Cadillac convertible for afternoon games.

A few years later, Madden would earn $5 a bag caddying at the prestigious San Francisco Golf Club, where he met future U.S. Open champion (1964) Ken Venturi, shagging balls for the young professional golfer as he practiced shots on the driving range. By this time, Madden was beginning to understand how the world worked. He had spent his entire life living among the working class in Daly City. But here, inside the gates of privilege, Madden was learning how the other half lived. These were men of wealth and power, doctors and lawyers, businessmen and star athletes. They drove fancy cars, wore fine clothes, smoked big cigars, and drank the top-shelf liquor in the bar after playing their rounds.

Madden listened, observed, and soon figured out that the men who walked these well-manicured grounds beneath the tall oaks and fragrant eucalyptus trees shared one common bond: they were all college graduates. The majority of the members were Stanford and Cal graduates, but every last one of them had a college diploma on his office wall. It was at that moment that Madden added another important life lesson into his personal catalogue, right alongside the one his father preached about never getting a serious job while he was young. He had to find a way to get through high school and go to college.

Robinson had arrived at the same conclusion. He was becoming a star player and student at Serra, where he would become an All–Northern California end. He was also excelling in the classroom at the parochial school, becoming a popular class president by the time he graduated. But while Madden realized that an education would lead to a better life, he didn't yet appreciate that there was a difference between simply going to school and excelling academically while he was there.

By his own admission, he was no scholar, at least not early in life. He was more than content to do what a lot of smart and gifted young athletes do: halfass his way through school, figuring out how little he actually had to do in order to squeak by in the classroom. Madden was getting quite good at sports, particularly football, where he was a standout offensive and defensive lineman at Jefferson.

There would come a time when he would decide to get serious about his education, but that was still eight or nine years away. For the time being, he determined that sports would be his golden ticket to a college education.

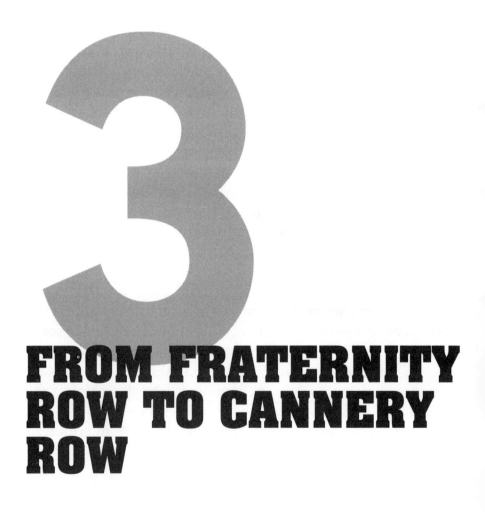

3
FROM FRATERNITY ROW TO CANNERY ROW

"Can you believe I wanted to be a lawyer?"

John Madden

IN THE SPRING OF 1954, JOHN MADDEN'S SENIOR YEAR ON THE Jefferson High School baseball team, he was catching in a big game against rival Sequoia High School of Redwood City. John Robinson didn't have a game that day, so he came by to watch and support his pal.

"Support" turned out to be strictly a relative term.

A Sequoia batter struck out, and when the ball went into the dirt, Madden got his big body in front of the ball, and it trickled a few feet in front of home plate. Madden could have zipped the ball quickly to first base to get the out, but he got a little too cute.

"I grabbed the ball, but I thought, *Hey, let him go, make him run, then* whoom, *I'll throw him out*," Madden recalled.

Well *whoom*, he didn't throw him out. The ball sailed way over the first baseman's head, rolled way down the right-field line, and by the time the right fielder had tracked it down, the batter who had struck out a few seconds earlier was rounding third and crossing home plate.

And there was John Robinson in the bleachers behind home plate, and his was the only voice that Madden could hear: "Hey, you threw a home run! You threw a home run!"

This was typical of the most basic, unforgiving law of the Madden's Lot tribe. If you screw up, you will take shit for it. Yet as embarrassing as that moment might have been, Madden was becoming good enough to draw interest from the New York Yankees and Boston Red Sox farm systems, who both offered him a minor league contract worth $75 per month. It was also further evidence that Madden might have been right about one thing: he wasn't thinking about becoming a coach that early in his life. He believed he was a player and that there was going to be somewhere else for him to play after high school.

Baseball was fun, and the minor league offers from the Yankees and Red Sox were quite flattering, but Madden was no can't-miss bonus baby. Besides, deep down in his heart, Madden knew he was a football player, plain and simple. He had grown to 6'4" and was starting to fill out to more than 200 pounds. He was a big, thick-chested youngster and a star on both sides of the line. His pal Robinson had also become an outstanding player, earning a football scholarship to the University of Oregon to catch passes for the Ducks.

Madden initially stayed closer to home, playing one season a few miles down the road from Daly City at the College of San Mateo before following Robinson to Oregon. Once they were reunited in Eugene, Madden and Robinson picked up where they left off when they were running the streets of Daly City.

IT WAS NEARLY 1:00 IN THE MORNING, and as was typically the case back in 1955, the gentle young coeds of the University of Oregon had a midnight curfew and were already in their dorms. But out in front of the frat houses on fraternity row, there was a commotion brewing. On the steps of the original Sigma Chi house at 13th and Adler streets in the heart of campus, Madden, Robinson, and Jim Bailey, a star miler on the Oregon track team from Australia, were among a crowd of frat boys and jocks talking trash into the wee hours of the morning. Bailey was a stud. A year later he would not only make the Australian Olympic team, but on May 5, 1956, in the Los Angeles Coliseum, he would become the first man in history to break the four-minute mile on American soil.

At some point during the night, the conversation got around to running. As the men sat there—probably with more than a few beers consumed—logic got a little fuzzy. Everyone on campus knew how good Bailey was, and everyone knew how big Madden was. For some reason, that led Madden to a remarkable statement. "I said I could run faster at a short distance than a world-class miler could," Madden says. "And now [Robinson] is out there egging me on and egging him on, and now everyone started wanting to lay down bets."

As a result of their Daly City childhoods, Robinson and Madden had the hearts of hustlers. "I think I was the pimp on this one," Robinson laughs. "I knew that because John was big, a lot of people didn't think he could run fast. Well, I grew up with him, and I knew he was a lot faster than he looked, so I start yelling, 'Hey, I bet John *can* beat Bailey in a race! I bet he can take him!'"

The hook was properly baited, and as someone stepped off 60 yards down the middle of 13th Street, there were as many as 200 young male students lining 13th Street from Adler toward Kincaid, and John Robinson was holding all of their money. He organized the betting, taking on all comers for him and his buddy Madden. There was only one small problem: Robinson had taken in more than twice as much money as either he or Madden had in their pockets. If Madden lost, they didn't have enough to cover their potential losses. "We didn't have any money," Madden says, laughing. "But John's telling everyone he can cover all these bets for me and him, and now it was like [retired pro golfer] Lee Trevino used to say: 'Pressure is trying to win a big bet and you're flat broke.'"

The pressure apparently didn't faze Madden. As the frat boys and jocks lined up near the finish line, the race went off. Side by side, the future Olympian versus the future NFL Hall of Fame coach. "And John smoked him," Robinson says, smiling like a Cheshire cat. "And we won a fortune. Maybe 10 or 12 bucks apiece!"

It was one of the few enjoyable moments that Madden would experience while in Eugene. The details are a bit vague depending on who is doing the talking, but Madden would leave Oregon by the end of the year. Robinson said his friend got sick. "He had a pituitary issue or something," says Robinson. "I don't know if he liked it up there or not. But I know after he got well, he transferred out."

In one of his books, Madden refers to a knee injury that sidelined him. In other interviews, he talks about how unhappy he was living among his far-more-advantaged classmates. Another longtime friend said he always got vague explanations of what happened in Eugene but had his own theory about what transpired based on his knowledge of how college football worked in the 1950s. He suspected that the Oregon coaching staff decided that Madden would be better off being stashed away for a year or two until he could get his grades together and/or he was healthy enough to play at the Pac-8 level. Ultimately, the most logical theory seems to be the typical reason most young college students leave school: Madden left because he just didn't fit in at Oregon.

He had grown up among working-class folks all his life. Now he was experiencing something he'd only seen while caddying at country clubs. He was surrounded by children of privilege. "That was the first time I was ever aware that I didn't have any money," he recalled. He came to Oregon with all his belongings in a couple of bags. His roommate in the Sigma Chi house had a closet full of stylish clothing, and his roommate wasn't the only one. Madden felt out of place. "It was easy for me to understand people who didn't have money but not the ones who did," he said. "Hell, I still hate to be presentable."

Robinson had no such problems. He adjusted easily and clearly aspired to the trappings of the upper class. He wanted to experience culture. He wanted to wear stylish clothes. He was learning to appreciate things like classical music and fine restaurants, all the things Madden spoke of as if they were stubborn pieces of broccoli stuck in his teeth.

Being enrolled in Oregon's prelaw program was another source of irritation. "Can you believe I wanted to be a lawyer?" Madden asks. "How stupid an idea was that? I didn't dislike Oregon. But I didn't care if I went back. I realized after the first year that I couldn't see myself wearing a suit and tie and sitting in an office all day. Sports had been my whole life, so I switched [my major] to education."

Madden heard of a nearby community college that he thought would be an ideal escape from Eugene. In the fall of 1956, Madden transferred to Grays Harbor College in Aberdeen, Washington, a small fishing and lumber town a few hours north of Eugene on the Pacific coastline. He would stay there for only one semester, but it turned out to be quite the adventure. Here was another one of those Steinbeck-like *Travels with Charley* moments that Madden would encounter repeatedly over the course of his life.

Aberdeen was a gritty town, now perhaps best known as the birthplace of the late grunge icon Kurt Cobain. But when a 20-year-old Madden arrived in the summer of 1956, Aberdeen's notoriety was based on its reputation as one of the rowdiest, most untamed towns on the West Coast around the turn of the century. In the early 19th century, they called Aberdeen "the Hell Hole of the Pacific" and "the Port of Missing Men" (because of its high murder rate).

Today the heart of the town is dotted with upscale bistros, boutiques, bed and breakfasts, and homey cafes overlooking the harbor, catering to the tourists who make the scenic one-hour drive down from Seattle. Yet in the early 1900s, Aberdeen was littered with saloons, whorehouses, and gambling joints catering to a gritty parade of immigrants, vagabonds, and mountain men who descended on the town because of the many saw mills, canneries, logging camps, and fishing opportunities that were abundant in and around Grays Harbor.

Aberdeen in 1956 was not quite the dangerous Wild West frontier town it used to be, but it was hardly the refined, gentrified oasis that it would eventually become. It was in Aberdeen that Madden tried figuring out where he was going to play next. Still unsettled by how much he didn't fit in at Oregon, life in Aberdeen and Grays Harbor College would be a dramatic change of pace from the pretentious fraternity life in Eugene. There were few signs of power and privilege in Aberdeen. The two-hour drive north from Eugene had essentially transported him from fraternity row to cannery row.

Grays Harbor College had an open-enrollment policy, so football coach Chase Anderson knew that his players were not going to be arriving with silver spoons in their mouths or trust-fund payouts in their pockets. His players had to work to earn their keep, so he found jobs for them at various establishments around town. Madden ended up working in a local drinking establishment called the Mint Cafe. To be kind, if the Mint Cafe existed today, it would be just the kind of hole-in-the-wall joint that the Madden Cruiser would park in front of for dinner.

There was a card room in the back of the place full of poker tables for the lumberjacks and cannery workers, and as young John Madden swept the floors every night, he enjoyed the company of these flannel-shirt, salt-of-the-earth folks who played draw poker, low ball, and something called fan tan. "The boss liked the way I mixed with the poker players," Madden recalled. "After that I was more of a shill than a sweeper."

Madden clearly enjoyed the company of lumberjacks far more than frat boys, and his semester at Grays Harbor gave new meaning to the phrase "adventures in higher learning." Soon his new "professors" were teaching him how to become a polished and incurable poker player.

PART TWO

THE MAKING
OF A COACH

"What seems to us as bitter trials are often blessings in disguise."

Oscar Wilde

WHEN JOHN MADDEN ARRIVED IN PHILADELPHIA IN THE SUMMER of 1959 to begin his professional football life, he was no different than any other million-to-one dreamer in the Eagles' camp. He was a 21st-round draft pick with a standard $7,000 NFL contract, yet young Madden believed that the sky was the limit for his career as an athlete. This was the culmination of a dream that began way back in Madden's Lot and carried through those idyllic summers in the Bay Area when he and his childhood pal John Robinson were hopping trains and hitchhiking up the highway to 49ers games and training-camp practices.

"I was going to play forever," he recalled.

The dream never included the unfathomable idea that his playing days could end prematurely. He was always looking for the next game, the priceless opportunity to move on to the next level. The path to the NFL had not been as smooth a path as he expected, but even his rather scenic route had ultimately gotten him to that place where he and Robinson often fantasized about being.

So now he was in the Eagles' training camp, wearing No. 77, playing offensive tackle, and attempting to work his way up the depth chart. But his career barely got started before it came to a crashing halt. It was the first week of August during a morning scrimmage when, in the midst of a scrum on a running play, a pile of chaotic humanity crashed into the back of Madden's left knee.

Immediately he knew something awful had happened. The only thing worse than the searing pain that raced through his body was the sickening feeling he felt in his gut.

"It's a bad one," the team physician told Madden. "You need an operation. You won't play this year, but maybe you can play next year."

He had torn ligaments and damaged cartilage in his left knee. The doctor thought he was sounding hopeful. But the only word that resonated with Madden was *maybe*. "'*Maybe* you can play next year'? That didn't sound too good to me," Madden recalled.

Madden's instincts were correct. This was long before the modern medical advances of today, where lasers and microscopes and other 21st-century magic can heal a knee miraculously, barely leaving a scar. In 1959 blown-out knees were dealt with via far more medieval methods, with giant scalpels and large surgical needles that left hideous long scars and automatically ended seasons and often careers. The Eagles put Madden on the injured list, and he spent the rest of the season in the bowels of Philadelphia's old Franklin Field, rehabilitating the catastrophically damaged knee.

He arrived first thing in the morning so he could get his treatment from the training staff and be out of the way by the time the healthy players showed up for work. Mostly, Madden spent a lot of time hobbling around on crutches or in the giant metal whirlpool tub, his knee dangling into the bubbling hot water. Then, as the buses rolled out of the parking lot to carry the rest of the Eagles off to afternoon practice at a nearby field, Madden would hunch over his crutches and maneuver the eight blocks back to his empty room at the nearby Penn-Sherwood Hotel on 39th and Chestnut.

It was all those idle hours in between the morning whirlpool and the walk back to the Penn-Sherwood when young John Madden had another one of those fortunate events that seemed to highlight his life path. Back in the late '50s, the pro football world was a less-glamorous nuts-and-bolts operation. This was a half-century before the advent of today's gleaming, high-tech multimillion-dollar palaces that the

NFL calls training facilities. The Eagles were housed inside ancient Franklin Field, which was opened in 1895 and was also home to the Ivy League's University of Pennsylvania. The Eagles played all their home games at Franklin Field but often had to practice at a variety of local high school or small college fields around the city.

The Eagles did not have a lot of space in the catacombs of Franklin Field. There were no special meeting rooms, no elaborate auditoriums, and no individual film rooms. Almost all team activities were done within the cramped locker-room walls. When the 23-year-old rookie wandered out of the trainer's room every morning and sat on a bench in the back of the dark locker room, he also found starting quarterback Norm Van Brocklin sitting in the front of the room with an old movie projector at his side, meticulously studying game film.

"Van was always there early," says Madden. "Every day he was there almost as early as me."

Van Brocklin would study film for hours, and Madden quickly became fascinated by the future Hall of Famer's diligence. The Dutchman seemed to be mesmerized by the action on the movie screen, and Madden soon became equally intoxicated with the whirling sound of the rickety old projector. "At first I would just watch him as I was getting dressed," Madden recalls. "I would just sit quietly in the back of the room. But as the season went on, after a while I would do less and less rehab and just sit in the back of the locker room watching him watch film."

Madden tried to be as unobtrusive as possible; he was the proverbial fly on the wall. Eventually, though, Van Brocklin began to notice that the big redheaded rookie was always lurking in the shadows. One morning, he surprised Madden. "Hey, Red," Van Brocklin said, motioning his arms toward the burly kid. "Come up here and watch it with me."

He didn't have to ask Madden twice. The big kid from California scooped up his stool, dragged it into position just behind the shoulder of the future Hall of Famer, and absorbed one of the most significant lessons of his football life. He was learning how to watch game film like a coach, not a myopic player. "I would sit by him, and Van was like the coach," says Madden. "He was putting game plans together."

As the film whirled and clicked and that warm streak of projector light beamed across the darkened room, Van Brocklin would narrate the action on the screen out loud. "I don't want to misconstrue that he was actually talking to me," Madden remembers. "I always figured he was talking to himself while watching the film. Every time he would see something on film, he would say, 'Well if [the opponent] does that I can put Tommy McDonald over there....' Or he'd say, 'Now see there's the post [route] right there. If I look the safety off, that play is there.' I never talked back [because] it wasn't that kind of thing. I was there to be quiet and learn. It was the first time I ever really learned the entire game of football. Up until then, I was just a lineman who knew what I did, or what the guy lining up against me might do. I only wrote notes down about what *I* did on film. I didn't know what the running back or receiver did."

With each morning film session with Van Brocklin, Madden would sheepishly keep his mouth shut, and with good reason. Initially, Madden had no clue what the quarterback was talking about when he would shout excitedly, "Did you see that?" *See what?* he often wondered.

It was like Madden was watching a complicated murder mystery unfold, and the only one in the room who could solve it was this intelligent veteran sitting in front of him. So Madden wisely chose to be seen but not heard. He never asked questions, never interrupted Van Brocklin's stream-of-consciousness monologues. Yet slowly he began to get it. Madden was back in a classroom, and he was being taught by a true football scholar. Van Brocklin was teaching Madden how to open his mind and understand how to watch football game film. As they sat in front of that movie projector, the quarterback taught the rookie how to look at the entire screen and understand that football was more than an isolated man-on-man battle in the trenches.

It was, in fact, a far more elaborate match played out repeatedly by 22 interconnected pieces.

"[Van Brocklin] was a master at it," Madden says. "He wanted me to understand the entire game, how to find every athletic and strategic advantage. He was constantly searching to find how he could put his best people in the best possible positions to do well."

And he was teaching John Madden the very foundation of what would be his own philosophy as a future head football coach, even if Madden didn't know it at the time. Van Brocklin had planted the first seeds that made Madden expand his mind and begin to analyze the game from a far more elevated coach's point of view.

For the first time in his football life, Madden was becoming a true student of the game. Van Brocklin taught him how to recognize everything an opposing defense could do. He taught him how to decipher zone, man-to-man, and combination coverages. He showed him how the secondary worked in concert with the linebackers. He revealed the secrets to attacking those defenses and took Madden on a crash course to understanding how every pass route could be used to pick apart holes in defensive coverages.

"I knew I was 10 years behind the Dutchman [in overall football knowledge]," Madden recalled. "But 10 years behind him was 10 years ahead of anyone else my age."

The seed had been planted, and now it was growing. For the first time in his life—mostly out of simple necessity—Madden was thinking about life after playing. He was developing a strong aptitude for coaching, and he liked the way all those Xs and Os danced in his head.

These daily film sessions with one of the NFL's greatest quarterbacks would provide Madden with invaluable information. As the season—and his injured knee—kept dragging along, Madden was coming to the realization that his playing days were over. He was still limping around with a brace on his knee in the off-season, and even when the fledgling American Football League began operations in early 1960 with the promise of new job opportunities for young guys like Madden, he knew he couldn't take the Los Angeles Chargers up on their offer to play.

"The Chargers had no idea how bad my knee was," he recalled. "I knew I had to move on. It was time to go back to school."

BY THE TIME HE RETURNED TO THE CAL POLY CAMPUS in early 1960, Madden's life was starting to change in every way imaginable. He had rumbled through his college years as a carefree jock, a self-confessed "weirdo." He did not take his academics seriously, instead devoting all his time to football, baseball, and goofing around with his similarly rowdy roommate Pat Lovell.

Yet as he returned to San Luis Obispo, Madden was determined to settle down and get his act together. He had met a young woman named Virginia Fields in a bar in Pismo Beach while he was still an undergrad at Cal Poly. She was smart and independent, funny and self-assured—the perfect foil for the affable giant—and they had gotten engaged shortly before he departed for Philadelphia's training camp.

When Madden returned to campus intent on enrolling in grad school to get his master's degree in education, Virginia was already teaching and working on a master's in the same field. In his mind, Madden was ready to bear down and grow up. But he still had to convince the chairman of the Physical Education department, a professor named Bob Mott, that he had changed his ways and was honestly prepared to be a serious student.

Mott was not convinced. Not only was he having second thoughts about admitting Madden to the master's program, the professor also actually tried to talk Virginia into breaking off her engagement to Madden, painting him as a hopeless ne'er-do-well who would only break her heart.

As part of the final approval to get into grad school, Madden had to sit down for an interview with Mott. This would prove to be the most important interview of his young life, and Madden had to somehow find the words to convince the resistant Bob Mott that he had changed his ways.

"I know I didn't study as much as I should've," Madden told him. "I didn't think I'd be back here so soon. I thought I'd be playing pro football for a few years. But now that I'm back, I'll work hard for my master's."

This was a familiar story for a lot of talented athletes who always had the intelligence to bear down in school but resisted until desperation became their greatest motivator. Often, it's a lesson learned too late. But Madden must have been sincere, because Mott gave him a chance. This time, John didn't disappoint him.

For the first time in his life, Madden could see the need to treat his schoolwork as seriously as he used to regard his burning athletic passions. "Education became a little more important to me," he says. "I knew I had to go back and get my master's and get a teaching credential." It became so important that he not only earned his master's but finished a few credit hours shy of earning his doctorate.

By now, there was one thing that was certain about the life of John Madden. Somebody up there clearly liked him, because here he was on the heels of another harsh setback only to see it turn into unexpected good fortune. Convinced that he was on a new path in life, Madden needed to find a way to earn some extra money while earning his degree. He applied for a student-teaching job at San Luis Obispo Junior High School and was hired immediately. It proved to be a right-place-at-the-right-time move.

The junior high school's athletic director, Phil Prijatel, had just fired his varsity football coach that spring and hired somebody new, a successful coach named Jack Frost from the Southern California area. But Frost would not arrive until later that summer, and with no coaching staff in place for spring practice, Prijatel was in dire need of someone to run those drills in the interim.

Prijatel knew Madden had played at Cal Poly and recently returned from his aborted stint in the NFL, so it seemed like a logical choice to ask Madden if he would coach the team, even though he had no prior coaching experience. Madden leapt at the opportunity. He would have 50 players under his guidance, with no assistant coaches to help him. Frost, the new coach, sent Madden his offensive and defensive play book, and Prijatel instructed him to teach all 50 kids what they needed to learn. Madden was too inexperienced to know what he didn't know.

"I was just back from [playing] pro football, so I thought I could do anything," he recalled.

Prijatel was not so naïve. He knew how difficult a job this was, so every afternoon he came out to the practice field and quietly observed from a distance. "I guess Phil wanted to come out and just watch to make sure I wasn't doing something crazy," Madden says. "I was pretty sure of myself back then. I was only 23 years old, and I'm sure I thought I knew a lot more than I probably did."

Whatever he did know would eventually be enough to sufficiently impress Prijatel and lead to another big break for Madden. A few months earlier, when he was looking for a job, Madden had walked into the office of the head football coach at a nearby junior college and asked for a job. Al Baldock, head coach at Allan Hancock College, did not appear to be terribly interested in a 23-year-old with no prior coaching experience and basically blew him off.

But now it was the spring, and Madden had spent three weeks coaching 50 kids all on his own. Prijatel had watched him every day and saw that Madden had a gift. He was a good teacher and a coach who had obvious love for and knowledge of the game. Whether kismet, destiny, or uncommon good luck, Madden seemed to have it in spades—because he was about to cross paths with Al Baldock again. Baldock was recruiting Prijatel's son Phil Jr., a running back at SLO High. During spring practice, he showed up at the high school to visit Prijatel Sr. and happened to mention he had a vacancy on his staff and was looking for a line coach.

"Do you know anybody?" Baldock asked.

"I have just the guy for you," said Prijatel. "He's running our spring practice."

This time Baldock hired Madden.

"I was a real coach now," Madden said.

5
TRACING THE SEEDS OF FEAR

"I've probably always had claustrophobia. I always sat at the end table. I hate elevators. Hell, I don't even like going to the movies."

John Madden

NOW THAT HE WAS "A REAL COACH," JOHN MADDEN APPLIED THE same obsessive behavior that he'd displayed as a player to becoming the best coach he could be. This was not a casual fling. This was a true commitment to his career backup plan. He knew he had received several lucky breaks that had shoved him on the coaching fast track, and he wasn't about to waste them.

It was 1960 now, and the 24-year-old's rise up the coaching ranks would prove to be meteoric. Within two years, Madden would have his first head coaching opportunity, and by the time he was 31 years old, he would be coaching professionals. By the time he turned 32, John Madden would be standing in front of a bank of microphones and a room full of TV cameras being introduced as a head coach in pro football. But the beginning of Madden's coaching life was far from glamorous. It was basic and humble.

Allan Hancock Junior College head coach Al Baldock had hired him as a part-time assistant. To make ends meet, Madden had to teach phys-ed at San Luis Obispo Junior High while splitting time at Hancock coaching the offensive and defensive linemen. And just as Madden's coaching life was getting started, so was John Robinson's. These two barrel-chested kids who had done everything together were now sharing another bond in adulthood.

Robinson's four years at Oregon did not lead to athletic stardom. In his last game in college, the 1958 Rose Bowl, the Ducks lost a thrilling

10–7 contest to Ohio State, and Robinson did not play until the final play of the game. He came in for teammate Ron Stover, who had set a Rose Bowl record with 10 receptions, "Just in time to get shot in the rear end with the final gun," said his head coach Len Casanova. The boys from Madden's Lot would not be playing for the Yankees in the summer and the 49ers in the fall.

"When we were kids, playing wasn't part of our lives. It was *all* of our lives," Madden would say years later. "When we realized all those years ago that we couldn't play forever, we decided the way we could was to coach. So now I think we're in it for life."

After six months in the army, Robinson went back to Eugene and was hired by Casanova to join the Oregon coaching staff, where he remained for the next 11 years. Robinson would learn his craft under Casanova and later Jerry Frei. "You loved being there," Robinson says. "Casanova was the father figure, always on my butt, and two assistants were like gods to me in their technical competence: Jack Roche and John McKay."

And now the boys were back together again, too. In the off-seasons when they weren't on the recruiting trails, Madden and Robinson were once again inseparable. "We were trying to be coaches. We were going around to all the clinics we could," says Robinson. "We talked all of the time about [coaching]."

One of the things they often talked about was the possibility that one day they would end up working together. They made promises that the first guy to get a head coaching gig would find a way to hire the other one as one of his top assistants. And now it was a race to see who would get there first. Robinson's association with John McKay at Oregon would provide him with his path to stardom. He followed McKay to Southern California in the early 1970s, and when McKay left USC for the NFL, Robinson was promoted and became a Trojan legend, taking USC to three Rose Bowl victories and a national championship between 1976 and 1982. He left for the pros in 1983 and promptly escorted the Los Angeles Rams to six playoff trips in his nine seasons there.

Madden, however, would be the first one to become a head coach. After two years as an assistant, Madden's boss Al Baldock left Hancock, and the 25-year-old Madden was promoted to head coach, where he led the Bulldogs to a 4–5 record in his first year and an 8–1 mark in year two. There would be no third year, because Madden was on the move again, hired by Don Coryell at San Diego State to be his defensive coordinator.

The two had met in another one of those series of fortunate events for young Madden. In 1960 Madden attended a coaching clinic headlined by John McKay, now USC's head coach. McKay was conducting a session on the I-formation offense. During this lecture, the coach admitted that he was not the one who had created this modern offense

"The coach who put it in our playbook is right here," said McKay. "Stand up, Don."

Don Coryell was McKay's backfield coach in 1960 but would soon be hired at San Diego State to run its program. After the lecture, while all the eager young coaches crowded around McKay, Madden chose to talk to Coryell.

"If McKay learned the I-formation from Coryell, then I'd rather talk to Coryell about it," Madden said.

No one else figured this out, so Madden was able to sit next to Coryell and talk uninterrupted for a good while, and they became friends. Whenever Coryell was recruiting in the Santa Maria area, he would stay with John and Virginia at their home. It was on those visits that Madden would sit up late into the night talking passionately about the game and soaking up as much knowledge as he could.

A pattern in Madden's life was finally becoming clear. These repeated "fortunate events" that kept following him around were not a product of luck or kismet or the football gods looking upon a favored son. This was all happening as a result of Madden's genuine thirst for football knowledge from wherever he could get it. The harder he worked to acquire that knowledge, the more good fortune seemed to find him.

So it was no accident that in 1964, when Coryell's defensive coordinator Tom Bass left San Diego State to join the AFL Chargers' coaching staff, Madden's coaching guru offered him the job, and Madden quickly accepted.

San Diego State was not a Division I football program back in the early 1960s, but it was one of the most elite small-college teams in the land, and everything else about San Diego State football was treated like it was the big time. They were able to recruit with most of the big West Coast programs and, unlike his last two years at Hancock, where the road trips were done mostly by bus, Madden had to get back on planes again.

This was going to cause a renewed bout of anxiety attacks, which began very shortly after an unpleasant road trip during his senior year at Cal Poly. While flying home from a road game, an unnerving moment occurred that would resonate throughout the rest of his life. Madden sat in the emergency exit row, next to the window. As the plane approached the local airport, Madden heard the pilot announce that the airplane's hydraulic system wasn't working properly. The landing gear wouldn't lower into place, so they had to circle around Santa Margarita Lake while they attempted to fix the problem. Then the pilot said if the problem couldn't be fixed, they would have to make an emergency landing. Madden remembers looking out the window, where he saw fire trucks and ambulances lining up on the runway. Already anxious about being in the plane in the first place, now Madden was positively petrified.

The anxiety that swept over Madden seemed to last for an eternity until finally he heard the grinding sound of the landing gear rumbling under his feet. The wheels were finally working, opening up from the belly of the plane and locking into place. There would be no emergency landing, no possibility of a crash landing, and, most of all, no need for all those emergency vehicles that were assembling below.

This was the first indelible scar that would damage Madden emotionally, making him forever fearful of the dangers of air travel.

The second would occur years later, and it caused the deepest emotional wound of all.

LATE IN THE AFTERNOON ON OCTOBER 29, 1960, Madden's old college team, Cal Poly, had just lost a road game 50–6 to Bowling Green University. Because their charter flight back home was leaving so late in the evening, many of the players spent time on Bowling Green's campus going to Halloween parties or hanging out in the student union building before the team buses loaded up and transported them to the nearby Toledo Express Airport. By the time the 48 passengers had climbed on board the C-46 aircraft for the Arctic–Pacific charter back home, many members of the Cal Poly travel party were wondering why anyone would even consider taking off in such dreary weather.

Under today's tougher modern aviation standards, it's unlikely the charter would have left the tarmac, at least not with this pilot. Never mind the questions about the dangerous zero-visibility weather conditions or the fitness of the antiquated C-46 aircraft, a relic from World War II. The larger question that remained was how the pilot, whose license had been revoked by the Federal Aviation Administration, could have been allowed into the cockpit in the first place. More than 50 years later, it is Donald Chesher's questionable judgment to take off in that foggy soup that is still being blamed for the tragedy that would occur just after the wheels of that rickety C-46 lifted off the runway.

Moments after the plane attempted to lift off, it exploded. The fuselage split into two pieces and came crashing back to the ground in a ball of flames. Of the 48 people on board, 22 died, including 16 members of the Cal Poly football team, a student manager, and a member of the booster club. It was called the first aviation disaster in U.S. history that involved an American sports team. Many of those young men who died were friends and former teammates of John Madden's.

The day after the crash, Madden drove over to the Cal Poly campus to console friends and families. As time has fogged over the actual details of that fateful night, it became urban legend that he was still playing for Cal Poly and was one of the survivors of the crash. It became the most logical explanation for his notorious fear of flying, even if the details weren't remotely accurate.

"Neither one is true," Madden told a reporter from the Associated Press nearly 50 years later. "I didn't like getting on planes before that. I got claustrophobic, and it got worse over the years."

In the subsequent days, weeks, and months after the Toledo tragedy, Madden would learn of the horrific details from survivors such as Ted Tollner, the Cal Poly quarterback who also ended up a coaching lifer in the NFL and college ball just like Madden. Tollner has retold this story before, remembering how he sat over the left wing, on the side where the engine gave out.

Just before the flight began, Tollner's teammate, wide receiver Curtis Hill, approached him in the aisle and asked Tollner if he would mind switching seats. Hill had gotten sick on the trip out to Ohio and for some reason figured it would be better if he moved from the back of the plane, where he was likely to feel more turbulence.

Tollner agreed. He unbuckled his seat belt, gathered his belongings, and moved a few rows back. A few minutes later, all hell broke loose as the C-46 military transport rumbled down the runway and attempted to take off in the thick fog. The pilot had spent the entire day flying the old twin-engine aircraft, having already hauled the Youngstown University team back from a game in Connecticut. There was a lot of discussion near the cockpit between Chesher, the tower, and members of the Cal Poly travel party. They were trying to decide if the plane should go or stay.

Tollner could look out the window and see that there was practically zero visibility. According to the Civil Aeronautics Board's investigation of the crash, Chesher made the ultimate decision to take off. Tollner said other teammates overheard several people tell Chesher, "Let's give it the ol' college try."

To this day, no one can definitively say if the plane ever actually was airborne. But within moments of initiating a takeoff attempt, the C-46 aircraft slammed into the ground on its left side, broke apart, and skidded into a nearby orchard. "After we hit, it was all a blur," recalled Tollner, who still struggles to understand why he survived.

The inexplicable fate that led Tollner to change seats with Curtis Hill had miraculously saved Tollner's life and tragically ended Hill's. "I was pretty much the cutoff," said Tollner, the former head coach at Southern Cal and a veteran assistant in the NFL. "About 100 percent of the people sitting in front of me were killed. Curtis was one of them. The people in my row and back mostly survived."

The orchard had turned into a chaotic scene full of charred fuselage, dead bodies thrown from the crash and still strapped into their seats, the stench of burning airplane fuel, and the horrific cries of confused and frightened survivors trying to make sense out of this catastrophe.

In this confusion, all the survivors who could walk began doing everything they could to assist those whose broken limbs prevented them from moving. Tollner had broken his foot and was dragged to safety along with several others while the survivors tried to go back to the wreckage and save as many people as they could. But as the flames grew more intense in the wreckage, several of the survivors started yelling and grabbing the players who wanted to continue to save the trapped passengers. "[They] started shouting that you couldn't go back in, the plane's on fire and is about to blow," Tollner recalled.

A few moments later, it did explode.

Eyewitnesses say the rest of the night was a haunting nightmare. Back on campus, members of the Bowling Green football team learned of the plane crash almost as soon as it happened, and many of them ran to their cars and drove out to the airport. When they arrived at the terminal, they were confronted with the staggering sight of emergency workers dutifully and respectfully stacking the bodies of the dead in blankets in a corner of the main terminal.

In the aftermath of the tragedy, Cal Poly canceled its final three games of the season, while the Bowling Green football team, still sorting through their own emotional wreckage, canceled their flight to their next road game. Instead, they took a two-and-a-half-day train trip to El Paso to play Texas Western a few weeks later.

Over the years, Madden has repeatedly attempted to minimize the impact of the Toledo crash as a contributor to his flight anxieties. To him, it was a simple case of claustrophobia and nothing more. He hated being confined to small spaces with no possibility of escape. "I've probably always had claustrophobia," he says today. "I always sat at the end table. I hate elevators. Hell, I don't even like going to the movies."

Yet in his first book, *Hey Wait a Minute (I Wrote a Book!)*, he did admit that the Cal Poly accident contributed to his fear of flying. "I think the Cal Poly plane crash…probably had a subconscious effect on my attitude toward planes," he said. "I thought about that crash for a long time…. I flew when I had to, but not when I didn't have to, not if I had a choice."

As the years went by, amateur and professional psychologists alike had a field day trying to decode the origins of Madden's fears. Clinically, what Madden suffered from has many names: aerophobia, aviatophobia, aviophobia, and even pteromechanophobia. Sometimes, fear of flying is a phobia that stands all on its own. However, it often is a combination of several other contributing phobias such as claustrophobia or acrophobia (fear of heights). Madden admitted to suffering from symptoms of claustrophobia for as long as he can remember, and he would also exhibit signs of a fear of heights in later years. But the trauma of sitting in that plane when the landing gear jammed (and seeing the emergency service vehicles on the ground from his window seat) coupled with the memories of the Cal Poly crash may have been the tipping points that solidified his intense aversion to flying.

This was only the beginning of a deep psychological tale.

6

GAME CHANGER

"It's been a long, a long time coming, but I know change is gonna come, oh yes it will."

Sam Cooke, "A Change Is Gonna Come"

AMERICA IN THE EARLY 1960s WAS SLOWLY CREEPING TOWARD a monumental cultural tug-of-war, with the aging establishment clinging mightily to a buttoned-down way of life deeply rooted in the ultraconservative 1950s, while a radical youth movement was determined to bring about a seismic shift in our social fabric. Everything that America had long preferred to whisper about—race, religion, sex, war—was about to be exposed like raw nerves. And nowhere were those uncomfortable conversations more prevalent than on college campuses across the land.

Oddly enough, San Diego State's campus was not exactly on the vanguard of the antiwar and civil rights movements sweeping across American campuses. Campus unrest did not begin to percolate to a full boil at San Diego State until much later in the decade. This afforded John Madden, approaching his late twenties, the opportunity to develop as a young coach without the additional burden of being overly engaged in generational turmoil. Even though there was no greater symbol of the American establishment than the quasimilitaristic, ultraconservative game of football, somehow the status quo remained intact in football a little while longer. This largely explains why the sports world was still run by stern authoritarians like Vince Lombardi and Bear Bryant. Perhaps it also explains why, in his formative years, Madden considered his coaching personality to be far more in line with Lombardi, whom he greatly admired and voraciously studied.

Madden loves telling the story of how he attended a coaching clinic at the University of Nevada–Reno in the early 1960s that advertised Lombardi as a featured speaker.

"I'll always remember the title of his lecture," Madden says. "'The Green Bay Sweep.' That's it. He talked eight hours about one play! Four hours in the morning, four hours after lunch."

It was the most thorough example of how superior Lombardi's football intellect was and how much further young Madden had to go before he could rightfully consider himself the true football scholar he aspired to be. Like most extremely talented and ambitious men his age, Madden was convinced at that age that he was much smarter than he really was or would eventually be. It took sitting through that one lecture from Lombardi to realize that he was only skimming the surface of coaching knowledge. To witness a man break down one play for eight hours was a revelation. With a piece of chalk in one hand, Lombardi feverishly attacked the blackboard, drawing elaborate football hieroglyphics and dissecting all 11 offensive players' assignments. Madden's eyes darted back and forth from the chalkboard to his notepad, recording everything. Lombardi was able to recreate every possible scenario for the play—blitzes, coverages, stunts—and explain how it would affect every player.

Madden walked away from that lecture realizing the most he could ever talk about a particular play nonstop was 20 minutes, a half hour, tops. So he did what he always did in moments like this: he dug a little deeper, worked even harder. It was a good time to be an aspiring coach at San Diego State. He would not completely escape the chaos of the generation (that would come a few years later when his career shifted to the professional ranks), but his time on the San Diego State campus would be predominantly spent doing what he loved most. Madden was becoming a true student of football, a serious young man with lofty professional aspirations. By the time he had ascended to a top assistant position on Don Coryell's staff at San Diego State at age 28, Madden had set his next career marker: head coach by age 35.

He was constantly in pursuit of ways to make all those Xs and Os dancing in his head work that much better, and he was in the ideal environment for such an education. Coryell was already blooming as a recognized offensive genius, experimenting with the concepts that would decades later be tagged with the colorful "Air Coryell" moniker and copied by some of the brightest offensive minds in the NFL. The Aztecs were a small-college power, going 8–2 in back-to-back years in 1964 and '65 before finishing the 1966 season 11–0 to win what was then called the Small College National Championship. Every day, Madden was observing how Coryell made it all work, while sharing office space with a talented coaching staff that included one other future Pro Football Hall of Famer (Joe Gibbs) and another coach who would end up as a future college and NFL head coach (Rod Dowhower). And just as he had done in Philadelphia with those early morning film sessions with Norm Van Brocklin, in San Diego Madden had befriended another valuable mentor from whom he could glean even more football knowledge.

Paul Vincent "Pitchin' Paul" Governali was the head coach for the Aztecs from 1956 through 1960. In his first year, the Aztecs went undefeated, but he could not sustain things, and he could never build San Diego State's football program to elite status. He was replaced by Coryell but stayed at the school in the athletic department as a tenured professor with an Ivy League (Columbia) PhD in education. Governali was a former All-American quarterback at Columbia University, the 1942 recipient of the Maxwell Award for College Player of the Year, and the runner-up for the Heisman Trophy. Legendary sportswriter Grantland Rice, who created all the larger-than-life heroes in college football's Golden Age, once wrote that Governali was "the closest approach to a one-man team that I have ever seen."

It didn't take Madden long to gravitate toward Governali and cultivate a student-teacher relationship. "Paul became a great friend of mine," Madden says. "He was like this wonderful football academic. Even though he hadn't been successful as a head coach, he was one of those older coaches who just knew things about the game. We used to sit around talking Xs and Os, discussing coaching philosophies all the time."

Madden had grown up a lot since those intimidating film studies with the Dutchman in the bowels of old Franklin Field. He was not presumptuous enough to regard himself as Governali's equal, but he was no longer intimidated by his status as the insatiable student. He would engage his mentor endlessly for any morsel of knowledge. There was plenty of give and take, as the student was challenged by the teacher to defend his ideas, to prove how his Xs could be effective against somebody's Os. Madden had already earned his master's in education at Cal Poly, but now he was immersed in a unique postgraduate environment. He was becoming a man of letters in the coaching profession, and Governali was his latest professor emeritus.

Madden had no idea that Paul Governali was also acting as his advance man. In the late '50s, another brash young football go-getter had also befriended Governali. His name was Al Davis. By 1966 Davis was already in charge of the AFL's Oakland Raiders as managing general partner. He was, in many ways, everything that Madden was—young, ambitious, and single-minded in his drive to be the best—but also many things Madden was not. In contrast to the rumpled, easygoing native Californian Madden, Davis was trim and polished, a stylish but calculating New Yorker who reveled in conflict and controversy.

The AFL was in the thick of its war against the established NFL, and Davis was the upstart league's most notorious field general. Davis loved scouting college players, particularly at the small colleges. Davis often bragged of his prowess at unearthing so many great college players who were not on the beaten path of the NFL scouts, so it was hardly a surprise that he often ended up watching San Diego State's practices. This was, after all, a small-college power with future NFL stars such as Haven Moses and Fred Dryer on its roster. And whenever Davis walked the practice-field sideline or sat in the stands, his good friend Governali was often by his side. When they watched practice, they would always talk. Mostly it was about players, but Davis also leaned on Governali's expertise as a great judge of coaching talent.

During one of those conversations in the fall of 1966, Governali pointed out the Aztecs' young defensive coach to Davis. Several decades later at a reunion of the Raiders' first world championship team, Davis would recall the first time he laid eyes on Madden on that San Diego State practice field: "There was a guy standing on that football field, wearing [high-top] shoes, almost up above the ankles. Baggy football pants. A jacket that—I don't know where he got it—it must have come from a rummage sale. A hat, a baseball cap, and he was pretty fancy 'cause he had a whistle on…. But goddammit, when I talked to him, I felt an emotional love of football and something about him that was a little different from those you normally come across."

Disheveled as always, Madden had made a good first impression on Al Davis. There was no pretension to him. In fact, his unmade-bed outer shell only cemented a belief by Davis that the only thing that truly mattered to Madden was football. And he was right. There was very little that mattered more to Madden than being on the field or in the locker room talking football. He was young enough to relate to the players of the day but old enough to appreciate the belief that hard work—not schmoozing or politics—would eventually get him where he needed to be.

Intrigued by Governali's subtle praise and Madden's outward presence, Davis went over to talk to him. The Aztecs were on their way to that perfect 11–0 season, but this particular week they were facing the top-ranked team in the small-college polls, North Dakota State. Madden was sitting on a bench scribbling away on a notepad. Madden had never met Davis, but he sure knew who he was. When the Raiders boss walked over to the bench, he casually asked Madden what he was doing.

The burly redhead looked up, smiled, and eagerly showed Davis what was on his notepad. He was trying to come up with a particular defensive scheme that would work against South Dakota State's split-T offense and the way the offensive linemen spread out with unusually large splits (the distance that separated the linemen from each other). The excited coach showed Davis his plan of attack.

"I was going to hit the gaps," Madden recalls. "We were going to hit all the gaps in the splits they gave us." Davis liked what he saw and even offered a suggestion.

"Why don't you take your guys and, just before the ball is snapped, jump them in the gaps?" asked Davis.

It was on that bench on the San Diego State practice field that another apparent chance meeting would once again help shape John Madden's future. Madden incorporated much of what Davis had suggested in his game plan against North Dakota State, and the Aztecs won the game. As the two men talked and traded thoughts on Xs and Os, Madden never considered that this was a significant moment in his life. Yet in the time he spent trading that pencil and notepad back and forth with Al Davis, Madden had just taken one giant step closer to realizing his ultimate football dream of becoming a head coach again.

"I didn't think of it that way at the time, but that was kind of an interview," Madden says. "So Al came out there and was talking to me about football, and that's all I thought of it. But in essence he was trying to find out what I knew to see if I would be someone he should keep on his radar."

IN 1966 AL DAVIS WAS NOT THE MONUMENTAL CHARACTER he would become in less than a decade. The man with the outsized character was Green Bay Packers coach Vince Lombardi, who had gone to Wisconsin in 1959 from the New York Giants and transformed a sagging franchise into an NFL dynasty. Madden had determined a while back that he should model himself after Lombardi, even though they shared little personality-wise. In his best-selling biography on Lombardi, *When Pride Still Mattered*, author David Maraniss tells many stories of how uncomfortable Lombardi was trying to relate to his players earlier in his career and how intractable he could be when faced with even the least bit of resistance. The players of the late 1950s were not exactly of a revolutionary spirit, but many of the New York Giants players viewed Lombardi in less than flattering terms. He was "loud and arrogant—a total pain in the ass," recalled running back Frank Gifford of those early years when Lombardi arrived fresh off of Red Blaik's West Point staff to become New York's offensive coordinator. Behind his back, the Giants called Lombardi "the Little General" or "Little Mussolini." They mocked him during late-night dorm-room sessions at training camp, hid his chalk before team meetings, and weren't above teasing him to his face, either.

Madden, by contrast, learned early on how to adapt. In his first year as a head coach at Hancock JC, Madden remembered how much he hated seeing players having a lighthearted moment before a game. As a player, he was a tightly wound, intense lineman who wanted everything about his pregame preparation to be stone-cold serious. As a young head coach, he'd get steamed if he saw players who wanted to listen to music or tell jokes in the locker room. He'd get that furnace-faced flush and shout, "This is serious! Football is serious!"

One of his players came up to Madden before a game and asked Madden if there was any way to compromise. Blair Sheldon, a thick-necked fullback, cautioned Madden that no two players were alike and everyone had their own way of putting their game face on. A few weeks later, Madden made an adjustment—two locker rooms before the game, one for the guys who wanted to be serious and one for the guys who wanted to joke and listen to music.

It was a breakthrough for Madden, and it would end up being that very quality that would eventually prove to be an even greater asset as he reached the pros. Leave it to Madden's best friend John Robinson to more accurately describe what that quality truly was.

"John was one of the first guys who could manage the chaotic stuff," says Robinson. "He wasn't one of those uptight, corporate-type coaches. He was the perfect guy for the perfect time. I was always one of those guys who always believed, 'Look out for the quarterback coach. They're always the handsome ones. They got their pants pressed.' That definitely wasn't John. Hell, he never pressed his pants or anything else. If I ever was asked to advise someone on who they should hire to be a head coach, I would always tell them to look for a guy like John. He was no damned quarterback coach. I always wanted to look for that old rat fucker kind of coach. John hung out [with] or liked or was friendly with the weird guys, the defensive guys.... He'd go stand around them in practice and bullshit around them."

This gift, that "old rat fucker" personality, was going to make John Madden rich and famous one day. In the meantime, becoming a head coach at the major-college level had become a Madden obsession. After the '66 season, when Coryell considered taking the University of Arizona job, Madden heard talk within the Aztec offices that he would be Coryell's successor. However, when Coryell decided to stay put, Madden seemed content to bide his time. He applied for, but didn't get, the vacant Utah State job (he was a finalist) but passed on jobs at Cal Poly–Pomona and Cal Western because he didn't think they were upward career moves.

So Madden decided that he would stay at San Diego State and continue to learn under Coryell. What he didn't know was that things were happening during the off-season up in Oakland that were about to change his life forever.

IN THE SPRING OF 1967, the short-lived Continental Football League had scooped up a talented young Raiders assistant running backs coach named Bill Walsh to become the head coach and general manager of its San Jose franchise, and now Oakland head coach John Rauch had an opening on his staff. Madden came home one night to find his wife, Virginia, holding a slip of paper with a note on it. Rauch had telephoned Madden and wanted him to call back as soon as possible. Madden didn't think it was a big deal. "I'll call him tomorrow," John told Virginia.

"No, he wants you to call tonight," Virginia said. "He specifically mentioned tonight."

Madden pooh-poohed the whole thing. A few weeks earlier, he had received another phone call from a pro head coach and had gotten prematurely excited—as it turned out, for no good reason. Tom Fears had just been named the head coach of the NFL expansion New Orleans Saints, and Madden excitedly thought this was the big phone call that would get him into the NFL. Madden wasted no time calling Fears back, but when he did, his heart sank when the only thing Tom wanted to talk about was getting some recommendations on some college players he was interested in as free-agent pickups.

Fool me once, shame on you. Fool me twice, shame on me. So when Madden was told that Rauch had called, he was not about to get overly excited about this message from the Raiders coach, no matter what Virginia's impressions were of the urgency in the coach's voice. Still, Virginia did a good enough job of convincing him to return Rauch's call promptly. When he picked up the phone and called, what he heard made his heart dance. With Walsh's departure, Rauch had been given the go-ahead to not only find his replacement but also expand his staff by one man. They were looking for someone to coach the linebackers and work with special teams, and Rauch invited Madden to Oakland for an interview.

What Madden didn't know was that Al Davis had insisted that Rauch make the call. There was never a move of any sort within the Raiders organization that did not have Davis' fingerprints on it, directly or indirectly. Rauch might have done the interviewing, but Al Davis was going to make the ultimate decision about who was on the coaching staff. When Walsh left for his new job with the Continental Football League, Davis began compiling a short list of potential candidates for the staff vacancies, and he happened to call his old friend Governali for help. When Davis asked if Governali knew about any good young coaches, the old football scholar reminded Davis about that big galoot he had met in one of his previous trips to the Aztecs' practice field. "You ought to hire John Madden," Governali told him, point blank. "He's a very good coach."

At the same time, Davis' personnel director, Ron Wolf, was also passing on a strong recommendation of Madden from Chuck Noll, who was an assistant coach with the Chargers. Wolf and Noll used to travel together on scouting trips, talking football and personnel. When Wolf asked Noll if he knew of a good young coach, Noll told him of his friend who was the defensive coach at San Diego State. Wolf heard the same words that Davis heard from Governali: "You ought to hire John Madden. He's a very good coach."

On May 22, 1967, the Raiders hired Madden. On the front page of the *Oakland Tribune* sports pages the next day, right next to the headline "DiMaggio Backs Oakland AL Bid" and below two other stories about the San Francisco Giants and San Francisco Warriors that spread across the top of the page, there was a small story announcing Madden's hiring. "Raiders Add Aide for Rauch," the headline proclaimed. It was no longer than eight or nine paragraphs, much of it detailing other issues with the Raiders. But the 31-year-old Madden had received his biggest career break yet. Only six years removed from volunteering to coach the San Luis Obispo spring practice for free, and barely seven years after leaving Philadelphia on crutches with his NFL playing career dashed, Madden was returning to the pros as an assistant coach with one of the better teams in the AFL.

NOTHING MADDEN HAD LEARNED UP UNTIL THEN IN FOOTBALL would sufficiently prepare him for the environment of the Oakland Raiders. Two years before Madden's arrival, Al Davis had given up coaching to move into the Raiders front office, and in April of 1966 he was named as Joe Foss' replacement as the AFL's new commissioner. Davis was planning an all-out assault on the NFL, plotting to raid the league of its best quarterbacks while continuing to throw money at college football's brightest stars. It took less than two months after Davis' appointment as commissioner for the two leagues to announce a merger.

Part of the merger settlement was that Pete Rozelle, the NFL commissioner, not Davis, would run the postmerger business. That meant Davis was coming back to the Raiders' new training facility and moving back into his oversized office on the top floor, the only one with windows looking out over the front of the facility. Once Davis returned, it left the man he had hired to replace him as the head coach, John Rauch, paranoid that Davis would take his job back.

Preoccupied with the real or imagined threat of Davis' interference, Rauch even offered to resign, but Davis wanted no such thing. He had outgrown wanting to be a coach. The daily grind of being on the field every day no longer interested him since he had been inside the corridors of power and the point man for the AFL in the waning days of the war with the NFL. His sights were set on becoming a larger-than-life figure in pro football. He had minority ownership and sought even more power. He wanted controlling interest in the Raiders, not to sling a whistle around his neck again.

Davis had even told owner Wayne Valley, "I can't be called 'coach' because that's demeaning."

"You can call yourself 'Mr. God,'" Valley ribbed him.

None of this could stop Rauch from letting his paranoia get the best of him. In 1966 Davis was off in New York serving as the new AFL commissioner, so he rarely visited the practice field. Yet his low profile seemed to only heighten Rauch's concerns that his Machiavellian boss was working in the shadows to undermine his authority. The Raiders' organizational culture seemed to be full of this sort of dangerous intrigue. Davis was a man of manipulation, but for the time being he seemed to be far more interested in winning the AFL-NFL war than returning to the team after the merger had been announced.

It was odd that Rauch would end up feeling such pressure because he was Davis' first hire when Davis took over as the Raiders' head coach in 1963. Davis pursued Rauch with the same zest he would a potential recruit. He kept calling the reluctant Rauch until the coach finally said yes. But now, four years later, Rauch was obsessed with the public perception that he was a puppet whose strings were being pulled by Al Davis. He believed Davis had signed and forced certain players on him, such as former Chargers tight end Dave Kocourek, and planted him as a locker-room spy. ("I might have been skeptical along those lines," Rauch once said. "I had to be skeptical of everything.") There were even rumblings in the locker room that the coaching staff had nothing to do with weekly game plans. According to the myth of Al Davis' meddlesome ways, the coaches would sit around the team offices on Monday and Tuesday nights killing time until a game plan would mysteriously appear under everyone's door—Davis' game plan.

Davis did nothing to defuse any of this. A few years before his death in June 2008, Rauch began to unload secrets to his son John Alan Rauch that he had kept bottled up inside for 40 years. Little by little, during conversations over cold beers on the porch of the family's Jersey Shore vacation home, the father began explaining the source of all his suspicions of how and why he believed Davis had sabotaged him. Was it paranoia or fact? The son wasn't sure. But he listened to his father's stories, and it all started to make sense. When Al showed up back in Oakland in '66, he immediately took over the office space that was supposed to go to the coaching staff, forcing Rauch to rent a two-bedroom apartment for him and his staff a few blocks from the practice field in Hayward, which was situated on the grounds of a condemned high school that sat on the San Gabriel Fault.

It was a horrible place to practice, but it wasn't unlike a lot of the rotten places NFL and AFL teams practiced all over the league in the '60s (the New Orleans Saints' facility, which sat on a plot of land that was below sea level and had high-voltage power lines running across the far end of the practice field, was so crappy that on the days it rained, the weight room was often two or three inches deep in rain water). Owner Wayne Valley paid to have the locker rooms in the old high school cleaned up and the plumbing fixed so the players could take warm showers. The apartment for the coaches was equally shabby, with Rauch using the kitchen as his office and the living room as the meeting room.

Rauch was so sure that Davis was out to get him that he convinced himself that Davis was stealing his game plans and offering them up to opposing teams. The coach had gotten so spooked that he started erasing the blackboard in the coaches' meeting rooms after every daily meeting, convinced that Davis would have one of his lackeys come in the middle of the night and copy it.

During one game in 1967, Kocourek was inactive because of an injury and watched the game upstairs with Davis. Just before halftime, Kocourek remembers Davis grabbing him by the arm and sending him down to the locker room with instructions for Rauch. "This is what you're gonna tell Rauch!" Davis shouted.

The old tight end listened carefully, tried to remember everything, and then walked into the locker room and awkwardly told Rauch what he'd been instructed to do by Davis.

"This is what Al told me," Kocourek said.

Rauch just stared at him with a confused and angry expression and walked away without saying a word.

IN 1967, AS THE RAIDERS WERE ON THEIR WAY to a team-record 13–1 season, their first AFL title, and a trip to Super Bowl II, Davis began showing up at practices wearing the same practice garb as the coaches. He would roam the practice fields with sovereign authority, boldly moving from drill to drill to offer unsolicited coaching to various players. The sight of this struck a raw nerve with Rauch, and he fearlessly (and some would say foolishly) took immediate issue with it. With no attempt to disguise his annoyance, Rauch stepped in and forcefully announced that Davis was causing a disruption.

"I'll never forget it," Raiders running back Clem Daniels told Davis biographer Mark Ribowsky. "Al said to somebody, 'You're doing that wrong,' and [Rauch] stopped him in front of the players and said, 'Hey Al, *I'm* the coach.'"

Davis stopped dead in his tracks, turned, and glared at Rauch. It was a steely glower that lasted but a few uncomfortable moments before Davis departed the practice field without saying another word.

Years of suffering in silence came bursting to the surface. Everyone who witnessed the event marveled at Rauch's guts for standing up to

Davis but questioned his intelligence for winning a fleeting battle at the cost of losing the war.

In the midst of all of this craziness, Madden's relationship with Davis was growing stronger. Rauch was convinced that Davis would visit with many of the assistants behind his back, mainly because everyone would inform Rauch every time Davis secretly cornered them for information on what the head coach was doing with his weekly game plans. It was a particularly silly and self-destructive exercise for the coach to be so consumed by his boss wanting to know what he was up to, and Rauch's constant grinding and chafing became a cruel form of entertainment for many of the players and coaches. His runaway paranoia was eating away at him, even while he was becoming wildly successful on the field (Rauch compiled a stunning 33–8 record with two consecutive trips to the AFL Championship Game in his three seasons in Oakland).

"[Rauch] did a helluva job, the record proved that," former Raiders offensive tackle Harry Schuh told Ribowsky. "But this wasn't your normal situation. Al knew the offense and he was the boss; and if you're Al, you don't just drop out of sight and not be heard."

7

THE PLAYERS' COACH

"I wanted John. He has the same temperament as Walter Alston of the Dodgers. As I've said, the Dodgers find Dodger-types... We look for Raider-types."

Al Davis

JOHN MADDEN WASN'T FAZED BY THE MACHIAVELLIAN machinations going on around him within the Raiders organization. He was 31 years old and a professional football coach, doing exactly what he had worked so hard to attain. There were no unseen demons distracting him from doing his job.

What was there to complain about? His remarkable rise up the coaching ranks had presented him with a chance to go to the Super Bowl in his first year in the pros. Whatever paranoia Al Davis might have created in John Rauch's mind did not prevent the Raiders' head coach from putting on a hell of a show in 1967. They opened the regular season with a 51–0 spanking of the Denver Broncos, a 35–7 trouncing of the Boston Patriots, and a thrilling 23–21 victory over the defending AFL champion Kansas City Chiefs before going to New York and losing 27–14 to Joe Namath and the Jets. It would be the last game the Raiders would lose until they reached Super Bowl II in Miami.

In the off-season, Madden and all the other Raiders coaches were on the scouting trail to evaluate college talent and prep for the NFL draft. Because most NFL teams were stingy when it came to travel expenses for these scouting excursions, the coaches often shared expenses with their friends from other teams. For Madden, that friend was another young coach he had befriended back in San Diego and the man who had recommended him for the Raiders' job, Chuck Noll.

Noll was an assistant coach on the Chargers staff when Madden was with Don Coryell at San Diego State. By now, Noll had moved on to Don Shula's staff with the Baltimore Colts, and he and Madden would coordinate their scouting trips so they could split hotel rooms, rental cars, and meals.

But things were getting weirder and weirder around the Raiders as Rauch's rage against Davis grew to the point where he was accusing his own coaches of being in on the conspiracy. All around the building, people were beginning to wonder how much longer Rauch would be able to last with all of the pressure he was putting on himself through his constant obsession with real and imagined spies lurking everywhere. Yet Rauch kept winning, following up the 13–1 season with a 12–2 record in 1968, again advancing his team to the AFL Championship Game in the bitter cold of New York's Shea Stadium against Namath's Jets. Yet no matter how much he won, Rauch could not escape his own demons. One day, late in the season during a meeting with his defensive coaches, Rauch was reviewing the game plan when he asked Madden an odd question.

"Where did this coverage come from?" he asked.

"That's the coverage we put in last night," Madden responded.

"No, we didn't."

"Yes, we did."

"No, no. Davis put that in," Rauch insisted.

This went on for several minutes before another assistant intervened and tried to remind Rauch that he was in the room the night before when all the coaches installed this rather vexing coverage.

"Oh yeah, I remember now," Rauch said.

For a man who loved winning as much as Davis, it remained a puzzle why anyone would believe that the man who proclaimed "Just win, baby!" would invest so much energy creating so many impediments for his head coach. Davis' supporters often bring that up whenever the subject of John Rauch's paranoia comes up. They all want to know why he would screw up a good thing when all he ever cared about was his "Commitment to Excellence."

John Alan Rauch may have wondered the same thing. He was only a teenager when his father left Oakland, and he was too busy being a kid to make any astute observations at the time. But he did ask his father about it as they bonded at the vacation house on the shore. "I think [my dad], he felt that Al, when he came into Oakland in 1963 and he had that first season when they went from 1–13 to 10–4, that he was the savior of the Raiders, and that's what situation he wanted to come back on," John Alan would recall. "Because they had an established team and he didn't want to just come in and bulldoze his way back in, but was hoping that the team would go down and that he could bring it right back up again, he could be the savior again. I think that's what my dad thought."

A few weeks after the odd confrontation in the meeting room—and with little warning to players or coaches—the Davis-Rauch nonsense reached its breaking point. The Jets defeated the Raiders on December 29, 1968, in the AFL title game, which meant Namath, coach Weeb Ewbank, and the Jets would get the historic honor of being the first AFL team to win a Super Bowl. Davis did not take this well. Angry at being robbed of the opportunity to stick it to the NFL first, Davis was quoted in the *Oakland Tribune* questioning Rauch's strategies against the Jets, going so far as to say, "We never should have lost."

Until that point, Davis kept his displeasure with Rauch inside the walls of the Raiders' complex. But during that Jets game he was heard openly ripping Rauch's decisions in the press box, slamming his fist on the table, and cursing loudly enough for any reporter to hear. This criticism got back to the coach, and there was no holding back from either man. To add insult to injury, according to Rauch's widow, Jane, Davis reneged on a promise to take Rauch and his family to Super Bowl III in Miami regardless of the outcome of that AFL Championship Game.

After the loss, Davis balked, telling Rauch the only one going to Miami would be Davis. Rauch took his family to Lake Tahoe for a skiing trip instead, and in the process began secret talks with the Buffalo Bills about their head coaching vacancy. Now both men were about to get what they wanted. On January 16, 1969, Rauch walked into a meeting room where the assistant coaches were preparing to evaluate prospective college players for the draft and announced, "I'm taking the Buffalo job."

The entire room was filled with stunned silence. Rauch was walking away from a team that had gone 25–3 in back-to-back seasons with two consecutive trips to the AFL title game, and was now a perennial championship contender. But Rauch was more than willing to toss that all away for his own peace of mind. Rauch simply didn't have the personality traits required to peacefully coexist with the outsized ego of the eccentric Davis. Buffalo might have looked like Elba to the rest of the football world, but after spending three tortuous seasons under the thumb of Davis, upstate New York looked like heaven to Rauch.

Rauch went on to Buffalo, and in a few years he was out of coaching. Years later, John Alan would often tease his father that he had walked away from a chance at coaching immortality when he quit the Raiders. "It's always kind of driven me crazy about how somebody could give up a situation like he had," says the son, "because I've always thought to this day that if he had been willing to put up with Al's interference… he could have gone for years and been one of the greatest coaches of all time. And it turns out Madden ended up being one of the greatest coaches of all [time]. You don't know how history would have gone, but you know, he was well on his way, he had the winningest record in all of pro football when he resigned."

MOMENTS AFTER RAUCH LEFT THAT COACHES' ROOM, Davis made his appearance. He reassured the coaches that anyone who wanted to stay would have a job with the Raiders. And then he said something that immediately caused John Madden's ears to perk up.

"We're all getting ready for the draft now. But after the draft, if anyone here thinks he should be the head coach, I'll talk to you about it," he said.

The coaches all sat there for a while trying to figure out what was happening but eventually went back to work breaking down draft prospects. But the moment they took a break, 32-year-old John Madden marched into Davis' office, closed the door behind him, stood in front of his desk, and boldly proclaimed, "I want to talk to you about the head coaching job."

Davis didn't say anything.

"I think I could be the head coach and be better than anyone," Madden said.

Davis mentioned how young Madden was, and Madden shot back, "What's my age got to do with it? If I can be the head coach, I can be the head coach now. I either have it in me or I don't. I'm either going to be good at it, or I don't have it in me, and I'm not going to be any good. And I said I have it in me, so it doesn't make any difference if we do it now or three or four years from now or five years from now."

Again, Davis brought up Madden's age. "You're only 32," Davis said. "What are your credentials?"

"Well, what were your credentials to get to be [the Raiders boss] at such a young age?" Madden responded.

The one thing that Madden understood and appreciated about Davis that Rauch never could was that Davis was a firm believer in the Socratic method. He wanted to turn every conversation into a heated debate. Davis' management style was to provoke someone into defending himself and scrutinizing his position by offering an often-harsh opposing viewpoint.

It was always business, not personal, unless you wilted under the intensity of the argument. Then it became very personal, because Davis saw that as a personal failing, and he hated weakness in the men he chose to be leaders.

He sensed that weakness in Rauch early on and relentlessly picked at it like it was an open sore. Madden would not make a similar mistake.

"Al liked a good argument," Madden says. "He would say things just to see how you really felt about it, and I enjoyed arguing with him, too. It always seemed to me like they were always academic arguments.

"'Would you trade Ken Stabler for Jack Youngblood?'

"'No fuckin' way.'

"All Al wanted to do was hear what you thought, find out if you really believed in something bad enough to defend it. That was his way of finding out what you knew and how much you knew."

So Madden fearlessly explained himself to Davis. "It was never 'selling,'" Madden says. "You didn't sell yourself to Al. You *explained* yourself."

Davis told Madden there was plenty of time before he would make his decision. They would meet again over the course of the next few weeks leading up to and following the January 28 draft, he said. In truth, Davis was buying time because he had other people outside the organization on his radar. Davis held Madden's good friend Chuck Noll in high regard (they had worked together with the Chargers in the early 1960s) and was hoping to fly him out to Oakland for an interview. But the Pittsburgh Steelers preempted that move when they hired Noll the day before the draft and only 11 days after Rauch's resignation.

The next day, Noll called Madden and offered him a job as his new defensive coordinator. Madden turned him down, choosing to take his chances on convincing Davis that he was indeed ready to be an NFL head coach.

Over the next three days, Madden met with Davis multiple times, and by the third meeting, he had convinced Davis to give him a chance. On January 30, the day after the two-day draft had been completed, Davis offered Madden the job but then did a rather curious thing.

"He told me to go away for a few days and not to tell anyone," Madden remembers. "He never told me why he wanted me to do that, but I went into hiding for three days. I went to a motel in Fremont and stayed there until he said it was okay to come back to Oakland."

Anyone who knew the way the ever-calculating Davis operated had to assume one of two things was behind this request: A) he was trying to stash Madden away to prevent any other teams from contacting him about potential jobs, or B) Davis was still interviewing people and didn't want Madden in the office while he was shopping around.

On February 4, 1969, the *Oakland Tribune* blared, "Madden's the One" across the top of the front sports page. Three other Madden-related articles dominated the page. Madden came out of hiding, stood before a bank of microphones, and was formally introduced as the sixth head coach in franchise history and the youngest head coach in professional football. A few days earlier, when Vince Lombardi stepped down as the Packers' general manager to become the head coach and GM of the Washington Redskins, he talked about how the most difficult thing to do in football was to successfully transform a losing franchise into a proven winner.

Davis, ever mindful of cultivating the image of his Raiders (and by extension, himself) as the new benchmark for excellence in pro football, purposefully engaged in a game of one-upmanship with his rival Lombardi. "The challenge confronting John Madden is a tremendous one," Davis said as he introduced his 32-year-old head coach. "It is much more difficult to maintain a high standard of excellence and continue on than to take a downtrodden organization and create excellence."

Madden, wearing a black sports coat, white buttoned-down shirt, and black-and-gold-striped club tie, was as neat as he would ever be in public. His bright auburn hair was carefully parted on the right side and slicked down with hair cream. His normally bushy sideburns were well trimmed as he spoke to a crowded room full of television cameras and notepad-toting reporters.

One of the reasons Madden immersed himself so much in anything related to Lombardi was because the living legend had taken the Packers from football irrelevance to dynastic supremacy in such a short period of time. As someone who aspired to become a head coach, Madden always figured whenever he did get his first shot, it would be with a bad team in need of a complete overhaul. So he studied whatever he could about Lombardi's approach to franchise reconstruction, never imagining that his first gig would be with a team fresh off back-to-back trips to the AFL Championship Game.

But John Rauch had just left the Raiders organization with the highest winning percentage in pro football, and Madden's first head coaching job in the pros was no urban-renewal project. His was a talent-rich football team with young, rising stars and legitimate championship aspirations.

If you took a quick poll around that hotel ballroom where his introductory press conference was being held, there were few people in that room on that Monday afternoon who believed that the inexperienced Madden would be able to truly maintain the sustained excellence that Davis was expecting.

The football world, cynical as always, thought that in the 32-year-old John Madden the puppet master Davis had finally found his willing marionette.

8

THREE SIMPLE RULES

*"They were all renegades, but John had a way of handling guys. My parents always told me, 'If you're going to lead...don't treat them the way you want to be treated, treat them the way **they** want to be treated.' In other words, you have to learn about other cultures. And John was good at that."*

Al Davis

WHATEVER SATISFACTION HE MIGHT HAVE DERIVED FROM FINALLY chasing off the belligerent John Rauch, whose greatest sin was not letting Al Davis do what he damned well pleased with his own football team, the Raiders boss was now in a very strange place emotionally as he began preparations for the 1969 season. Losing the 1968 AFL Championship Game fueled Davis' public disgust with Rauch. Davis had spent the better part of the 1960s in the trenches of the bitter AFL-NFL wars, and the loss to the Jets had ultimately robbed him of what he surely felt was his destiny.

In this AFL-NFL battle, Davis had been as great an agent provocateur as any man. In his heart, he felt that it should have been the Raiders racing off the Orange Bowl field on January 12, 1969, as the first AFL team to take down the NFL in a Super Bowl. But Rauch had ripped that page right out of Davis' legacy and sent it to Joe Namath for a Hollywood rewrite. To make matters worse, the AFL-NFL merger was complete, and the AFL's final season was only a few months away. The war was ceremonial now, and Davis was expected to lay down his weapons and make peace. It was not an easy thing to do. "To Al, they were the enemy," John Madden remembers. "I mean, Al was out there taking players and hiding them, putting them in motels and taking them to different places. He was signing players under the goalpost."

As the AFL commissioner, Davis came up with the aggressive plan to go after all the NFL's quarterbacks and sign them to big "futures" contracts, a move that infuriated the NFL owners and coaches and was the final blow that forced the established league to a merger. And now they were expecting Davis to forget about all of that and play nice.

Davis didn't know how to play nice.

So a lot was going on in the summer of 1969 when Madden took over as the new Raiders head coach. The two leagues had nervously sized up each other from a distance and were a year away from interleague play in the regular season. For the time being, the only way to measure up was during preseason games. This was the third year the Raiders had scheduled an NFL team for the preseason, and of course it was the cross-bay rival San Francisco 49ers. One evening during the off-season, Madden was invited to dinner by Davis and another owner, Ed McGah. At one point during the meal, Davis had to leave the table to use the phone. As he politely excused himself and walked away from the table, McGah leaned across the table, stared Madden in the eyes, and spoke in the urgent tones of a man wanting to reveal a deep secret.

"You know, there's really only one thing that you have to do to ensure that you'll keep your job," McGah told Madden. "All you have to do is beat the 49ers."

Because he had witnessed the intensity of the battle during his first two years with the Raiders, Madden had already been properly indoctrinated in the AFL's underdog mentality. He'd felt the indignant lash of the NFL, too. He'd listened to the constant look-down-their-nose superiority of the NFL establishment and the snide remarks from the pro-NFL reporters, too. Now his marching orders were being laid out by McGah.

"It was just a preseason game," Madden says. "But back then it was a lot more than that. [Davis and the other owners] had lived this life with Oakland kind of being secondary to San Francisco and then the AFL being secondary to the NFL. It was that important to them. In those days, it was so competitive between the owners that once they got a chance to face the NFL teams in the preseason, those games were big games, in many cases bigger than some regular-season games."

In the fifth and final game of the Raiders' 1969 preseason, before more than 53,000 witnesses in the Oakland Coliseum, the Raiders defeated the 49ers 42–28, and Madden passed his first test as head coach.

AS THE RAIDERS BEGAN TRAINING CAMP in Santa Rosa that summer, Madden was taking over a championship-caliber team that had won 27 of its last 32 regular-season and playoff games. It was a veteran team with its own peculiar personality. The renegade Raiders were just beginning to find their wild and unconventional spirit, and 33-year-old John Madden was not about to screw things up.

In Kansas City, Hank Stram was sending out letters to all his players informing them that whatever cool hair and mod fashions they had acquired during the off-season, when they reported to training camp, it would all have to go away. No mustaches, no goatees, no sideburns that fell below the ear lobe—but most of all, no damned long hair. Everything had to be trimmed so that it did not fall below the bottom of the helmet. He also had them wearing a dashing costume when they traveled to road games: custom-made black blazers with the Chiefs logo stitched onto the breast pocket, gray slacks, white shirts, and black ties. Uniformity was the order of the day for the Chiefs, right down to the precise way Stram insisted they huddle up like a church choir.

Contrast that to the culture of the Raiders. Madden had grown up with old-school, traditionally authoritarian coaches all his life. Yet when he was given his chance to take over the Raiders, he had been around long enough to understand that wasn't the Raiders' way of doing business. The first thing he did was streamline his authority down to threadbare simplicity.

He only had three rules for the wild and rowdy Raiders.

Rule No. 1: "Be on time."

Rule No. 2: "Pay attention."

Rule No. 3: "Play like hell when I tell you to."

This moment should have been documented as a historic turn in American sports culture. With his CliffsNotes approach to football, Madden had signaled the first seismic shift in the way modern coaches would conduct their business. "John Madden's style of leadership was based on a logic of emotion rather than on a logic of will," former Raider Pat Toomay would write years later. With little fanfare, Madden had quickly evolved into professional sports' first "player's coach," shattering "my-way-or-the-highway" institutional control. He was making a mockery of the buttoned-down control freaks who were quite successful on sidelines everywhere else. Madden was the perfect coach for the most imperfect team, a man who was young enough to relate to the rapidly changing sensibilities of the time without giving a shit what other people thought.

"What I always remember is that as a player I was a little rebellious about things I thought were stupid," Madden says. "I always thought some of those traditional drills teams did before games were a waste of your energy. I never wanted to do them. But most of all, when I was looking at these grown men I had to deal with—a lot of them were weirdos—and I knew the only rules I was going to have for them were rules that pertained to winning and losing. I didn't care what they wore. I didn't care about their facial hair. So I didn't ask for it much. Be on time. Pay attention and play like hell when I ask you to. There was nothing else I needed.

"Think about it. There really is nothing else you need. I saw teams back in those days; you had to fly in coats and blazers. That was the dumbest thing I ever saw. I hate shirts and ties. I wear sneakers everywhere, and I don't tie my shoes. So why would I force my guys to do that? We didn't have any pregame warmups, either. That was the dumbest thing. I hated that. I just let guys warm up on their own. What was the need for that stuff?"

Madden knew that with a group as outrageous as he had, the more rules you gave them, the more likely they were to break them. "And then you get into a problem with guys, because then they start thinking too damned much," Madden says. *"Okay, now that I broke that rule, is this one all that important?* When you narrow it down to three rules, there is no thinking. There are no questions. You don't have to weigh one rule against the other 25. It's very simple when you give them only three. They can't screw that up."

In an ego-driven business like coaching pro football, it takes an extraordinary man to have the self-confidence to not want to control every step and breath that his players take. Madden quickly proved himself to be that extraordinary guy. As new players arrived and witnessed the madness of the Raiders environment under Madden, their initial reaction was shock. Their second reaction was usually, "Oh crap, what have I gotten myself into here?"

When linebacker Monte Johnson showed up as a rookie out of Nebraska in 1973, he was certain that he'd fallen into some chaotic dream. "Oh, man! It was like the boy who had never left the farm and went to the big city," Johnson remembers. "It was a *big* change. We were so used to the discipline and following the leadership of the coaches. It was a 'Yes, sir' and 'No, sir' and 'Where, sir?' kind of a response. Then all of a sudden you land here, and you're hearing players yelling at coaches and screaming at the owner and calling them names. It was a ragtag crew. They were the misfits of the NFL. It was amazing [because] John Madden did such a great job of allowing individuals to take their personal issues that would have not been understood or even tolerated by other teams and let them goof around from Monday through Saturday, but as long as they showed up and performed on Sunday, that was what he was interested in."

Johnson remembers Madden telling the players very specifically what mattered most to him. "He told us, 'I'm *interested* in what you do Monday through Saturday. But I *care greatly* what you do on Sunday.'"

BECAUSE HE WAS NO OUTSIDER, MADDEN HAD A BUILT-IN EDGE. The players already knew him, already understood how he worked. When Davis promoted him, they didn't bother thinking about his young age or his lack of NFL head coaching experience.

"It wasn't a problem for us," says George Atkinson, who was in his second year with the Raiders in '69. "We all knew John before, knew he was a demanding guy even as an assistant. We also knew he was ready to be a head coach. Plus, he always treated us like men. Shit, we had guys on the team who were just as old or older than he was. George Blanda, Billy Cannon, Cotton Davidson. How are you gonna come in and start trying to treat these guys like we're back in college or something? It would never have worked. That's why we respected [Madden] right away because of what he brought to the table. He didn't come to the table with any of that gung-ho stuff. He came as a head coach and laid out what his expectations were, treated us like professionals."

Coming in to run a free-spirited defending championship team—and a team where the aura of Al Davis loomed as large as a threatening storm cloud or impressive monument (depending on your perspective and degree of paranoia)—required a certain amount of finesse, which Madden had in spades. As Atkinson would so eloquently put it, he wasn't going to be some punk-ass pushover, but Madden had an innate gift for knowing when to play the engaging big oaf and when to be the no-BS boss.

"It wasn't chaos," Atkinson recalls. "From the first day, he took charge. He knew what was important and what was silly bullshit, and he tried hard to never worry about the silly shit. He made sure you knew he was the guy, but the thing that he did that was so smart with this group was he empowered the players. We policed ourselves. He laid out the simple three rules and then we buttressed his rules with the ones we laid out too in the locker room."

Atkinson had met Madden the first day he arrived in Oakland as a rookie seventh-round draft pick out of tiny Morris Brown College. Atkinson had flown in from Atlanta for camp, and the Raiders 32-year-old linebacker coach met him at the gate and drove him around town. They clicked immediately. "George was always one of my favorite guys," Madden says. "Once I became the head coach, he was one of my go-to guys. If I needed something handled, if I thought there was a problem, I called George into my office, laid it out for him, and George took care of things. He was no snitch. This wasn't one of those deals where I had a locker-room spy. No way. George was a leader. He was a part of the core group of guys that made this all work. Because of guys like George, Art Shell, Gene Upshaw, Jim Otto, it was easy [getting the players to all go in the same direction]."

It was the perfect leadership blend. Madden's laws wove in seamlessly with the players' unwritten rule, which was you adjusted to the way the core worked or you got the hell out. "You had to hustle, you had to work hard, you had to know the system," Atkinson said. "There was no slouching off in practice. You had to practice hard. You could do a lot of crazy shit when you were away from the practice field, but when you got to practice, you had to understand that we were about winning."

OUTSIDE THE WALLS OF THE RAIDERS' LOCKER ROOM, America was changing rapidly. The counterculture movement that was sweeping across the national landscape in the '60s had somehow failed to pierce the authoritarian shield that encased football. But by the late '60s, even that was changing. Football's ultimate hero of the '50s and early '60s was Baltimore quarterback John Unitas, who came out of the Pennsylvania coal-mining country with his signature crew cut and black high-top cleats. Now he was being replaced by a mod, longhaired playboy quarterback in New York named "Broadway" Joe Namath. Namath was another child of Western Pennsylvania coal country, but he was as radical a departure from Unitas as possible. With his gleaming white low-cut cleats on the field and his fur coats off the field, Namath was the embodiment of a new world order.

Other symbols of change were less public, yet no less alarming to the pro football establishment. Drugs, booze, free-spirited hippies, and socially aware black athletes were coming into the league in larger numbers. While the Raiders were clearly different from most franchises, even well beyond the cutting edge in coping with these modern realities, they were not always a social utopia.

"There was a lot going on socially at that time that John took over," Atkinson recalls. "So there was a lot that John had to deal with at times because we had a lot of us [both black and white] who came in from the South, a lot of us were in the midst of all that civil rights uproar in college." And many of them came into the organization with a lot of dangerous emotional baggage. Black players who had never been teammates with whites and whites who had never associated with blacks were now being expected to play side by side, eat together, and, in some cases, room together. They came to Oakland with prejudices, hang-ups, and unspoken racial reservations that had built up over a lifetime of segregation.

In 1969 the Raiders were not that far removed from a potentially deadly nightmare. At their 1966 training camp, Rauch had to step into the middle of a racial skirmish in the locker room that involved one angry gun-wielding player.

The Raiders players were dressing for a workout when Rauch got a phone call in his office. When he picked up the receiver, equipment manager Dick Romanski was screaming on the other end of the line: "Somebody better get over here! There's a guy in here with a gun and he's threatening to shoot!"

Rauch raced out of his office and across the motel complex. He dashed into the locker room, where he found the most disturbing sight he could imagine. There were white players on one side of the locker room and black players on the other side. A player was standing in the middle of the room waving a gun, and Rauch was sure something awful was about to happen if he didn't act decisively.

"I had never experienced anything like that before, so I just walked into the middle of the thing and said, 'What are you guys doing? Are you all crazy?'" Rauch told writer Mark Ribowsky. "Like a fool, I reached out and said, 'Give me that gun,' and the guy handed it to me."

As suddenly as it started, the riot was over. Rauch then shouted at the top of his lungs that everyone was expected on the practice field in 30 minutes and anyone who was late would be fined. Years later, he revealed the back story that had led to this volatile moment:

"This had stemmed from what happened in the dining hall involving a black guy and a waitress, some bitch of a waitress, and one thing led to another, and we had a couple of white guys on the team that were notable rednecks. But here's the thing: it happened, and 24 hours after that there was a little talk about it here and there, but we never saw anything more of it, and I think Al had a lot to do with that."

Davis wasted no time addressing the situation. He called a team meeting after practice and laid down the law. He wanted everyone on the team to know that he was not going to tolerate racial hatred. "He really stuck his neck out and took a stand that wasn't all that popular with the white guys," recalls running back Clem Daniels.

Three years later, the Raiders front office took a sanguine approach to racial tension. In the coaches' office, there was no such blithe optimism. As a child of the more tolerant West Coast, Madden had black teammates most of his life. At a time when most college football teams were lily white, you could look at Madden's 1958 team photo in his senior year at Cal Poly-San Luis Obispo and see that he had six black and at least two Hispanic teammates.

But he was not so foolish to think that within three years intolerance had just vanished like someone had flipped a magic switch. This wasn't exactly lower Alabama, but like Atkinson said, there were a lot of Southerners in that locker room, and old habits and attitudes die hard.

"Sure, we had some issues, but it didn't last long," Atkinson recalls. "If John suspected something was wrong, he'd call me into his office, and we'd talk. He knew I was a guy who said what I meant. I didn't BS with anyone. If something bad happened, John asked me to address it. He oversaw everything, he delegated well. Guys knew it. It's how he got things done."

IF MADDEN HAD NOT ALREADY BEEN WITH THE RAIDERS for two years—or if he had the uptight, despotic traits of his head coaching contemporaries—the players' push-it-to-the-edge, walk-on-the-wild-side behavior could have been perceived as a direct threat to his authority. But this wasn't Madden's first trip to the puppet show. He knew all the characters and every one of their eccentric habits, and he was comfortable enough in his own skin to give whoever wanted some latitude as much as they needed.

During that first training camp, the 33-year-old Madden made one of his first celebrated bargains. Madden found it almost silly to insist that 42-year-old backup quarterback and placekicker George Blanda, who began his playing career in 1949 with George Halas' Chicago Bears, abide by the midnight curfew he had instituted for the rest of the team. "John figured that would be like putting his dad on curfew," recalls former Raiders defensive end Ben Davidson. "So Madden always deferred to Blanda.... Now, George liked to enjoy himself, so he would show up for morning practices bleary-eyed and out of sorts. So Madden decided George didn't have to be at morning practice. John also had a rule that we weren't to hang around the pool in swimsuits. Sunburns, ya know? George ignored that. Instead of practicing, he'd sit around the pool working on his tan."

After several days of observing the benefits of being George Blanda, Davidson, Tom Keating, Jim Otto, and a few other adventurous veterans who decided they too needed some latitude came up with a plan. "[We] figured out that if we hung out with George at night, Madden really couldn't do much about it," Davidson remembers.

Madden was not a big sleeper, and he would often be seen in the middle of the night roaming the parking lot of the motel. The players at first thought he was checking up on them (he was). But it was just as much because he was claustrophobic and a workaholic and stayed up all hours watching game films and practice films. One night when Madden caught the entire gang rolling in with Blanda well beyond curfew, Davidson looked at Madden, shrugged his shoulders, and let a devilish grin curl out from beneath his bushy handlebar mustache.

"Hey, somebody's gotta be [Blanda's] bodyguard, right?" he said.

ON THE FIELD, THE 1969 SEASON WAS GOING SMOOTHLY. The Raiders opened the regular season unbeaten through their first seven games with six victories and one tie. On October 19, before 54,418 witnesses at the Oakland Coliseum, quarterback Daryle Lamonica set a pro football record with six touchdown passes in the first half of a 50–21 victory over John Rauch's Buffalo Bills. They would lose only once all season, on the road in Cincinnati (31–17), and rolled into the AFL Championship Game off a 56–7 destruction of the Houston Oilers. Even with the largely disappointing loss the following week to the Chiefs (when an injured Lamonica threw three interceptions and Blanda came in and threw one more and missed three field goals), Madden's rookie year had been a critical success.

He was named *The Sporting News*' Coach of the Year. But the bigger prize, the Associated Press Coach of the Year, mysteriously went to a man who won only four games in 1969, Paul Brown, who led the Bengals to a 4–9–1 record in their second season of existence. To George Ross, an *Oakland Tribune* columnist, this was the unfortunate cost of doing business as an Al Davis subordinate. Ross was livid that anyone other than Madden could have been given the AP award but chalked it up to the fact that the writers who cast their votes could not get beyond Al's enormous shadow. "The curse on Madden seems to be he is Oakland's coach," wrote Ross. "The price of success here is the bum rap that Al Davis turns all the cranks, pushes all the buttons, calls all the plays. It simply is not so. At the outset with John Rauch in 1966, Davis called the shots a few times when the panic flags were flying. It's his system, and he can see from the press box when it is being loused up. The man in charge of the football in 1969 is John Madden."

Ross was stunned that the vote wasn't even close. Of the 30 AP voters, only nine cast their first-place votes for Madden. "It's past due for someone to blow a bugle or beat a drum," he said. "John Madden, his coaching staff, and his players deserve to hear someone say, 'They're Number One' in the American Football League."

Davis' imposing aura was impossible to escape, but Madden wasn't bothered by Davis' presence. In fact, he embraced whatever contributions someone of Al's vast football knowledge had to contribute. Madden was only 33 years old and still had a lot to learn. It would have been foolish (and self-destructive) to resist Davis' contributions. "Al and I were a lot alike," Madden says now. "We were closer in age than most coaches and owners. He was a young owner, I was a young head coach, and the reason it worked for us was because there were no layers between us. Between the coaches and front office people, there were only seven, eight, or nine of us. It wasn't like we had to have a big meeting anytime we needed to get something done. Al's office was not far from mine. As much as he knew about football, it would be dumb not to use him as a resource, and that's what I did all the time. We would talk every week, and he would have three or four things he thought were very important ideas, and I would listen to them. Never on game day, always at practice."

Because Davis was always there, always roaming the practice field, moving easily from one drill to the next, talking to players—essentially doing the same thing he had done when Rauch was there but without any of the outward resentment—cynical media types kept furthering the perception that Davis was drawing up the plays, organizing the game plans, and calling down to the sideline to tell Madden what plays to call.

"I read that shit that he would call plays in games, call down during games," Madden says. "Well, there was no way it could have happened. First of all, I never wore a headset. Look at any of those old NFL Films tapes and tell me when you ever saw me with a headset on. It never happened. The quarterback always called the plays in our offense. And the real truth was, while I gave the quarterback all the power to call the game the way he wanted to, I had done my work training them all week, every week since the start of training camp, to think exactly the way I think. So Kenny [Stabler] or Lamonica or Blanda may have been calling the plays, but it wasn't 'their plays.' It's *your* plays and it is a whole-week process where you are basically feeding the information into their heads every day in meetings and in practice. Short-yardage situations, this will work. Two-minute offense. Red zone. This is where working with Stabler was great. You could give him something, and it was in his head. 'This is the first goal-line play we want to use. This is the first play-action you want.' I was able to prioritize all of these for him so that whenever he got into a particular situation…*BOOM*…it's in his head.

"I would assume nowadays, it's the same way. The only difference is the offensive coordinator calls the plays, but the head coach has already made it clear what he wants. So let me make this clear: anyone who says Al was calling my plays is full of shit. Unless you were there, you can't know what was going on with us."

The perception of how much Davis meddled or controlled things behind the scenes—and how much he wanted the world to believe he was the puppet master—was radically different from the truth. First of all, Davis trusted Madden far more than he did Rauch. And he also knew that whatever "suggestions" he sent Madden's way would not be regarded with fear and loathing.

Did Davis send plays to Madden during the games?

Well, technically, no.

"He treated John respectfully," says Mike Ornstein, who served as Madden's administrative assistant for several years in the mid-'70s. "Al would have an offensive guy on the staff and a defensive guy on the staff who he could intimidate. He may not go to John Madden and tell him what to do. But he would tell somebody who'd be in that meeting, and everybody knew who that guy was. And he wasn't above sending messages to the coaches' box either during games. Al would write something down, give [it] to me or whomever, and tell us to run up to the guy and say, 'Al says [to] run this play' or, 'Al says [to] look at this.'"

By whatever means necessary, Davis got his message to the right people, and if it somehow filtered down to Madden through some elaborate chain of command, the coach didn't seem to have a problem with it. "Look, we all worked together," Madden says now. "Al was a coach and a damned good one. So if he had ideas, you take that up. Did I take suggestions from Al? Hell yes. I took suggestions from everyone."

Davis also respected Madden's ability to lead this wild bunch of renegades without any fear that it would somehow come unglued, and he hated to see Madden get shortchanged when it came to credit for the team's success.

Early in Madden's fifth year in charge, the Raiders had gotten off to an unusually slow start. Entering the fourth game of the regular season, the team would arrive in St. Louis with a 1–2 record to play the Cardinals. Lamonica had gotten off to a terrible start in those first three games. He completed only 13 of 30 passes for 183 yards, no touchdowns, and two interceptions in a 24–16 loss to Minnesota. He managed only seven of 10 passes for 63 yards and an interception in a monumental 12–7 win over Miami before a record crowd of more than 74,000 at the University of California. Four George Blanda field goals broke the Dolphins' 18-game winning streak. The week before the Cardinals game, Madden pulled Lamonica in the second half of a 16–3 loss to Kansas City when he completed only four of 12 passes for 53 yards and an interception.

On the Wednesday before the Cards game, NBC play-by-play man Jay Randolph received a surprise phone call from Davis.

"I know, Jay, that you've been assigned our game this week, and I wonder if you can do me a favor?" asked Davis.

"Sure, anything, Al," replied Randolph.

"Can you have breakfast with me Sunday morning?" Davis asked.

As Randolph looks back on it, he remembers that this was a rather unusual request. NFL owners rarely, if ever, invited the network announcers to breakfast the morning of a game, mainly because they had to assume the guy would be working in the morning prepping for the broadcast. "So before I agreed to do it, I called my producer in New York and ran it by him," Randolph remembers. "Well, he said if Al wanted to talk, I really had no choice, just as long as I could get to the stadium by 9:30 or 10:00 for the noon game."

So arrangements were made and Randolph arrived at the Marriott Hotel across the street from Lambert Airport, took the elevator up to the top floor, and knocked on Al Davis' suite door promptly at 8:00 AM.

Randolph and Davis talked for about half an hour over bacon, eggs, bagels, and coffee.

"Jay, I've got a problem with my coach," said Davis. "We've lost a couple of tough games, and it's really wearing on him. It's just awfully tough on him when we lose, and he's doing the best coaching job he's ever done, but no one seems to want to give him credit."

"Well, Al," said Randolph, "when you're talking about the Oakland Raiders, whatever decisions are made, on or off the field, the focus is on you. You're the owner, the general manager, coach, cook, and chief bottle washer."

"Well, I wonder if after a good play, maybe a first down, a nice drive to kick a field goal or score a touchdown, if you could find maybe 35 or 40 seconds to kind of point out that John is doing a tremendous job with this team?" Davis asked. "I'm not asking a lot. But I want the fans out there to know that John really is doing a hell of a job."

"I guess I can do that," Randolph said. "If you tell me he's doing a good job, I believe you."

Midway through the first half, Randolph found a moment to keep his promise. The Raiders had just kicked a field goal to cut the Cardinals' lead to 7–3. Randolph mentioned the way Madden had managed the quarterback situation and kept the team from falling apart. With Kenny Stabler as his starter, Madden's Raiders would go 9–2–1, win the AFC West, and advance to the AFC Championship Game.

"What I said wasn't a big deal," Randolph recalls. "I think whatever I said took all of 10 seconds. But the next day I get another call from Al. 'Jay,' he said, 'What you said yesterday really helped. John heard it, and he's in a much better mood this week.'"

9
THE RAIDERS' MYSTIQUE

"The autumn wind is a Raider, pillaging just for fun. He'll knock you 'round and upside down and laugh when he's conquered and won."

"The Autumn Wind," NFL Films, 1974

BY THE START OF THE 1970 SEASON, WITH HELP FROM HIS ancient quarterback, George Blanda, and the strength of NBC's cameras, John Madden and the Raiders were about to become one of America's favorite football teams. Because they were so consistently good, and because they were the most telegenic AFC team on the West Coast, the Raiders found their way onto NBC's late-afternoon doubleheader national schedule nearly every Sunday.

Coming off their sensational '69 season, the team started the '70 campaign with a disappointing 2–2–1 record. Much of this could be blamed on the inconsistency of quarterback Daryle Lamonica. Unlike a lot of coaches of his era, Madden was unafraid to treat his starting quarterback like a major league starting pitcher. If he played well, he could get a complete game. If he struggled, Madden wasn't above yanking Lamonica in favor of 43-year-old Blanda. On October 25, in the first quarter of a 7–7 tie with Pittsburgh, Blanda came into the game to relieve Lamonica and went on one of the most sensational five-week runs in sports history. Considering everything about Blanda—his age, his gruff appearance with those bristly salt-and-pepper sideburns, and his weekly late-game heroics—the aging quarterback and the Raiders were putting on the sorts of shows that would help to cement pro football's burgeoning popularity in American culture.

In his first relief appearance, he threw three touchdown passes to spur a 31–14 rout of the Steelers. The next week, at Kansas City, the

Chiefs were up 17–14 late in the game. The contest should have ended there, but Oakland's Ben Davidson was called for a late hit on Len Dawson on a third-down conversion. This caused a big brawl on the field that offset Davidson's cheap shot. When the play was replayed, Kansas City didn't convert the third down. They punted, and the Raiders moved the ball into field-goal range for Blanda, who kicked a 48-yarder into the wind to give Oakland a 17–17 tie.

The next week, the heroics came at home against the Cleveland Browns. With four minutes left and trailing Cleveland 20–13, Blanda came off the bench once again. With the ball on the Cleveland 4-yard line, the Raiders called a timeout.

"[Blanda] comes over and I'm going through [play calls]," Madden recalls. "'Let's do this. Let's go far right 16…. No, no, no, I don't want to do that. Let's go far left 7…. No, no, let's go near left 65….' So I'm just bumbling, stumbling, trying to find a run down there on the goal line, and George said to me, 'I'll tell you what, Coach, if you let me throw three slants in a row to Warren Wells, I'll guarantee you a touchdown.' I said, 'You'll guarantee it?' He said, 'Yeah, I'll guarantee it.' I said, 'Well, that's a hell of a lot better than anything that I have.' So first down, he throws a dirt ball on a slant to Warren Wells. Second down, he throws a touchdown. That was George Blanda. I'm the coach, and I'm thinking, *Goal-line run, this is what I want*. He's thinking, *What the heck are you talking about? Just put the ball in my hands, and I'll win the doggone game for you.*"

The Browns got the ball back and were driving when, with 34 seconds remaining, the Raiders got an interception. A few plays later, the drive stalled, and Blanda was looking at a 52-yard field goal for the victory. If he made it, it would be the longest successful kick of his career.

Money.

Raiders win again.

On the radio, the flamboyant Oakland play-by-play man Bill King proclaimed, "George Blanda has just been elected the king of the world!"

The next week at Denver, ho hum, Blanda stepped in again. Late in the game, with the Raiders trailing 19–17, Blanda threw the game-winning TD pass to Fred Biletnikoff with 90 seconds still on the clock.

Week Five: the Chargers and the Raiders were tied 17–17. Four seconds left. Blanda knocked through a 16-yard field goal. By now, his popularity had peaked, and the Raiders were must-see TV. Johnny Carson even performed a monologue about Blanda's ageless wonders. *Sports Illustrated*, *Time*, and *Newsweek* put him on their covers. Blanda's star status was also providing the furnace-faced, red-haired giant Madden with newfound national popularity. NBC's cameras loved zooming in on the combustible coach on the sideline, frantically leaping and waving his arms and looking like some excitable dancing bear in those baby-blue stretch Sansabelt slacks with his sideline pass flapping under his jiggling belly.

Sometimes he was celebrating the Raiders' good fortune, but mostly he looked like a stark-raving lunatic verbally assaulting the referees. By now properly infused with Al Davis' "us against them" mentality, Madden spent most of his Sundays raging against game officials he was certain were wretched souls whose entire goal in life was to screw the Raiders.

The TV cameras always caught him performing but rarely captured the X-rated audio to go along with the comic video. "We're playing Denver in Denver one year, and the side judge is a guy named Jack Fette," Madden recalls. "Well, Jack Tatum comes right on our sideline and hits a guy so hard—in bounds—he knocks him out of bounds and over our bench, and Fette comes in and throws a flag. Well, now [I] start yelling, 'You cocksucker! That wasn't a foul.' The ref marches off 15 yards on us, then he comes back to me and says, 'Hey, who did you call "cocksucker"?' and I say, 'There's only one cocksucker out there, and that's fuckin' you!'"

Out came another yellow flag.

Then Fette marched off 15 more yards, and Madden was beside himself with anger. He couldn't let the bleepin' ref get in the last blow. Madden had to take one more verbal swipe.

On the next play, Denver's quarterback Craig Morton threw an interception right into the hands of Oakland linebacker Phil Villapiano, and on the very next play the Raiders went in for a touchdown. Madden began racing down the sideline flailing his arms, hoping to get Fette's attention.

"Hey, Fette!" Madden shouted. "Well, that [touchdown] just proves you're a cocksucker!"

The next morning, Madden was on the phone to the NFL offices in New York because he knew a fine was sure to be coming his way for his vulgar insult of the referee. But as a preemptive measure, he called the supervisor of officials, Art McNally, to explain himself.

"Art, let me ask you something," said Madden. "Should a guy be penalized for telling the truth?"

"Well, that depends, John," said McNally.

"I want to tell you what happened between me and Jack Fette," Madden said. "See, I did call him a bad name, and I'm sorry for that. I shouldn't have done that. But he comes back to ask me who I was talking to when I cussed. Now, I could have lied and said I was talking to my equipment man or another player, a coach, the trainer, the ball boy. But he asked me to tell him who I was talking to, and I did, and then I get penalized, and I gotta tell ya Art, that just ain't right, is it?"

McNally paused for a moment.

"Well, John," McNally said, "that's just a man being a man."

For all his antics, that was the only 15-yard penalty Madden ever received in his 10 years on the NFL sideline. And he never received a fine for his uncomfortable version of the truth.

While the rest of the football world was discovering Madden to be a wonderfully likeable lug of an everyman, NFL referees and opposing players saw the coach in an entirely different light. He was not a warm and fuzzy guy. He was a possessed competitor who needed to win as badly as he needed to breathe. Tom Jackson was a three-time Pro Bowl linebacker who played 14 seasons for the AFC West rival Denver Broncos, which meant he faced Madden's Raiders twice a season.

"I didn't see that 'loveable lug' guy everyone sees now," Jackson recalls. "I sensed a guy who was very driven to win. He knew what the expectations were for that organization, and that was 'Just win, baby!' I thought Gene [Upshaw], Art [Shell], Jim [Otto], and Biletnikoff were all extensions of John on the field. I thought all the dirty shit they pulled out there was because that was the way John expected them to play. Those were his marching orders. We had a bitter, bitter rivalry with them, and for too long it was all one-sided because we couldn't beat them. From the time I arrived in 1973 until 1977, when we finally turned the corner against them, we lost six out of eight games to the Raiders.

"I will say this, and I will say it clearly. I still don't like him, I don't like them as a team. Fuck him, fuck them, I still hate the Raiders. But that is a mutual respect thing now. I found it easier to play against them because I didn't like them. And even to this day, when I see them at Hall of Fame functions or at the Super Bowl or wherever, we all just give each other that little head nod, like 'Yeah, what's up? And fuck you still,' because we all remember the wars the Broncos and Raiders went through, and a lot of that was sparked by Madden's direction."

A lot of people who didn't know any better always blamed Al Davis when the Raiders perpetrated their wicked ways on the football field, somehow absolving Madden from any culpability. Jackson never bought into that innocence routine. "The Raiders did lead the pack—along with the Chiefs—in that attitude of living outside the boundaries," he said. "And we all understood and accepted that those were the rules of engagement. I remember when young guys would come into the league on our team, I would always sit them down and tell our guys, 'When you get ready to play the Raiders, you better be prepared to protect yourself at all times and meet their attitude with the same brute force.'"

And what was the best word to describe that attitude?

"Oh that's easy," says Jackson, who is now an Emmy-winning TV commentator for ESPN's NFL coverage. "It was *bully*. But shoot, it's okay to be a bully on a football field, and the Raiders were clearly the bully on the block. They knew it, they carried themselves like it, and they were very successful at it."

During one game against the Raiders, Jackson grew so tired of being held by Upshaw, Oakland's Pro Bowl guard, that he complained strenuously to an official.

Jackson was screaming at the ref, "He's *holding!* He's *holding!* You can't let him do that!" when he heard shouting above the noise of the crowd. It was Upshaw, standing in the Raiders huddle and grinning at Jackson.

"Tom! Tom! *Tom!*" Upshaw yelled, finally catching the linebacker's attention. "If you're not cheatin', you're not trying."

Jackson laughs when he recalls the scene, and curses Madden under his breath. "Shit, all those folks want to blame it all on Al Davis," Jackson says. "But I knew better. I saw that man on the sideline encouraging his players. His message was pretty clear to me. That 'Just win, baby!' stuff meant, 'Do anything you want, just as long as we win. You win, I'm good to go. If it gets to the point where you might have to do something outside the boundaries, I'm good with that, too.'" And that, Jackson explains, is why in the closing minutes of Denver's 1977 20–17 AFC Championship Game win over Oakland, Jackson stood out near midfield, angrily waved his fist in Madden's direction, and screamed, *"It's all over, fat man!"*

"That comment wasn't meant as a swipe at him or them," Jackson recalls. "It was more of an, 'Oh my goodness, we finally overcame this enormous hurdle.' To me, that was our way of saying we put an end to the Raider swagger."

THAT IS THE SPIRIT THAT MADDEN HOPES PEOPLE WILL REMEMBER MOST about his Raiders, not the acid freaks (Chip Oliver), rapists (Warren Wells), convicted criminals (Jess Phillips), and other assorted lunatics and goofballs who filtered through the club's revolving door and created the anything-goes aura around the Renegade Raiders of the late '60s and early '70s. Thanks to Davis and personnel man

Ron Wolf, this was a talent-rich football team. There were nine future Hall of Famers on the Raiders while Madden was head coach: Jim Otto, Gene Upshaw, Bob Brown, Art Shell, Fred Biletnikoff, Willie Brown, Ted Hendricks, Dave Casper, and George Blanda. In addition to this Hall of Fame talent, there were at least 13 others who earned a minimum of one Pro Bowl honor during the Madden years.

"Here's the thing about reality and perceptions," Madden says today. "The reality was I had a good group of solid, strong-character guys; I mean, genuine solid citizens, and that's what made it work. Because when I brought in someone who wasn't quite as solid, they had to fit in with the solid guys, or they were gone. Gene Upshaw was as solid as they get. Art Shell? Solid. Jim Otto, Dave Casper, Willie Brown, and George Atkinson? They knew the difference between right and wrong. I just think a lot of things over the course of history get blown out of proportion. We had good guys, solid guys who created an environment where they were feared and respected. The weird ones all knew that if they didn't blend in, their asses were gone."

To men like Madden and Ron Wolf, who were responsible for assembling this menagerie of talent and attitudes, it was always quite simple. "Those [crazy] guys we had, they were never that vital to what was going on," says Wolf. "The Raiders had great locker-room presence. The leaders of that team were Jim Otto and Gene Upshaw, and later Dave Dalby. They controlled the locker room. The crazy guys wouldn't step too far out of line because of Jim and Gene."

But Wolf says it wasn't out of respect. "[It was] out of fear. They were afraid of Otto and Upshaw because they would have beat the shit out of you if you stepped out of line and caused anything to happen that prevented the Raiders from winning."

But people weren't just making up the stories about the wild behavior that went on within the Raiders family. Things could and often would go buck wild at the team's camp.

"It was a pretty tight ship in one way but a fairly *untight* ship in so many other ways," recalls Betty Cuniberti, who covered the Raiders for the *San Francisco Chronicle* during the 1976 Super Bowl season.

"Let's face it, they were the coddlers of guys who were not totally unfamiliar with the criminal justice system. In that way, it was a very loose ship. But because John always made it all about football, he didn't care about anything else. Nothing. If you could perform on Sundays, allowances were made for the rest of the week. You were fine if you did that, but you had to do it. I believe he looked the other way on a lot of things like [drugs and boozing]. I don't think he gave a shit about stuff like that."

So it bears repeating once again what Madden believed: "I'm *interested* in what you do Monday through Saturday. But I *care greatly* what you do on Sunday."

In the beginning, it seemed like an original thing to do. But by the early 1970s, as the drug culture was growing in football, it was a necessary evil for keeping his coaching sanity.

When defensive end Pat Toomay was traded by the Dallas Cowboys to the Raiders, he remembers the jokes that were always told around the NFL about the Raiders environment: "You didn't have to be a convicted felon to play for the Raiders, but it helped."

The Raiders laughed at those jokes, too, but it was with the uneasiness of knowing someone was hitting a little too close to home with their biting satire. Toomay, a football intellectual and published author, saw some noble truths to the Raiders' outlandish image. They weren't coddling scoundrels and reprobates. Al Davis and John Madden were offering them a second chance at football salvation.

But you better be able to play. They weren't opening up their doors to all the tired, poor, and huddled masses yearning to be Raiders. Exceptional talent was the value in this Faustian bargain. One of the most notorious reclamation projects Madden had to take on was defensive end John Matuszak. By the time the Washington Redskins were ready to kick him to the curb in 1976, head coach George Allen famously offered this explanation for why he was cutting Tooz: "Vodka and Valium, the breakfast of champions." Matuszak's rap sheet stretched back to his college days, when he punched and nearly killed a man he suspected had foolishly hounded around with his girlfriend. While playing for the Chiefs, Matuszak was arrested for marijuana possession and overdosed on booze and sleeping pills.

The Raiders were willing to take a chance on Tooz because Madden had three defensive linemen go down to season-ending injuries in 1977. If he could stay straight for six or seven months, Matuszak would be the short-term solution to the Raiders' troubles.

Or another headache.

When Madden took on these high-risk cases, he didn't spend a lot of time worrying about their rap sheets. He was more concerned with the present and future than their pockmarked pasts. As affable as Madden could be with his players, he was absolute about what would happen if the guy couldn't help. If he was a nutcase and he could play, he was an eccentric. If he was a boozer, criminal, or pill popper and couldn't contribute, he was an asshole soon to be unemployed.

Tooz was a special challenge for Madden. The public's impression of Matuszak was that he had come to Oakland and gotten his life in order. Behind the curtain, Toomay saw the truth. Tooz was always teetering on that fine line between good and evil. Madden reportedly had to kick two of Tooz's "dates" off the team charter when the three of them showed up at the airport buzzed and disoriented. Toomay was the victim of an up-close and disturbing episode on a road trip to Cleveland before the fourth regular-season game of 1977.

Matuszak and Toomay had been paired as roommates on the road, and the fun began as soon as they got to the team hotel after landing in Cleveland on Friday night.

"I grabbed a bite from the team buffet before heading up to the room to relax," Toomay wrote in an article for ESPN.com in 2007. "My roommate, I noticed, had met some friends in the lobby. After making only a token appearance at the buffet, Tooz headed out with them."

As the clock hit midnight, things disintegrated into an all-too-typical Tooz-day.

"Up in the room, I read, watched TV, until around midnight, when I started to drift off," Toomay said. "Then a key sounded in the lock, the door flew open, and in staggered Tooz. He was ripped. Hardly able to stand, he was slurring his words. *Quaaludes* was the word that popped into my mind. Weaving as he stood there, Tooz looked around, as if to get his bearings. He had the appearance of a man who'd been hit on the head with a hammer. To his right was our open closet, in which hung a single shirt. The shirt belonged to me. A Pendleton flannel, it was one of the few nice shirts I owned and the only one I'd packed for the trip.

"'Ohhhh! What a puuurrrty shirt!' Tooz exclaimed. At which point he took off all his clothes, yanked my shirt off its hanger, and tried to pull it over his head. Of course Tooz was 6'8" and weighed more than 300 pounds, while I was 6'5" and weighed a little under 250, so my shirt wasn't going to fit him—and it didn't. As Tooz struggled to squeeze his massive biceps through the shirt's skinny sleeves, both armpits ripped out, leaving the shirt in tatters. I groaned as Tooz, still naked except for my shirt, wandered out into the hallway and began banging on doors.

"In the room, I lay there, wondering what I should do. Before I could make a decision, however, Tooz was back, only now he seemed more disoriented than ever. Staggering over to the window, he tripped, losing his balance. For an instant, it appeared he might slam his head against the wall, but he recovered, grabbing the curtains for support. But then the curtains ripped away, and down went Tooz, crashing through the table to land with a thud on the floor. I helped him up, pushed him toward his bed. Collapsing on the mattress, Tooz reached for the telephone. 'Gotta…call…Tammmmmpaaa…' he mumbled. Then he murmured the name of his ex-wife."

Toomay just wanted to figure out how he was going to get a good night's sleep while trying to prevent Matuszak from indulging in further stupidity. Eventually, they were able to marshal up some support. The team doctor showed up, the trainer arrived as well, and they relieved Toomay of his responsibility as his brother's keeper.

"By now it was almost 1:00 AM…. Another knock sounded at the door," said Toomay. "I opened it and there stood [team physician] Doc Fink, grinning as he held up his little black bag. *Thank God*, I thought. *Finally, some real help.* But Doc Fink was a little giddy himself, since he'd also been down in the bar, drinking with George.

"'Tooz, you big dummy, what are you doing?'

"'Valiuuum,' Tooz groaned."

Toomay changed rooms and went to sleep. As he walked down the hallway the next morning to go to the elevator and get breakfast, he saw that the team trainer had slept in a ball in front of Matuszak's door to make sure he didn't go on another night crawl. "This was nuts," Toomay observed. "But it was also oddly touching. Sad, too, in a way. But touching all at the same time. And nuts. Mostly, it was nuts." As he sat in the ballroom eating breakfast from the team buffet, Toomay saw Madden enter the room and slowly make his way to his table. "He had a pained expression on his face, as if he'd swallowed something sour," said Toomay. "I'm sorry about what happened last night," Toomay recalls Madden saying. "It won't happen again. From now on, you'll have your own room."

It was Saturday morning, and Tooz had survived the night. By Sunday afternoon, whatever regrets Madden had harbored were forgotten when the Raiders routed Cleveland 26–10. Matuszak was a key contributor in the victory, and the Raiders' image had been burnished with another outlandish tale for the ages.

And Madden could reconcile it all by clinging to this one fine thread of truth: "Those crazy guys were never the core of our team."

10

THE "CONTROVERSIAL PASS DEFLECTION"

"No matter what happens, when they tear Three Rivers down, a monument ought to be built there. Even if they end up building a hockey rink there, they should put some kind of a monument to that area where the Immaculate Reception took place."

John "Frenchy" Fuqua, Steelers running back

ON THE EVENING OF DECEMBER 23, 1972, PITTSBURGH WAS IN THE grips of one of the most glorious bacchanals this blue-collar city had ever known. Rip-roaring drunk was perhaps the best state of mind to be in to truly comprehend what so many Steelers fans had witnessed a few hours earlier on the artificial turf of Three Rivers Stadium when, by a last-second miracle (or, depending on your perspective, sordid treachery by Pete Rozelle's feckless minions), the hometown Steelers had dispatched the Raiders 13–7 in a first-round AFC playoff game that would go down as one of the most remarkable and controversial games in NFL history.

With 22 seconds remaining and the Steelers trailing 7–6 on a fourth-and-10 play at their own 40, Pittsburgh quarterback Terry Bradshaw faded back to pass, rolling to his right to avoid two Raiders pass rushers. Bradshaw desperately flung the ball as hard as he could throw it across the middle to running back John "Frenchy" Fuqua, who was 25 yards downfield crossing the left hash mark. As Fuqua and the ball arrived at that hash mark, a third party joined them at this fateful intersection. Raiders safety Jack Tatum raced up with serious intent to separate man from ball. A violent collision occurred. Pretty much everything after that remains subject to debate.

The ball went flying backward, and for the briefest second, it looked like the play and the game were over. Then everything turned into a hazy, slow-motion dream.

There was Franco Harris, Pittsburgh's star running back, instinctively reaching down to pick the ball out of the air before it hit the artificial turf....

And there was Harris galloping down the right sideline, shedding one tackler and racing into the end zone for....

For what?

A touchdown?

A pointless frolic?

Just what the hell was it?

Hours after the game, colorful Steelers broadcaster Myron Cope was sitting at his desk in the WTAE television studios preparing for his 11:00 PM sports commentary. There were revelers all over town soaking in the suds and celebrating what by now everyone in America knew was a miracle finish for the Steelers. Pittsburgh 13, Oakland 7 is what was recorded in the books at the end of the game.

Cope was sitting in front of his typewriter trying to come up with the poetic phrases to properly describe what everyone had witnessed. Meanwhile, across town in a bar called The Interlude, a twentysomething Steelers fan named Michael Ord was toasting the team's victory. He stood up on a chair in the middle of the bar, grabbed a piece of silverware, and tapped it furiously against the side of his beer mug until it made a loud enough chime to pierce the deafening jubilation.

With his glass raised to the heavens, Ord looked out into the boozy masses.

"This day," he said, "will forever be known as the Feast of the Immaculate Reception!"

It was brilliant and blasphemous and the consummate phrase to capture as incomparable a moment in sports as anyone could ever imagine. Luckily for the slightly tipsy Ord, his good friend Sharon Levosky immediately recognized the genius of it all.

"We gotta call Myron Cope!" she screamed.

When his phone rang in the WTAE studios, Cope listened intently to the excited Levosky and knew almost immediately that this was indeed something beneficial.

"The *Immaculate Reception?* Tasteless?" Cope would recall in his autobiography *Double Yoi!* "I pondered the matter for 15 seconds and cried out, 'Whoopie!'"

When he went on the air that night, Cope put that lyrical label out there. Here was a worthy nickname that poignantly captured one of the most unique moments in NFL history.

Everywhere you went, people were now calling Franco's catch the "Immaculate Reception."

Everywhere, that is, except Oakland.

In the Raiders locker room, it was castigated in vulgar tirades. To this day, in the "Raiders Historical Highlight" section of the team's official media guide, they call it the "controversial pass deflection."

But in some angry circles in Oakland and cynical ones around the NFL, they were calling it yet one more example of how John Madden's Raiders were no different than John Rauch's Raiders.

They couldn't win the "Big Game."

While Rauch's teams in '67 and '68 went 25–3 in the regular season, they ended each season in defeat (a 33–14 loss in Super Bowl II to Green Bay and a 27–23 loss to the Jets in the '68 AFL Championship Game). Now here were Madden's Raiders, 38–12–6 in his first four seasons, and they had lost an AFL Championship Game, an AFC Championship Game, and this bitter first-round loss to the Steelers.

"Yeah, I heard that stuff about how Madden couldn't win the big game," Madden remembers. "But I used to say, 'Before the game, tell me when there's a little one.' We won a lot of big games. A lot of regular-season games, playoff games, games to get into the playoffs. We never lost to a bad team. We lost to some of the greatest teams in the history of the NFL."

Over the course of his first seven seasons as head coach, Madden's teams would end up playing in some of the most famous games in NFL history. Entering Super Bowl XI after the 1976 season, the Raiders played in 13 postseason games, winning seven of them. Unfortunately, it was the losses that people remembered. Gut-wrenching, controversial defeats that helped to define the ever-growing popularity of the NFL as America's new favorite pastime but cast Madden as the one who could get his teams *to* the mountaintop but never *over* it.

They lost to the New York Jets, who won Super Bowl III; the Kansas City Chiefs, who won Super Bowl IV; and the Baltimore Colts, who won Super Bowl V.

However, none of those games mattered more or captured an NFL-obsessed country's fanaticism more than the brutal, superb wars with the Pittsburgh Steelers. "Games that changed the game," former NFL quarterback and *Monday Night Football* analyst Ron Jaworski called them. From 1972 through 1976, the Raiders and Steelers faced off five straight times in the playoffs. Steelers versus Raiders had become one of the best rivalries in sports in the 1970s, maybe *the* rivalry in sports, because the games were intense, nasty, physical, and violently competitive contests that forged the AFC's reputation as the superior conference to the more established NFC.

"It was almost like the Steelers and Raiders *were* in the same division, because we met them so often in the playoffs," said Tom Flores, Madden's receivers coach. "It was an incredible rivalry because it was the same guys basically playing year in and year out. You'll never see that again, with the way free agency is and the salary cap. They had Noll, and we had John Madden and pretty much the same assistant coaches all throughout the '70s. And there were only seven coaches back then, too. So the philosophies of the teams did not change."

The hatred was deep and without any made-for-TV hype. Long before there was ESPN or NFL Network stirring things up artificially, Raiders vs. Steelers was perhaps pro football's grandest war. "It was a blood feud," Lynn Swann said. "We disliked the Raiders. We had no respect for them."

The foundation of the blood feud was essentially the Immaculate Reception.

THE OLD COACH ONCE AGAIN ROAMED THREE RIVERS STADIUM.
His fiery red hair had long since faded to a more distinguished white

mane. The stands were nearly empty as Madden and his CBS broadcast team walked the stadium turf the day before a 1994 game. Michael Silver, a writer with *Sports Illustrated*, was tagging along for the show because he was preparing to do a story on the old coach. As Madden mingled with the crew in between Pittsburgh's Saturday walk-through, Silver was talking with CBS reporter Lesley Visser.

"So Les, which end zone did the 'Immaculate Reception' happen in?" Silver wondered.

She shrugged her shoulders. "I don't know," she said before shouting across the field to Madden.

"Hey John, which end zone did…"

She barely got half the sentence out of her mouth before the old coach was transported back in time.

"It was wild," Silver says. "Lesley didn't complete her question, but she didn't have to. John knew. Boy, did he know. I mean, it was like he'd gone back to 1972 again. He was waving his arms wildly, pointing toward the end zone where Franco ran in for the score. Now he's cussin' up a storm. It's this steady stream of 'bullshits' and 'MFs,' one after another, interrupted only by these wild-eyed accusations of how the NFL screwed them. I swear you had to see it to truly appreciate how mad that play still makes him."

To go back to that game, to be asked to relive the haunting memories, was nothing new for Madden. The game's controversial result had never left the pit of his gut. He could flash back to it instantly, remembering every awful detail with vivid, angry detail.

If you are looking for omens that would foreshadow the despair of that regrettable Saturday, wind back the clock to 24 hours before the game. All week long, as Pittsburgh football loyalists prepared for the Steelers' first-ever playoff game, members of Franco Harris' "Italian Army" goofed that if presented the opportunity, they would swoop into the Raiders' hotel, the downtown Hilton, and kidnap the now 36-year-old Madden.

On Friday night, December 22, a sizable, unruly, and decidedly overserved mob of Steelers fanatics took their downtown pep rally to the front of the Hilton and proceeded to damn near create a spontaneous riot. Madden, as always, was hanging out in the lobby that evening, and he couldn't believe the sight before him. Several hundred out-of-control fanatics started banging their fists on the plate-glass window, and then someone tossed a beer bottle that crashed into a second-floor window.

It started one of those crazy chain reactions, with a city police officer falling down while trying to hold the crowd back and the cop getting stepped on and trampled. Police reinforcements were called in, and before you knew it, they were hauling anyone they could get their hands on in the crowd off to jail, including two of Madden's own players, who just happened to get caught up in the madness as they were returning from a movie. One of them, tight end Bob Moore, got beaten over the head by a riot cop's nightstick.

Through all the confusion, Madden watched the craziness at first with a bit of amusement that rapidly devolved into worry when he learned that Moore had his head cracked open and was about to be thrown in a Pittsburgh jail cell the night before a playoff game. Madden marshaled up whatever influence he could find on short notice to rescue his player and wound up at police headquarters trying to plea-bargain with the police chief and mayor to let his guys go free.

After much angry negotiating, Moore was released. As he and Madden returned to the team hotel, the coach had no inkling that this was only going to be the second-worst thing to happen to the Raiders on this eventful road trip.

The next day, as the game moved into the final minutes, things were finally starting to look up for Madden. Trailing 6–0 in a gripping defensive battle, the coach once again pulled Lamonica from a big game, this time replacing him in the fourth quarter with rookie quarterback Ken "Snake" Stabler. On three successive third downs, Snake produced a big conversion, and with 1:17 to go he raced into the end zone for a 30-yard touchdown that put Oakland ahead 7–6.

With 22 seconds remaining and facing a fourth-and-10 on their own 40, the Steelers only had time left for a miracle. In his autobiography, *It's Only a Game*, Steelers quarterback Terry Bradshaw recalled, "I wouldn't have wagered my momma's tooth on our chances." Chuck Noll sent in a pass play that he thought might be able to pick up the necessary yardage for kicker Roy Gerela to win the game with one swipe of his powerful and accurate leg. It was a play designed for rookie wide receiver Barry Pearson to go over the middle and pick up the first down. But on the snap of the ball, Bradshaw was immediately pressured by two Raiders pass rushers. He scrambled to his right and let fly a desperate fling across the middle to Fuqua.

Anyone with even the faintest sense of NFL history knows what happened next, or at least what the NFL "officially" said happened next. *Bam!* Tatum drove his shoulder into Fuqua. The ball sailed backward as if it had been shot out of a cannon. Harris scooped it up and raced into the end zone to make history with the Immaculate Reception.

And that's when things got nuts.

Referee Fred Swearingen never signaled that it was a touchdown. Instead, there was a long delay as Swearingen and his crew tried to figure out what to do. According to Madden, Swearingen told both he and Chuck Noll that he didn't know what happened and was going to call upstairs to the booth to see if he could get some help.

In the press box, reporters were being told that NFL officials upstairs were making a ruling on the play, but after the game, those same officials denied that story.

Now Madden was on the field screaming at Swearingen, who was telling him to get off the field because they didn't know what happened.

"I know you don't know what happened!" Madden screamed back at Swearingen.

Madden was enraged not because he thought Harris never caught the ball or that Fuqua touched the ball instead of Tatum. He was steamed and on the verge of losing his mind because he knew that something unprecedented in football history had just happened. "My argument was, the officials didn't call anything," Madden says. "They didn't call touchdown. They didn't say it was a touchdown. They didn't say it wasn't a touchdown. They didn't say any damned thing. Instead, they went and they had a conference. And that's why I ran out on the field. I mean, we're fighting for our lives...we're in Pittsburgh...and they're out there conferencing?"

So Madden went ballistic, and rightly so. It made no sense that Swearingen could not give him an answer or that NFL game officials—supposedly the best and brightest at any level of the game—were paralyzed and unable to make a decision. "In the history of football, a man crosses into the end zone and a referee either raises his hands over his head to signal a touchdown, or he waves it off. Period," Madden says. "They call a touchdown or they don't, and the damned game is over. But they didn't call it anything. How the hell can that be? Then they go over to the side of the end zone, and they have a conference. Then the referee leaves the conference and he goes over and he talks to someone on the telephone. If it's a freakin' touchdown or isn't a touchdown, you don't have to go through all this other drill."

Thirty-nine years later, Madden is still exasperated. "To this day, I don't know how they decided it was a touchdown when they didn't call it a touchdown when it happened. How do you do that? It still pisses me off," he said.

Raiders conspiracy theorists believe that some NFL suit in the press box told Swearingen what he was going to call. As he called up to Art McNally, the supervisor of officials, Swearingen finally decided (or was told to decide) that it was a touchdown. He put the phone down, came back on to the field, and thrust his hands in the air to signal a score, and the entire stadium erupted, but none louder than Madden or Davis. They knew they were getting knifed in the back and that somehow the evil influences of Pete Rozelle were working in the background to drive the implement even deeper.

Sitting in the end zone in NBC's makeshift postgame studio behind home plate, network anchor Jay Randolph was staring into a TV monitor watching the play roll back over and over again. He had seen the play live and wasn't sure what had happened. And now, after watching at least 35 replays roll back on his monitors from countless angles, he was no better prepared to go on the air for the postgame show and tell his viewers whether it was a legitimate touchdown or a botched referee's call.

Inside the Steelers' locker room on the other side of the stadium, Fuqua had showered, dressed, and completed his postgame interviews, so the Morgan State College graduate stopped by the visitors' dressing room to console his old college teammate, Raiders tight end Raymond Chester. Chester had to know. He looked at his buddy Frenchy.

"Did you touch the ball?" Chester asked.

"Yeah," said Fuqua. "I touched the ball."

By now the NBC crews were wrapping things up after the postgame show, and Randolph and his producer Roy Hammerman shared a cab to the old Pittsburgh airport to kill time before their flights home. They went to the United Airlines lounge for a few preflight drinks.

"As I walked into the room, there off to my right were Al Davis and John Madden," Randolph remembers. Davis immediately popped up and walked over to Randolph and Hammerman.

"Jay, did he catch the ball or didn't he?" Davis asked.

"Al, I don't know. I just don't know," Randolph replied.

Davis didn't have much to say after that and walked back across the room to rejoin the despondent coach, who Randolph said was suffering visibly from the loss. "I mean, he just looked awful," said Randolph. "He never took losses well anyway, but this one was the worst of all."

Randolph took a two-hour flight back home to St. Louis and was in bed before midnight. Hours later, he was awakened by the sound of a ringing telephone. Drowsy and out of it, Randolph had no clue what time it was. A few seconds later, his wife entered the bedroom and with an urgency in her voice said, "Jay, Commissioner Rozelle's on the phone."

It was 8:30 AM in New York, and Rozelle had already read clips from the Oakland and San Francisco newspapers. He wanted to talk to Randolph about something that he'd read that deeply disturbed him.

"Good morning, Commissioner," Randolph said.

"Good morning, Jay," Rozelle replied. "Could you relate to me exactly what you said to Al Davis at the Pittsburgh airport?"

Randolph retold his conversation verbatim.

"Well, [Davis] took your 'I don't know' to be a 'yes,'" Rozelle said.

According to Rozelle, shortly after Davis disembarked from the team flight back home and was met on the tarmac by local media, his opening remarks were that "Jay Randolph of NBC told me absolutely it was not a catch."

DAYS LATER, TIME HAD NOT DULLED THE AGONY OF DEFEAT for Madden. In fact, four days after the game, he outlined for the *Oakland Tribune* everything that was done wrong by the NFL officials at the end of the game. First and foremost, the real mistake wasn't ruling that it was a catch by Harris. The real mistake was ruling that Harris was an eligible receiver since, according to Madden, Jack Tatum never touched the ball, only Fuqua, which meant that no Steeler could have touched the ball legally.

Over the course of the previous four days, Madden said he had heard any number of explanations from the NFL, none of which satisfied him. "It's all a bunch of double-talk," he said.

Swearingen had claimed that he was not calling upstairs to get help on the call, only to inform McNally what his call was. "None of it makes sense," Madden said. That morning, the *Oakland Tribune* ran a frame-by-frame photo display of the play on its front sports page. Madden looked at the photo montage and broke it down as if he were examining the Zapruder film. Madden would glare at it over and over and over and over again, searching for some confirmation that would convince him that the Raiders' demise was a result of anything other than an insidious NFL conspiracy against Al Davis' Raiders.

"If you've ever seen a ball hit a shoulder pad, you'd know that ball couldn't be hitting Jack because of what follows in the next two frames," Madden told the *Tribune*. "It would make it impossible for the ball to drop down as shown in the next picture. It's an optical illusion created by the camera…. Fuqua's arm is there too. You can see it. I maintain that the ball is on Fuqua's arm and it flew out when Tatum hit him from behind. I still say Tatum doesn't touch it."

The Raiders would never forget the agony of this defeat or the way the lost weekend in Pittsburgh would devolve. "There's a riot outside the hotel the night before the game, one of our players gets clubbed in the head and arrested by the cops, then we lose the damned game on Sunday," Ron Wolf remembers. "Then we get to the airport, and there are blue laws in Pennsylvania, so all the bars in the airport are closed. How could the bars be closed after a game like that, huh? And it's Sunday, so there's nowhere to eat, either. And then we had plane trouble, and they couldn't get it fixed for like three or four hours. And now we finally get on the plane, and it takes forever to get home, but when we land, it's now December 24. It's Christmas Eve. You're supposed to be happy on Christmas Eve, but none of us were happy."

11

ALWAYS A BRIDESMAID, NEVER A BRIDE

"Defeat is a bitch."

John Madden

AT THE START OF THE 1973 SEASON, CHANGES WERE UNDER way within the Raiders franchise. They were the sort of changes that would signal a shift in the public's perception of John Madden's role in the organization and ultimately lead the Raiders to where they had never been before.

But it wasn't going to be easy. With change would come turmoil, with turmoil more championship failure. But Madden knew that for the Raiders to take the final step to winning those big games that had eluded them so many times in the past, he would have to go with his instincts—and for the first time publicly buck the long-standing philosophy of Al Davis.

After five years of serving as an apprentice, the 1973 season would be the breakthrough year for Kenny Stabler. This would be the season when he would become the permanent starting quarterback. It probably should have happened sooner, but Stabler knew from locker-room gossip that he was stuck behind Daryle Lamonica because Al Davis favored Lamonica's big arm. Davis wanted his quarterbacks to throw deep spirals downfield. He wanted the Raiders to use a fearless vertical passing attack that did not worry about what the defense was doing. Stabler was not that kind of quarterback. The lefty was an accurate nibbler who could throw ropes as receivers ran quick seam routes or perfectly timed slants.

By the end of the 1972 season, everyone in Oakland but Davis thought it was time for a change from Lamonica to Stabler. There was a crisis of confidence in Lamonica within the Raiders locker room now, as veterans noted how many times over the past few years Madden had pulled Lamonica after poor performances and went with either the aging George Blanda or the young Stabler. In the 1973 preseason, Stabler was convinced he had won the starting job. He hadn't. Lamonica would begin the season as the Raiders starting quarterback, but the team got off to an unusually slow start. Entering the fourth game of the regular season, the team arrived in St. Louis to play the Cardinals with a 1–2 record. Lamonica had played poorly in all three games. The week before the Cardinals game, Madden pulled Lamonica in the second half of a 16–3 loss to Kansas City when he completed only four of 12 passes for 53 yards and another interception.

On the Tuesday after that game, during which Stabler came off the bench in a can't-win situation, he confronted Madden in his office and complained about how he was being used. "John, that situation you sent me into on Sunday, down by 13 with just a few minutes to play, I don't want to go into one of those again," Stabler told Madden. "Start me, and I'll go all the way. But you can't count on me to go into situations like that again. I think I'm playing well enough to start, and I want to."

Madden, cool as ever, had a sharp reply. "I hate to hear you say I can't count on you in those situations," he said, staring right at Stabler as he brushed his hands through his thick red hair.

After an awkward moment of silence, Stabler said, "You can count on me, John, but you can count on me to play regular and do the job. I just don't want to go in and mop up somebody else's mess."

Again, no emotion from Madden. Just a firm answer that let the young quarterback know that the coach didn't respond well to player ultimatums. "Well, I'm sorry you feel that way, Ken," Madden said. "But we haven't decided to change our starter. That's the way it is right now. What you have to do is go out there in practice and just keep working hard."

Stabler went out to Tuesday's practice, worked with the second unit, ran the St. Louis Cardinals offense against the Raiders first-unit defense, and played out of his mind. The next morning, Madden called him into his office for another chat. This one was less confrontational. Madden informed Stabler that the next time he went into a game to replace Lamonica, it would be a permanent decision: "Win or lose, it's gonna be your ball, Kenny."

True to his word, Madden gave him control of the offense for good and was immediately rewarded for his faith. The Raiders went 3–0–1, and in his fourth game as a starter, Stabler set an NFL record by completing 14 passes in a row in a 34–21 victory over the Baltimore Colts.

With the sting of the Immaculate Reception still lingering, the Raiders would face Pittsburgh twice in the '73 season, losing the regular-season rematch in Oakland 17–9 in early November. They would meet again in the first round of the '73 playoffs, one day shy of the one-year anniversary of the "controversial pass deflection," and the Raiders kicked the Steelers' butts. This time, Madden's offensive game plan was brutally simple: run the ball all day over the left side of the line behind his trio of future Hall of Famers—Otto, Upshaw, and Shell. It was as dominant a running show as the Steelers had ever seen against their heralded Steel Curtain defense: 55 running plays for 232 yards in a 33–14 victory.

But the 1973 season ended just like every other season under Madden did, with the Raiders being eliminated from the postseason by the ultimate Super Bowl champion. This time it was Miami in the AFC Championship Game.

Fast-forward to the start of the 1974 season. The Raiders were primed for a great season. On paper, this was one of the best teams that Davis and Madden had ever assembled. The third week of the season, they traveled to Three Rivers Stadium to face Pittsburgh and seal yet another dominant Oakland victory, a 17–0 shutout with the Raiders once again relying on a potent running game that accumulated nearly 200 yards.

"That loss [in November] could have shattered our hopes and confidence," Steelers defensive tackle "Mean" Joe Greene told Ron Jaworski in the book *The Games That Changed The Game*. "That was the same team that beat us so bad the prior season in the playoffs— they booted us right out. Oakland had become our nemesis."

The Raiders left Pittsburgh and went on a rampage, winning 10 of their last 11 games to finish 12–2, the best record in football in 1974. Oakland won the AFC West, Miami won the AFC East (at 11–3), and Pittsburgh was the AFC Central champ at 10–3–1. The three best teams in the NFL had to trample each other for the ho-hum chore of wiping up the NFC champ in Super Bowl IX.

In the first round of the AFC playoffs, Pittsburgh would face wild-card Buffalo (9–5), the runner-up out of the AFC East, while the Raiders would host Miami in a game everyone was billing as Super Bowl VIII ½. The Dolphins hadn't lost a playoff game in three years, had been to three consecutive Super Bowls, and had won the last two in a row. The Raiders and Dolphins—and everyone else in pro football, for that matter—treated it like it was *the* championship game.

The game lived up to the hype, too.

After being on the wrong end of one of the most remarkable finishes in NFL history two years earlier in Pittsburgh, the Raiders experienced their own Immaculate Reception game when Stabler led the team to a 28–26 victory in the famous "Sea of Hands" game. Scrambling out of desperation, and with Miami defensive lineman Vern Den Herder dragging him down by his ankles, Stabler flung a ball into the end zone toward one black jersey and what seemed to be a million white Dolphins jerseys. Somehow Clarence Davis outwrestled two Miami defenders, caught the ball, and gave the Raiders the go-ahead touchdown with only 26 seconds remaining.

After the game, Phil Villapiano raced over to Madden and handed him the game ball. Madden clutched it in his thick right hand; thrust it in the air toward the stands; and did a rather odd-looking, awkward, high-knee prance as he was mobbed by fans and players.

Caught up in the postgame excitement, Madden was quoted as saying, "When the two best teams in football get together, great things will happen."

Years later, Madden says that was one of his biggest mistakes as a coach. "Now, beating Miami was big…. We were so excited and so happy about stopping their streak and beating the Dolphins, I got carried away," Madden recalled. "And I think the players got carried away, because beating Miami was big…. To beat a [Don] Shula team in a playoff, coming off a second straight Super Bowl win, we thought we had won a championship. I still look back at it and I think I made a mistake of letting us celebrate it too much. I got carried away, the players got carried away, because the next week, we had to play the Steelers in the real championship game. I think the lesson was, 'We haven't done anything yet.'"

Back in Pittsburgh, the Steelers noticed what transpired in Oakland, and head coach Chuck Noll—Madden's old friend—gave his players all the bulletin-board material they could digest. In a team meeting the Tuesday before the AFC Championship Game, Noll did not yell. He barely raised his voice. But when he noted what Madden and others said about the Raiders' victory, Noll spoke clearly so that no one in the room would misinterpret his message.

"The best team in the NFL didn't play the other day, and the Super Bowl wasn't played the other day," Noll said. "It's being played in two weeks, and the best team in the NFL is sitting in this room."

So now the real championship game was ready to happen, amidst the backdrop of an already contentious rivalry between two bitter opponents that had no qualms about displaying their hatred for each other.

This game would have all the delicious subplots you could want. The Raiders were the perennial championship bridesmaids, with four consecutive AFC Championship Game appearances and no victories to show for it. The Steelers were from a football town that for 42 years had never produced a single championship victory. And, oh yes, this was the third consecutive year that they'd faced each other in the playoffs—not to mention that the sting of the Immaculate Reception loss was still stuck in the guts and heads of every last Raider who competed in that game two years earlier, while the pain of Oakland's two consecutive dominant victories over the Steelers was certainly a prime motivator for Pittsburgh.

On December 29, 1974, before a sold-out crowd of 54,000 Raiders crazies in the Black Hole, another memorable Raiders-Steelers duel was about to occur.

This time, Madden was sure his team would break their championship losing streak. This was the best team he had coached, even better than the one-loss squad from 1969. This time there was no worry about cold weather or bad field conditions or crazy riots outside the team hotel. This time there were no distractions like having one of your players arrested the night before the championship game. This time, it was all set up nicely for the Raiders to break through and reach the Super Bowl for the first time since 1967.

Pittsburgh 24, Raiders 13.

Unlike the game in September, when the Raiders shut out Pittsburgh's offense and rolled over their defense on the ground, this championship game saw everything flipped. The Steelers pounded the ball on the ground (224 yards rushing), but more impressive was the way they completely dismantled Oakland's ground game (29 yards rushing for the Raiders). Said linebacker Andy Russell to Jaworski: "They appeared to have figured out our offense. This was a crushing loss. We came out of that thinking, *We've got to revamp this whole thing.*"

That's exactly what the Steelers did, promoting Terry Bradshaw to starting quarterback on offense and doing something that would prove to be revolutionary on defense, allowing Greene to take a practice experiment—lining up at a 45-degree angle off the shoulder of the opposing center instead of heads-up on the opposing guard—and use it in games.

They called it the Stunt 4-3 defense, and its impact completely disrupted the Raiders' running game as Greene kept shooting through the gap before anyone could get a hand on him. Still, it was not a blowout. The Raiders led 10–3 going into the fourth quarter, and with only 1:14 remaining in the game, they trailed 17–13. A week earlier, Stabler took the stage near the end of the game to produce a miracle finish. He had thrown 26 TD passes in the regular season and four more against the Dolphins a week earlier. Could he do it again against Pittsburgh? A holding penalty against Steelers cornerback J.T. Thomas nullified a sack of Stabler and instead gave the Raiders a first down on their own 32-yard line. The boisterous crowd in Oakland Coliseum was on the edge of their seats anticipating yet another Snake miracle finish.

In the Steelers' huddle, Thomas' teammates were telling him to not only forget about the penalty, but keep on playing as aggressively as he had done on the previous play. On the next Stabler pass, Thomas made an interception, raced 37 yards the other way, and hushed the manic crowd.

Two plays later, Franco Harris galloped into the end zone with 52 seconds remaining for a 21-yard touchdown. The Raiders were AFC Championship Game losers once again.

"We had the lead," said linebacker Phil Villapiano. "We were on top. All we needed was 15 more minutes of solid play. We just didn't come through. There's no crying this year. We just got whipped."

After the game, reporters crowded around Madden and his players. They were as gloomy as they had ever been. Madden understood what was coming next. The same criticisms he'd heard the past five years when a highly successful regular season ended in a postseason defeat, just shy of the Super Bowl. The rumblings about Madden not having what it took to get the Raiders to a Super Bowl would not be silenced now.

"Defeat is a bitch," Madden told reporters after the game. "Any time you lose, it's a big disappointment. There's no relativity to it. I can't say this loss is harder or easier to take than last year's loss in Miami and the one two years ago in Pittsburgh. A loss is total disappointment. I have to live with it and the consequences that go with it. When you lose, you're open to anything they want to say about you. Until you win the Super Bowl, you have to just sit there and take it.

"This was our best team. It was sounder and deeper than any we've had, and we had the playoff and championship game at home. It was our best chance to go all the way. That's what makes defeat difficult to accept. A whole year's work boils down to the fourth quarter. The draft, training camp, exhibitions and a 14-game schedule, the playoffs, and then this game. All of that time, and we're 10–10 with 15 minutes to play. I thought we would pull it off. I really did."

12

"WE'RE GONNA WIN IT ALL THIS YEAR..."

"I work 18 hours a day during the football season. I don't own a mountain cabin. I believe that a successful coach must be totally dedicated. I don't even play golf. If I don't give this job 99 percent, I'm a dead coach."

John Madden

FRUSTRATIONS WERE BUILDING ALL AROUND THE RAIDERS organization at the start of the 1975 season. Outside, there was labor unrest between the NFL players and owners. A failed 42-day players' strike in 1974 produced nothing but anger for the players, who were beginning to understand how underpaid and limited they were without free agency in their sport. It had been five years since the AFL-NFL merger, and with it came the absence of the bidding wars that created higher salaries. In 1975 average salaries in pro football were roughly $35,000 per year.

A year earlier, the upstart World Football League had emerged, and free spending started again. Shortly after Ken Stabler signed a new contract with the Raiders that would pay him $37,500 for the 1974 season with an option for the '75 season, Snake signed a "futures" contract with the Birmingham franchise of the WFL that would begin in the 1976 season, giving him a $50,000 signing bonus and guaranteed salary for seven years totaling $825,000 plus attendance bonuses that would give the Alabama native even more money based on how well the team's attendance did with him in uniform.

Snake knew this news could create a potential nightmare when he arrived in camp. Never mind the reaction that Al Davis would have, since Stabler had been afraid to inform the Raiders owner of the deal. Stabler said he didn't tell Davis about the negotiations because he didn't want him thinking he was using the WFL to get more money from the Raiders. "But I didn't think [Davis] could have changed my decision," Stabler wrote in his autobiography, *Snake*. "I wanted to get back to the South because that's where I felt my future lay. But I also knew Al Davis would be upset with me…. Like everyone else, I was always a little afraid of the man."

Stabler figured by signing a "futures" contract, that would give him two years to win "a couple of NFL titles" with the Raiders. But he was still anxious about how he would be received. He'd already received several pieces of hate mail from fans who were convinced that he would simply tank the next two seasons because, "You've got yours…you won't give a damn about the Raiders." Instead of being angry with him, Stabler's teammates were supportive, much of it coming from the strong clubhouse voice of team union rep and future NFLPA president Gene Upshaw. The failed '74 strike was not able to shake up the owners, but maybe these WFL contracts would. "Blame Snake? I think what he did is super," Upshaw told reporters. "I'd sign with the WFL, too, except I'm on a multiyear contract. But this is going to stir things up."

As Stabler reported to Santa Rosa in July 1975, Upshaw's prediction of how "this was going to stir things up" came true. When the Birmingham franchise defaulted on two payments due to Stabler in early 1975, he took them to court and his contract was voided. Davis, who couldn't find an adequate replacement for the AFC Player of the Year, did not act vindictively. He quickly re-signed Stabler to a new three-year deal that paid him $200,000 per season.

There were other dramatic changes happening within the organizational environment, and some within the Raiders fortress would say the changes were not all for the better. Jim Otto was finally forced to retire because his knees could no longer hold up. He was replaced by another stud center and team leader, Dave Dalby. Middle linebacker Dan Conners also ended his 11-year career before training camp. Those were natural transitions that John Madden was prepared for. There were other more significant changes that he wasn't thrilled about.

It was starting at the top, where Davis was noticeably changing. The pre-merger Al Davis was a pure football man, locked in on a maniacal personal quest to make his team and his league the best of the best. If that meant swooping in and hiding a valuable potential draft choice in some out-of-the-way motel so that the NFL couldn't find him or sign him, Al would do it. If it meant watching endless reels of film as preparation for a brilliant trade, then that's what he would do. If that meant taking a chance on a young coach from San Diego State with no NFL experience and grooming him to be his 32-year-old head coach, then that is what he'd do, too. Everyone who knew Davis in the early and mid-1960s said all his efforts were geared toward making the Raiders the greatest organization in pro sports. His commitment to excellence wasn't lip service. It was as real as real could get.

That Al Davis was one of the most uniquely talented men to ever come along in professional football. Coach, scout, general manager, league executive who helped foster a merger, and an owner who may have been overqualified for his job. That Al Davis was a living football legend who would end up in Canton, and deservedly so. But some of those same people who readily praised Davis for all of his contributions to the Raiders' success were now quietly questioning his motivations.

The same man who took pride in his ability to discover great coaches and unknown players had become not nearly so concerned with that as he was with finding sycophants who would tell him nothing but how great he was and willingly do his bidding, no matter how distasteful it might be.

It stopped being about the team and started being all about Al. Davis was beginning to do things that he had never done before. He was sprinkling yes-men throughout the organization, some of them on the coaching staff. He could easily intimidate these men and make sure that they did his bidding. Like Madden's executive assistant Mike Ornstein would say, there were men in that coaching booth that Davis knew he could manipulate.

He didn't have to go through Madden during games; he simply sent slips of paper into the coaching booth through his gofers. But

Madden was also learning how to fortify his position. He had already won five division titles along with more than 70 percent of his games, and he had taken the Raiders to an AFL Championship Game, three AFC Championship Games, and been named the AFC Coach of the Year. His Raiders teams had won more than twice as many games as any Davis-coached teams. And now people were starting to notice.

"Remember how when John first took the job it was 'Al Davis' Raiders...*with John Madden*,'" said John Robinson. "Then it was 'Al Davis *and* John Madden.' Then with the more success that John had, people started saying it was 'John Madden's Raiders...*with Al Davis*.'"

In 1975 Madden kept a longtime promise to his buddy Robinson. When they were both starting out in the coaching business, they often talked about how one day when one of them got a great head coaching job, he would hire the other guy on his staff. So when Madden needed a running backs coach in 1975, he brought Robinson in from the University of Southern California, where he was an offensive assistant to John McKay. Madden needed Robinson around. He was a friend, first and foremost, and his loyalties weren't in question. Robinson was able to see things going on around the organization that his best friend was too preoccupied to notice.

Robinson's bluntness would fill a void on the coaching staff, which was overrun with assistants who were too insecure to challenge Davis' strong opinions, even if privately they disagreed with them. Right off the bat early in training camp, Robinson displayed his loyalty to his best friend over Davis when Davis was hell-bent on making sure that a player he drafted in 1974—a sixth-rounder from UCLA named James McAlister—made the team.

Davis had a problem. In Robinson, he had someone on the staff whose loyalties were to Madden first, and Davis went out of his way to display how much he didn't particularly like it. It was over McAlister that Robinson had his first spirited confrontation with Davis, and McAlister was one of those players the old Al Davis would never have signed, but the "new" Davis would.

McAlister was a big and fast former world-class track man and a star running back at UCLA who was a first-round pick by the World

Football League's Southern California franchise. Davis saw him play that one season in the WFL (531 yards rushing, 65 catches for more than 700 yards) and determined that McAlister would be perfect for the Raiders. Robinson had scouted McAlister in high school and coached against him in college. So while Davis thought he had discovered another one of those world-class sprinter/football players who would be a star in his offense, Robinson knew otherwise.

"He wasn't a great football player," says Robinson. "He was a track guy. Not a tough guy. Not a very good football player at the pro level, and I could tell that right away during two-a-days. But Al loved him. So one day early in camp, he and I start talking about the running backs on the roster, and he starts going on and on about McAlister, and he asks me what I think of him.

"I said, 'He can't play, Al, and if we're smart we should try to make a deal for him now before the preseason games start and everyone else finds out what a stiff he really is.'"

Davis exploded. He took the criticism of McAlister as a personal attack on his ability to evaluate players and bombarded Robinson with a vulgar tirade.

"You cocksucker, you fuckin' cocksucker. I just want you to know something! I hire all the assistant coaches. I hire them all, but I didn't hire you! You're John's guy, dammit, and you know what that means? That means you better be right about McAlister, because if you're not, I'm fuckin' firing your ass! Do you hear me? I'm gonna fuckin' fire your ass if you're wrong!"

Robinson wasn't wrong.

McAlister never played a down for the Raiders. His NFL career lasted three unspectacular seasons, two with Philadelphia and one with New England. He gained a grand total of 677 yards rushing and scored three touchdowns.

ROBINSON WOULD ONLY SPEND THE 1975 SEASON in Oakland before heading back down the West Coast to Los Angeles, where he was named head coach at Southern California. But in the short time he was with the Raiders, Robinson could see that his buddy, who used to laugh and smile and be the most normal human being he knew, was suddenly miserable. He was angry and uptight and growled at the media and everyone else because of the pressure that Davis had put upon him.

"John had a tough workplace. Working for Al Davis takes an additional 10 years off your life," said Ron Wolf, the longtime Raiders personnel director. "I remember thinking on a few of those nights driving him home from work, *Shit, if it's this bad, why are you doing it?* I never told him that, but I was thinking it. He was sucking down bottles of Pepto-Bismol. Oh, it was awful. Al would wear your butt out. But it worked. They were very successful."

Madden was always the first one in the building every morning. Robinson would pick him up every morning around sunrise, and on the drive to work, he could already see how miserable Madden was. This wasn't the John Madden he grew up with and knew all his life. This wasn't the guy who was always the life of the party. This was a man who was suffering, and Robinson did all he could to lighten up Madden's mood.

"I used to laugh at him when we were driving to work," says Robinson. "He got all uptight and would be sitting in the front seat just grumbling about everything."

Robinson begins imitating Madden's voice, and it isn't the famous, stream-of-consciousness bundle of joy America would easily recognize.

"'I'm not talking to anybody today. I'm mad about this…I'm mad about that…. Arrrrgggghh…. Grrrrrrrr…rrrrrrrrr.'"

Robinson would look across the front seat at Madden and laugh. Then he would slow the car down and make Madden look out the window at the people on the street.

"Hey, look over there, John," Robinson would say. "Look over there on the bench at the bus stop. There's a woman and her children. She's a cleaning woman, and she's on her way to work, but she's getting her kids off to school first. They're normal people, John. They have real jobs and real problems. Look at 'em, John, look at 'em."

And what was Madden's reaction?

"Oh, he just grumbled some more and called me names," says Robinson. "But I understood what was going on. This was pressure coming out of him. This was all that pressure, and Al put all that on him. Al would tell him, 'Don't do interviews, don't talk to anyone.' And I think some of that was as a result of how their statures were changing around the franchise.

"And when that happened, I think there was a little tension there. But the thing is, even with all this tension, I can't explain it, but they were always good friends. Al had great respect for John and, to this day, you can see how close they both are. You can't fake that friendship and respect that they still have for each other to this day."

But the tension was real, and it was tearing Madden apart. After five years on the job, his friends were seeing the results of how working for Al Davis was taking its toll. When he walked into the building around 7:00 AM, Madden was usually the first one from the football side of the organization to arrive. There were player meetings in the morning and practice in the early afternoon. And that was the best time of his long day, because he was either on the field or roaming the locker room talking to players. But just as the players were leaving the building in the afternoon, Madden would go to his office to get away from it all, steeling himself for the grueling late night that he knew lay ahead.

Coworkers knew that sometime around 3:00 PM each day, Madden would go to his office, close the door behind him, and take a three-hour nap to get ready to deal with the ritual late-night encounters with Davis. The football people in the building knew how nuts this was, how Davis would grind John and the coaches for three hours from 6:00 to 9:00, then they'd take a dinner break for an hour before Madden would have to return for more one-on-one meetings with Davis that would last until after midnight.

Every night, Madden would leave the Raiders' offices with either Robinson or Ron Wolf or someone else to drive him home, and he would sit in the car even more miserable than he was on the ride to work, drinking entire bottles of Pepto-Bismol like they were soda pop. The players would see him walking around the facility with that familiar pink bottle close at hand, and they saw him biting down on towels during practice, and they knew that he had an ulcer.

Madden was in the early stages of turning into a coaching burnout victim, only he didn't know it at the time. He had developed all the worst symptoms, but it would take a few more years—and several significantly disturbing life-altering events—to push him over the edge.

After he became a famous television broadcaster, Madden was struck when he saw those same symptoms in another hard-driven, obsessive head coach named Dick Vermeil. Vermeil was in his first NFL coaching stint as the head coach of the Philadelphia Eagles, and during a visit to Philadelphia to prepare for a CBS broadcast, Madden recognized that Vermeil was on the verge of burnout, too. "There's a certain sort of personality," Madden would say, "that worries about things he can't control. He's going to burn out. I don't give a damn how long it takes. It's going to get him. With that kind of personality, you can coach for 10 years in the pros. That was my limit. Dick Vermeil was a little less than 10. Sid Gillman's the other type. Sid just thrives on it…. His age tells him he can't live with it, but his mind says he can't live without it. George Allen [was] the same type. They can't live without it."

Here he was, only six years into his head coaching career, and the 39-year-old John Madden was privately wondering how much longer he could keep up this sort of grinding and self-destructive pace.

MADDEN FOUND SANCTUARY IN BEING AROUND HIS PLAYERS.
In the locker room, in the meeting rooms, on the practice field—these were the best times of the day for Madden. "He loved being around the guys," says Fred Biletnikoff, the former Raider and NFL Hall of Fame receiver. "John was a head coach who loved hanging out in the locker room. You'd see him walk in there in the morning with a cup of coffee and a newspaper stuffed under his arm. He'd grab a stool and just listen to the guys tell stories. He wanted to know what happened

the night before when the guys had Camaraderie Night. He'd pull up in the middle of it all and go, 'Okay, what happened?'"

This was his refuge from the increasing pressure that he was feeling whenever he had to deal with everything and anyone else. Even when the players were acting nutty, being around them seemed to be a soothing tonic. So, in the early days of training camp in 1975, when Ted Hendricks joined the Raiders, the man they called the Mad Stork was quickly embraced as another lunatic who added the proper amount of spice to this crazy gumbo of humanity that Madden had assembled. Midway through two-a-days, the team moved practice to nearby Sonoma State College to change the setting and break the monotony of working every day on the motel's practice fields. Just outside the school gates, an equestrian show was going on, and there were beautiful horses trotting around the adjacent fields. As the players assembled on the far end of the stadium field to begin stretching, Madden noticed that one player was not there.

Ted Hendricks was breaking one of Madden's three simple rules: Rule No.1: Be on time.

"So where the hell is Hendricks?" Madden's voice boomed across the practice field. His question was met with a lot of shoulder shrugs and troubled expressions.

A few seconds later, Madden got an answer to his question. Down on the other end of the field, the gate opened wide. In a cloud of dust, the entire team saw something that even by Raiders standards was an unusual sight at practice. Ted Hendricks, in his full practice uniform and wearing a German helmet with the No. 83 painted on both sides, sitting astride a horse, came galloping onto the field, rode right to the 50-yard line, and dismounted.

There were several immediate reactions that rippled through the team upon the Mad Stork's arrival. One was instantaneous laughter.

"We all just looked each other and said, 'Yep, fits right in,'" recalled Ken Stabler.

That was immediately followed by a quick glance over at Madden. On any other team in professional football, this sort of outrageous stunt would have been regarded as a needless distraction. The typical authoritarian coach of the day would have fairly exploded in a no-fun-allowed rage.

But that wasn't John Madden's approach. He stood there laughing, just like everyone else.

"Stuff like that never bothered me because [Hendricks] always played his ass off," Madden says. "I actually kind of knew he was going to do something like this. So here he comes across the field riding a horse, and yeah, everyone's looking for a reaction. What was my reaction? 'Yeah, that's great Hendricks, that's just great. Now get rid of the horse and get the fuck out here for practice.'"

The team exploded into even more hysterics because Madden handled it perfectly. "John never got worked up over stuff like that," says George Atkinson. "He had as much fun with it as we did."

Hendricks quickly dispatched with the horse, and practice went on without a hitch. "It's things like that where it's just easier to go along with it," says Madden. "You have to remember back then, we were in training camp for over two months. We had six preseason games. Every practice was in pads, and there were two-a-days every day. So sometimes you needed things to break the monotony of training camp, and that sure as hell did."

In the early 1970s, professional football players were not exactly raking in the big bucks. Even in the aftermath of the old AFL-NFL salary wars—and with the brief appearance of the World Football League—the salary explosions were not widespread around the NFL. The players might have been stars on television, but they were blue-collar stars who weren't concerned about endorsement deals with sneaker companies or guaranteed salaries and bonuses. In 1975, after a two-year labor dispute with the owners, the players won a major decision when the federal courts struck down the so-called Rozelle Rule, allowing hints of free agency in the NFL for the first time.

The salary boom was on its way to football, but for the time being, it was still a blue-collar sport, and the Raiders epitomized that common-man attitude in every way possible, enjoying the most obvious perk of the profession—being able to live life on the edge as true celebrities in their football-crazed town.

"They were great guys," says Robinson. "But since they weren't making money, they were wild off the field. They played hard, they partied hard. They drove trucks and motorcycles, and they created a lot of chaos, and John understood and tolerated it because he knew once they came to work, he would push them hard. So off the field, like I said, he tolerated a lot of stuff. That is, until he said, 'Okay, let's go!'"

Not everyone saw it that way. In May 1975, Daryle Lamonica, who had been benched in 1974 by Madden and finally escaped the Raiders by playing out his option to sign with the World Football League Southern California Sun, ripped into Madden on his way out the door. "Madden has completely lost control of the situation there," Lamonica told the *Oakland Tribune*. "He doesn't have any discipline over the team and as a consequence, the players don't have the pride it takes to go all the way."

"Man for man, Oakland has the best talent in the National Football League," Lamonica charged. "Pittsburgh shouldn't have been the Super Bowl champion last year, Oakland should have. But players came to meetings late in Oakland and think everything is a big joke. They don't fear Madden and the players should fear the man they're playing for. There's no team spirit anymore. Can you believe there hasn't been a team meeting in two years? It's no longer a team. It's a bunch of individuals…. I won't say I wouldn't play for Oakland again, but I wouldn't play as long as John Madden's there. I won't let anyone take my confidence again."

Inside the locker room, the players who remained behind didn't quite see it Lamonica's way. Veterans like Willie Brown, Atkinson, Stabler, and Biletnikoff said Madden expected you to practice and play your butt off with no reservations. What Lamonica saw as "lack of control," they saw as Madden always treating his players like grown men, even when they gave him little reason to treat them that way.

"John could be intense when he needed to be," says Biletnikoff. "You could see that by the way he acted on game days. But with us, he was an extremely understanding guy. There was no real comparison between the personalities of John Rauch and John Madden. You see, John knew there were times when he had to loosen up the practices. Whether it was eliminating an afternoon meeting or whatever. John had a great feel for that. He had that great sense what the team needed. It wasn't like he was giving everyone the keys to the cell."

Repetition was Madden's thing. He wanted no mistakes. He prided himself on how disciplined his teams could be. "We didn't make mistakes," he says. "And if we had penalties, it wasn't because of a lot of mental errors. No offsides, no illegal motion. Our teams were smart, our teams were disciplined. I wanted them to understand exactly what we were going to do in every situation."

In five of Madden's 10 seasons as Raiders head coach, his team was among the least penalized teams in the NFL. In 1975 they were the least penalized, in '74 the second-least penalized, and in '77 and '78 only two teams had fewer penalties called on them than Oakland. In 1973 they slipped to ninth, but the point is, Madden did run a disciplined team despite their renegade reputation. The players knew he would keep them on the field forever if they weren't paying attention. He would stand on the sideline with that towel wrapped around his neck, and he would curse his head off if the play wasn't run exactly like he wanted it. Presnap penalty? Run it again. Ball not thrown to the proper shoulder? Run it again. Any missed assignment, any lapse in attention? Run it again.

The only object was to get everything exactly right so that there would be no surprises. Madden was a firm believer in Al Davis' philosophy that you don't take what the defense gives you. You take what you want, even if they know what you're going to do, because the Raiders will always outexecute you.

"No matter who we played, no matter what time of day, wake us up and we'd play," says Willie Brown. "If they want to play us in the parking lot, we knew the way John had prepared us, we would win the football game."

John Madden fulfilled his boyhood dream of becoming a professional football player after being drafted by the Philadelphia Eagles in 1958. A knee injury during training camp ended his career.

Hired as an assistant coach by the Raiders
in 1967, Madden took over as the team's
head coach in 1969. At 32 years old, he
was the youngest coach in professional
football.

Known as a players' coach, Madden's rowdy Raiders lost five AFC Championship Games in his first seven years. Getty Images

Madden's commitment to the Raiders often left him little time to spend with his wife, Virginia, and two sons, Mike and Joe.

Madden, Al Davis, and the Raiders finally reached the mountaintop after the 1976 season, defeating the Minnesota Vikings 32–14 in Super Bowl XI.

Madden retired from coaching after 10 seasons and entered the second phase of his football life as a color commentator for CBS Sports.

The former coach's football knowledge and everyman personality gave him credibility with viewers and made him a fan favorite.

Madden's crossover appeal led to numerous promotional appearances, including hosting Saturday Night Live in 1982.

A crippling fear of flying caused Madden to crisscross the country hundreds of times in his own customized bus, dubbed the Madden Cruiser.

Madden's eponymous line of video games is one of the best-selling titles of all time and is closing in on 100 million copies sold as of 2011.

After being denied entry for years, Madden was finally inducted into the Pro Football Hall of Fame in 2006. His fellow honorees that year included Troy Aikman, Reggie White (represented by his wife, Sara), Warren Moon, and Rayfield Wright.

Madden was presented in Canton by Raiders owner Al Davis, and the coach thanked his former boss for his decades of friendship and support.

For three decades, Pat Summerall and John Madden formed arguably the most popular sports broadcasting team in American history.

After three seasons working on NBC's Sunday Night Football *with play-by-play man Al Michaels, John Madden announced his retirement from the booth in 2009.*

KENNY STABLER WAS BEING GROOMED ON THE FIELD and off the field by George Blanda. The ageless quarterback took an immediate liking to Stabler, and in the kid's early years with the team began to show him how to think the game. Since Stabler did not have a cannon arm, Blanda tried to teach him to rely on his accuracy as a passer and his knowledge of his own offense and every imaginable defense he would face. Off the field, Blanda knew how to have a good time. He preferred a hard liquor diet in the evenings and even stashed bottles of mixed cocktails in Maalox bottles in the trainer's room.

He was the perfect tutor for Stabler, who also loved the nightlife, chased skirts, and enjoyed strong beverages. They were part of the Rat Pack culture of the times, chasing women and drinking booze. Since Madden couldn't bring himself to put a curfew on Blanda, the best place to be if you were a notorious carouser like Stabler was with Blanda on the road.

"I remember one of our road games [in 1975], I think it was Denver, and I had bed check duty," recalls Robinson. "Well, Kenny and Blanda and Pete Banaszak were all late. I had to go tell John, who was always nervous anyway. They're all out 45 minutes after curfew, and when I tell John, he starts cursing up a storm. So now we're both out in the courtyard of this hotel just waiting for them. And here they come strolling in like they didn't have a care in the world. Well, John starts screaming at them."

The high-strung Madden was cursing at everyone, angry not necessarily because they were late but because he was worried out of his mind that something bad had happened to three of his important players.

"What the fuck were you thinking?" he screamed.

Robinson stood right beside him, watching. Before Blanda or Banaszak could say a word, Stabler interrupted the Madden tirade. In his cool Southern drawl—and with his breath reeking of liquor—Stabler grinned at his red-faced coach. "Don't worry about it John, we'll kick these guys' asses easy," Stabler said, grinning as he casually stumbled away and headed to his room.

A few hours later, Oakland did beat the Broncos easily. It was a lopsided 42–17 victory, and Stabler completed 11 of 15 passes for 166 yards, two touchdowns, and a 121.1 pass-efficiency rating. This was the sort of compromise Madden seemed to be willing to make with his players. If you could stay out half the night and play like hell on Sunday, that was an allowance he could afford. The art to coaching the Raiders was to deal with the craziness if it directly or indirectly led to winning football games. Madden believed there was something in the culture of pro football that bred men who loved living on the edge. If you took that renegade edge away from them, restricted them with too many rules and regulations, it might take away some essential trait in their competitive personalities. So even if it drove him to nightly anxiety fits, he'd just grab a bottle of Pepto-Bismol and deal with the angst.

"I think there was part of that kind of behavior that John actually liked," says Robinson. "He fostered all that sort of thing."

Biletnikoff, who also flirted with a few curfew violations in his time, didn't necessarily believe that Madden fostered the behavior as much as he tolerated it as a necessary evil of the job. "He just wanted guys to act mature, like a pro football player," says Biletnikoff. "And he did not like having problems off the field."

Whatever maladjusted nonsense he tolerated, Madden knew his team was among the best in the game. Their misfortune was that, at their peak, they were playing in the Golden Age of the AFC. Think about the teams they were facing in the late '60s and early '70s. The Kansas City Chiefs were innovative, intimidating, and loaded with future Hall of Famers. The Jets were the first AFL team to win a Super Bowl. The Miami Dolphins went to three consecutive Super Bowls between 1971 and 1973 and finished the '72 season a perfect 17-0. And then there was the Pittsburgh Steelers, winners of four Super Bowls in the decade.

In each AFC Championship Game that the Raiders lost between 1968 and 1974, the team that beat them went on to win the Super Bowl. And by the end of the 1975 season, the Raiders were back in another AFC Championship Game, facing the Steelers again. And once again it ended in bitter defeat and angry controversy, forcing Madden to feel that numbness of another season's hard work ending without the fulfillment of a championship.

In the bitter cold in Pittsburgh, with a sheet of ice on the playing field that slowed down the Raiders' high-octane offense—and amidst charges from Al Davis that the Steelers had intentionally frozen the field—the Raiders lost a very violent 16–10 contest that only heightened the hatred between the two franchises. The game was memorable for many reasons, not the least of which was Atkinson knocking out Pittsburgh wide receiver Lynn Swann with a wicked clothesline blow.

The Atkinson-Swann conflict would turn even uglier the next time the two teams met. This was a mere preamble to a tempestuous blood feud that would wage over the course of the next 12 months.

After the game, Stabler kept telling himself, "We didn't lose. Time just ran out on us. Again."

A few weeks later, in the middle of January, the Steelers were preparing to win another Super Bowl. While trying to console Madden during a phone call, Stabler told his coach exactly what Madden already knew: "Well, we're gonna win it all this year, John."

13

THE ROAD TO SALVATION

*"He was way too intense. And the more I saw the kind of
long hours he was putting in, the more I kept thinking,
This guy can't keep going on this way."*

Betty Cuniberti

AS SOON AS THE 1976 NFL SCHEDULE WAS ANNOUNCED IN late January, everyone on the Raiders saw that the schedule-makers either had a wonderful sense of humor or a flair for the dramatic. Opening the season at home on September 12, the Raiders would get another crack at the Pittsburgh Steelers right out of the gate. Talk about your "must-see" TV. The Raiders and the Steelers would be the late national game on NBC to open the regular season, and a football-obsessed nation would be tuned in anticipating a continuation of the mayhem that had by this point become a signature of this fantastic rivalry. And while Pete Rozelle might have disliked Al Davis' franchise, he also was a natural-born PR man and knew a good thing when he saw it.

Raiders vs. Steelers was a truly great football rivalry. This was something even a blind man could sell.

The NFL image-makers understood the essence of fascinating athletic theater. There was real animosity fueling this match, not the cartoonish pouting of pro "wrasslers," but genuine fear and loathing of two equally matched combatants who used violent intimidation as one of their primary weapons. "Pittsburgh was just like us, very tough, very intimidating," said Ken Stabler. "I've seen Joe Greene kick guys, stomp guys, and he's a Hall of Fame player. I've seen Mel Blount pick Cliff Branch up and toss him like a rag doll and dump him on his head."

The 1976 season was going to be all about the Raiders and the Steelers, plain and simple. They would spend the entire season measuring each other up close and from a distance, constantly linked as their seasons progressed. John Madden didn't make a big or emotional speech when the '75 season ended so abruptly in Pittsburgh following the AFC Championship Game. His speech was simple and to the point. He told the players how well they played, how tough it was to lose. He told anyone who was nicked up or injured to go see the trainer. But before he walked away from the center of that morgue-quiet locker room, the last thing he said would set the tone for the next 12 months: "We'll be back, and we're going to win it all next season."

After delivering that message, Madden walked over to a quiet corner of the locker room and plopped his big body down on a large black equipment trunk that had been placed in front of his locker stall. His long red hair was wet and matted, and he was emotionally drained. He had taken off all his cold-weather gear and was now in his short-sleeved dress shirt, his skinny brown-and-black club tie loosened slightly. The only noise in the room was the distant hiss of the showers and the muffled sounds of players packing their belongings.

He sat there on the edge of the trunk, his face buried in his meaty hands, and he seemed to be staring off into some faraway place, oblivious to all the activity around him. Minutes passed. When the doors were opened and the press was allowed in the room, Madden rose to his feet. As the media horde surrounded him, he began the painful act of performing an autopsy on this emotional defeat.

One of the first questions that came from the crowd just added insult to injury: "Were the turnovers, Al…"

Without glancing in the direction of the offending inquisitor, Madden didn't miss a beat. "My name is John," he said.

The response was delivered with the smooth improvisation of a quick-witted comic. Only, Madden clearly didn't think this was funny. He dropped his head slightly, rubbed his neck, his face flashed an exasperated expression. "It's a hell of a time, I know…but anyway, John thinks that…."

The internal and external pressures were weighing heavily on Madden by now. He tried to minimize a lot of the slights, yet even as successful as he had become at such an early professional age, they kept piling up. Remember what he said after the loss in 1974: "When you lose, you're open to anything they want to say about you. Until you win the Super Bowl, you have to just sit there and take it."

So he had to take the Freudian slips from the media who still believed he was Al Davis' puppet. He had to take the bitter, distant jabs from Daryle Lamonica, who said he wasn't in control of the team. He had to cope with the external insults, both subtle and direct, that labeled him and his team as big-game chokers. "But the thing that bothered me about all those insults was how many big games we did win," Madden says. "We played against some of the best teams and best coaches in the history of the NFL, and we more than held our own."

ENTERING THE 1976 SEASON, MADDEN HAD COMPILED A SUPERB RECORD against the eight future Hall of Fame coaches he had faced as a head coach (27 victories, 14 defeats, and four ties). He was proud of that record, proud that he could say he was 4–0–1 vs. Sid Gillman, 3–2–1 vs. Don Shula, 8–5–2 against Hank Stram, 4–2 vs. Paul Brown, 3–0 vs. Weeb Ewbank, and that he beat Tom Landry and George Allen in the only games his Raiders played against their teams.

He had winning records against all of them except his old friend Chuck Noll. In his seven seasons as head coach, Madden was only 3–5 vs. Noll and his Steelers. Noll was nearly four years older than Madden, but he started his coaching career one year later. After a six-year NFL playing career as an offensive lineman with the Cleveland Browns, Noll retired at age 27 in 1959 and a year later landed his first coaching job as an assistant with the AFL's San Diego Chargers. A year later, he met then-25-year-old Madden, who had just joined Don Coryell's staff at San Diego State.

When Madden made it to the Raiders as an assistant coach in 1967, Noll was working on Don Shula's staff with the Baltimore Colts, but he and Madden remained close. The NFL was a little different then, not nearly as layered and complicated. When the Steelers hired Noll as their head coach in 1969, Noll thought so highly of his old friend that he offered Madden the defensive coordinator position. Madden, of course, turned him down and was promoted a few days later to being the Raiders head coach. But the competitive nature of the Steelers-Raiders rivalry would prove to be a stern test for that friendship, a test where the rivalry ultimately won out over the friendship.

"Yeah, things changed," Madden says, his voice full of resignation. "Unfortunately, things did change."

CHANGE WAS THE BUZZWORD IN TRAINING CAMP as the players arrived in Santa Rosa in July. There would be plenty of changes around the team, starting with the fifth-round drafting of a left-footed soccer-style kicker from Boston College named Fred Steinfort. With that simple move, the Raiders were signaling that the ageless 48-year-old kicker and hero of the 1970 season, George Blanda, was finally being ushered toward retirement. Trouble was, Blanda wasn't very good at taking hints, and he stubbornly showed up at training camp anyway.

Remember, this was the same George Blanda to whom Madden couldn't bear to give a curfew. Now Blanda was coming to training camp two months shy of his 49th birthday, expecting to challenge the kid soccer kicker for his job.

Ben Davidson, the old Raiders defensive end, happened to be in New York on business the weekend of the team's third exhibition game against the Jets on August 13. He got Davis' executive assistant Al LoCasale on the phone, asking if he could come to the game, then hitch a ride back to Oakland on the team charter.

"He said, 'Sure,'" Davidson recalled.

What Davidson saw stunned him. Blanda hadn't played in the first two games against Dallas and St. Louis, and now in this third game in Yankee Stadium, the Raiders kept him on the bench again. "I asked around, and it turned out the Raiders had written him off after the 1975 season," Davidson said. "Well, either they didn't tell

George, or he didn't listen. He could be very stubborn.... How do you tell George Blanda he can't play anymore? Nobody wanted to, so they rushed around and got him a locker and a uniform. But he wasn't in the Raiders' plans at all, and they weren't about to play him in the preseason because if he played and got hurt, they would have to pay him for the entire season.

"So the team is flying back to Oakland, and I'm sitting on the plane, minding my own business, and here comes George down the aisle. He kneels next to me and for the next 30 minutes proceeds to tell me how the Raiders are screwing him, how Al Davis lied to him, what a dirty deal he was getting, and so on. I had to tell him, 'George, you've been around long enough to see a thousand guys get cut. It happens to all of us.' But he just would not believe he was finished. He was a fighter to the end. Hell, he would have played linebacker just to stay in the league."

On that long flight home, Davis also sat next to Blanda, and they had a long talk. Davis finally told him the words the old kicker and quarterback had avoided for more than 25 seasons. The party was finally over. It was time to retire gracefully or be cut unceremoniously.

"I'm just glad for George's sake and the team's sake that George didn't bump into a sportswriter coming off that plane," said Davidson. "Man, he was so mad he would have told the world. The idea of a team not wanting him was just too much for him to get a handle on."

A few days later, just a month shy of his 49th birthday, Blanda quietly left the team. "One day George was there, and the next day his locker had been cleaned out," Stabler recalled.

The revolving door kept spinning. Marv Hubbard retired with a bum shoulder that wouldn't stay in its socket. Horace Jones and Art Thoms suffered season-ending knee injuries in the preseason. Defensive end Tony Cline was waived with a bad knee before the season started, and tight end Bob Moore departed for Tampa Bay in the expansion draft. When the injuries to Jones and Thoms made the defensive line too thin, two more changes came about: Madden would incorporate more 3-4 fronts into the Raiders' traditional 4-3 defense, and Al Davis would bring another renegade into the tent when he acquired John "Tooz" Matuszak. This move was made once everyone realized that rookie second-round pick Charles Philyaw (a 6'8", 285-pound specimen) was built like Tarzan but played like Jane.

Another change at the start of training camp in '76 would cause Madden to make a few social recalibrations. All over the country, the faces in the press box were changing. Female sportswriters were beginning to make inroads into the domain once dominated by older white males. Shortly before training camp began, Madden received a phone call from the sports editor of the *San Francisco Chronicle* to inform him that the Raiders would have a new beat writer in Santa Rosa.

Her name was Betty Cuniberti. Like most NFL clubs, the Raiders had never had a female reporter covering the team on a regular basis. All the usual fears that accompanied a woman showing up in the press box, practice fields, and locker room played into the reservations within the Raiders organization—"organization," of course, meaning "Al Davis."

"There was a phone call made to the *Chronicle* not to send me," Cuniberti remembers. "This was more Al Davis than John, although John never defended me. Al Davis didn't want me on the team plane, never mind that the other male writers were on the plane. You know that old navy superstition about how a woman is bad luck on a ship? Well, Al thought I would be bad luck on the plane. Never mind that there were female flight attendants and never mind that Al brought his wife. But the *Chronicle* said, 'Nothing doing. You put the *Tribune* guy and the *Examiner* guy on [the plane], so nothing doing.'"

Madden recalls a phone call, but it was from the *Chronicle* to him, not from Davis to the paper. As he remembers it, the *Chronicle* sports editor called him shortly before training camp began.

"Our beat writer is going to be a woman."

"Okay."

"She's going to be at practice every day."

"Okay."

"She's going to travel with the team."

"Okay."

"She's going to be going into the locker room at training camp."

"No, she won't. The locker room at camp is too damned small. Barely enough room for the players. No writers come into the locker room at camp."

Madden says there was no long argument, and he had no issue with a woman covering the team. Cuniberti saw it differently. "Like most men in sports at that time, particularly in football, he was very upset that I was with the team at all," she remembered. "It started as soon as I showed [up] at training camp."

Madden watched her carefully from the start. He was an old-school kind of football guy, and he wasn't sure what sort of dynamic would be created with a young female sportswriter stepping into the outlaw Raiders environment. He was suspicious of everything she did and skeptical of her knowledge of the game. Most of all, he was just a victim of his generation's chauvinism. Essentially, the attitude of the day was, the only women allowed inside the boys club of professional football were groupies or cheerleaders. Cuniberti was neither, and she rejected all those archaic chauvinistic attitudes.

All she wanted was to do her job in relative peace, which was not always an easy thing to accomplish. One day at practice, Cuniberti had to leave early to drive back to San Francisco for another assignment. Midway through the morning practice, she began to walk off the field.

"Where are you going?" Madden shouted at her from across the field.

"I have to go. I have another assignment," Cuniberti replied.

"You can't fuckin' leave! Practice isn't over!"

"Well, yes I can, John, I'm not one of your players."

Madden grumbled about Cuniberti's version of this story. "All I remember is that she started out coming to all the practices, but little by little she stayed less and less," he says.

Madden would have more issues with Cuniberti before camp ended. Two months in Santa Rosa made for a lot of idle time for the Raiders. They practiced hard, and they played even harder off the field. When the sun set over the El Rancho Motel, the bad boys in silver and black went out on the town for drinking and other forms of debauchery. They had bowling tournaments that really weren't bowling tournaments since they were played on a machine in a bar. But the biggest event of the summer was an air-hockey tournament that was a ritual event held the week of the final exhibition game. It was bigger than Rookie Night, and it was the sort of team-bonding event that Madden absolutely loved.

It was an event that was pure Raiders. It had very specific rules. Among the most notorious:

Cheating is encouraged.

It's only cheating if you get caught.

Drunkenness is mandatory. Urine must be clear.

Verbal abuse of opponents is encouraged.

This off-the-field drunken revelry was an unspoken—and far more importantly, unwritten—part of the Raiders' camp legend. Until Cuniberti showed up at camp, no sportswriter bothered to chronicle this colorful aspect of camp life. But in her first summer in Santa Rosa, Cuniberti wrote a feature story full of the colorful and often raunchy details of the air-hockey tournament. The story ran on the front page of the sports section on the morning of the exhibition game with the Rams. Perhaps no other part of the story frosted Madden more than this opening quote from Phil Villapiano: "If I was the coach, I'd say, 'The hell with the Rams. Let's just practice for the tournament.'"

The morning of the game, Madden stormed into the team's cafeteria, kicking the door open with his foot and shattering glass all over the floor. He made a beeline for Villapiano and started shouting. "You don't worry about the Rams? Why don't you get the fuck out of here?" he screamed.

Next, he went after Cuniberti. She was summoned to Madden's office, and he went on a tirade. "I can't believe you wrote this story!" he shouted. His face was red, his arms waving uncontrollably. "It has nothing to do with football! This is why women shouldn't cover football. This has *nothing to do with football!*"

"Well, yes it does, John," Cuniberti said. "I said it has everything to do with football. It has a lot to do with football. It has a lot to do with these guys working hard all through training camp, sticking together, and looking forward to this tournament every year. This is part of team cohesion."

Madden wasn't angry with the players for having fun. In fact, he encouraged that sort of mischief because he knew how long and grueling training camp could be. He just didn't understand why anyone was writing about it.

Cuniberti and Madden went at it for a few minutes, and neither one stepped back from their point of view.

A few days later, Madden summoned Cuniberti back into his office, and he brought up the story again. "You know what I really hated about that story?" Madden asked.

"Now I'm like, 'Ohhh gawd, are we back to this again? No, John, what did you really hate about that story?'" Cuniberti recalled.

"My wife really loved it," Madden said.

More than 30 years later, recalling that conversation still makes Cuniberti laugh. "I think that was John's way of a little surrender, okay? It was a little olive branch, but not much. He was still a little hard on me, but little by little as the year went on, he loosened up and began to respect me. He realized I knew what I was doing. But he really had a hard time with me being there.

"But I have to tell you, the John Madden I knew was not the guy I would eventually see years later on television. When I heard that he was going to be a broadcaster, I thought this was the biggest mistake of all time. He was not a guy who laughed and joked. He was a guy who was always on the edge. And then when I saw him as a broadcaster, I was like 'Who is this guy?' I never saw that coming. Now, part of that was because I was only there a year. But another part of that was, in my mind, because I was a girl and he didn't want me there. For all I know, he was always that guy, jolly and joking with other male reporters. By the end of the year, it was clear that he respected me…. But I have to tell you, I never saw this jolly guy, this everyman that you see on TV now."

Again, Madden's response was a quick and dismissive shrug of the shoulders.

"She is right," he said. "She wouldn't have seen that side of me because she was never around."

AFTER JOHN ROBINSON LEFT TO TAKE THE PRESTIGIOUS HEAD COACHING JOB at Southern California, there was no one around to tell Madden he was killing himself, at least no one he would listen to. Whether it was the pressure applied by Al Davis or Madden's own neurotic behavior, he was driving himself toward a potentially unhealthy conclusion. There were never enough hours in a day, never enough film to watch, never enough time to come up with another game plan or new offensive or defensive scheme. "I really do believe if he hadn't stopped coaching when he did, he wouldn't have lived long," says Cuniberti. "He was so intense. He was working so hard, he couldn't even go to sleep."

Cuniberti recalls returning to training camp in Santa Rosa in the middle of the night after returning from an assignment in San Francisco. She pulled into the parking lot of the El Rancho Motel around 2:00 AM, only to be greeted by the sight of a bleary-eyed Madden emerging from the shadows.

"Whoa, what are you doing?" she asked him.

It startled her to see the big man coming around the corner, hair uncombed, sneakers untied, seemingly patrolling the motel grounds. Cuniberti originally figured Madden was making the rounds to see if any of his notorious late-night carousers were either sneaking in or sneaking out. That would have made sense, considering the mayhem his players were capable of once the sun went down.

"I've been up watching film," he told her.

He said it was his normal nightly routine. He would watch practice films, then take what he would call a relaxing stroll in the still of the night. Only it didn't look so relaxing to Cuniberti. "I could never put my finger on it," she says. "Why would he be up that late every single night? Why was he working such ridiculously long days? Was it insecurity? I don't know. He was way too intense. And the more I saw the kind of long hours he was putting in, the more I kept thinking, *This guy can't keep going on this way."*

If Cuniberti's impression did not exactly fit the contemporary caricature of Madden as the disheveled, loveable lug, Mike Ornstein's image surely did. Ornstein came to the Raiders in the winter of 1976 after being hired by Al Davis to be Madden's unpaid executive assistant. Ornstein was a hustler, trying to do whatever he could to break into a pro football organization, so if it meant working long hours for little or no pay, he would do it. He met Madden on his first day on the job, but the coach was leaving for vacation. The next day, Ornstein came to work, went into Madden's office, and found it to be either a biohazard or the desk of a brilliant but cluttered mind. "He was a very bright man but a very disorganized man," says Ornstein. "So while he was on vacation, I decided I'd clean John's office and file things off his desk. He had game plans stacked in piles that were 10 years old, dirty bowls full of chili on the bottom of the pile that had turned green and yellow and red."

Ornstein spent days decluttering the mess. He created a filing system for the game plans and every other piece of essential paperwork that Madden had relied on throughout his coaching career. He organized everything and even tried to give the office a special touch by hanging team photos on the walls. In the process, he also made himself quite important to Madden because Ornstein was the only one who understood the filing system. "He became very reliant on me because I put everything in files and he didn't know where they were," Ornstein says. "John appreciated me, I think, because there was some organization."

As training camp broke and the team reported back to Oakland, the Raiders had a week to prepare for the highly anticipated season opener against the Steelers. This incredibly bitter rivalry had produced great football and legendary animosity. After the AFC Championship Game, all anyone wanted to talk about was the clothesline hit that

George Atkinson used to knock Lynn Swann out of the game. By the end of this season opener—another remarkable comeback engineered by Stabler when the Raiders trailed by two touchdowns in the fourth quarter—everything was overshadowed by an even more vicious blow landed by Atkinson to the back of Swann's head.

Atkinson had leveled Swann away from the ball, knocking him cold. After the game, Noll was livid. "You have a criminal element in all aspects of society," he said. "Apparently we have it in the NFL, too. Maybe we have a law-and-order problem."

In a television interview, Swann continued to stoke the flames. "The ball wasn't even thrown to me," he said. "If he was making a play on the football, he would have tried to make a tackle on Franco Harris, who was running right past him. The blow was illegal, delivered with some sort of malice. It is our contention it was basically criminal."

Because the game was on national television, a large sports-loving audience witnessed the hit, and the incident was replayed constantly during the game. It created a furor. By the end of the game, Noll and several Raiders players got into a confrontation under the stands, and commissioner Pete Rozelle was probably pushed by the growing unfavorable public reaction— and a phone conversation with Steelers president Dan Rooney—to do something about it.

It took more than a week, but on September 20, Rozelle's office announced it was fining Atkinson $1,500 for a "flagrant" hit. In a letter informing Atkinson of his fine, Rozelle told the cornerback, "In 16 years in this office I do not recall a more flagrant foul than your clubbing the back of Swann's head totally away from the play.... Our sport obviously involves intense physical contact, but it requires of all players discipline and control and remaining within the rules. Every player deserves protection from the kind of unnecessary roughness that could end his career."

Ever the shrewd politician, Rozelle also hit Noll with a $1,000 fine for his "criminal element" remarks, citing an NFL bylaw that forbids public criticism of member teams by someone in the league. Rozelle sent both Madden and Noll a letter decrying the violent tone of their rivalry: "A full review of the available films and television tapes of your Sept. 12 game indicates that your 'intense rivalry' of recent years could be on the verge of erupting into something approaching pure violence. There is, of course, no place for that in professional football and you both know it.... Aside from the specific incidents of flagrant action, there are any number of plays in which the actions of many of your players can be questioned. No action was taken in these instances because reasonable doubt exists in my mind as to the intent and motivation of the individuals involved."

All that did was make matters worse between the Raiders and the Steelers. Rooney sent Rozelle a letter ripping his decision to not come down harder on Atkinson and the entire Raiders organization, accusing them of "direct premeditated, unemotional efforts by the Oakland Raiders to seriously injure Lynn Swann."

Rooney battered the Raiders, saying, "I believe it is a cowardly act to hit someone from behind with his back turned. I also believe, because of the number of Oakland Raider players making such attacks on Lynn, the Raiders must have an opinion that Lynn is vulnerable and can be forced out of the game, which makes such acts premeditated and involves the Raiders coaching staff as well as the players." Rooney sent along film clips to illustrate all his points and also blamed the Raiders coaching staff and Davis as a shadow conspirator.

Madden tried to stay out of it but found himself embroiled in the mess as Atkinson's character witness. He just wanted to coach his football team, win games, and find a way back to the Super Bowl. He couldn't understand why the Steelers, of all organizations, were making a big stink about the violent nature of the game. "Come on, this was the Steelers, dammit," Madden recalls. "Mel Blount, Mean Joe, Ernie Holmes. How did they play? They were nasty guys, and they want to just stick it to us? Are you kidding me? Besides, football was played differently back then. We used to be able to clothesline. It was legal. You watch George, you watch Tatum, you watch [Baltimore linebacker] Mike Curtis, [Hall of Fame cornerback] Dick 'Night Train' Lane."

The Raiders could not understand why they were being singled out and not Pittsburgh. This just fueled Al Davis' "us against them" mentality.

The distraction of the Atkinson controversy was not going away. This was a fire that would continue to get stoked from one coast to the other. In Oakland, Davis was working behind the scenes to turn this thing into an inferno. He did not like what was being said about his players and his organization, and he was going to fight it like he always did, as if it were trench warfare. "You guys wrote as though the Pittsburgh game was the My Lai Massacre," Davis told the *Tribune*. "You guys are the problem. You want us to win. You want us to be tough, but when we're in a vicious game with the Steelers, a team that is notorious for busting up opponents, you seize on an incident involving one of our men and you hammer away."

He might have been upset with the media, but he saved most of his real anger for Noll and Rozelle. Behind the scenes, Davis was steaming, and he launched his own counteroffensive against them both. On October 6, clearly with Al Davis' support, George Atkinson filed a $2 million slander lawsuit against Noll. The language of the suit is classic Davis: "Pro football is on trial here. If a jury rules that Atkinson is not slandered by being called part of a 'criminal element,' then the term 'criminal' has been judicially certified as a viable, proper, accurate definition of the game. After this, every time a player is injured...he could bring a criminal suit for assault. Hell, you could bring a class action suit against showing the 'criminal' violence of football on TV. Pro football could be X rated."

To put a capper on it, the attorney said the case would zero in on "the contention that there was a conspiracy on the part of the Rozelle-Rooney establishment to get the outcast upstart Oakland crowd led by Al Davis," according to *Sports Illustrated*.

Rozelle would charge that, "Davis financed and ran the case. Al didn't care how he did it. Hurting the league didn't bother him at all."

The trial would not go to court until June of the following year, but the buildup to it would be part of the carnival of the '76 season that would serve as the backdrop to the inevitable rematch in the 1976 AFC Championship Game. It was also an additional aggravation to add onto Madden's ever-growing pile.

Three weeks later, the Raiders would lose their only game of the regular season, a lackluster 48–17 defeat at the hands of the New England Patriots, before reeling off 10 straight victories to end the season as AFC West champs. Along the way, however, Madden's fear of flying was getting worse than ever. On the plane ride back from Denver in Week 6, there was some particularly heavy turbulence. Most of the players knew that Madden would be a nervous wreck on even the calmest of flights. With turbulence, he was an anxiety attack waiting to happen. On every team flight, Madden sat in the first row, on the aisle. On the team charters, he liked to get up and roam the aisles to keep from feeling claustrophobic. But on this particular flight, with the plane bouncing up and down, the pilot had already gotten on the PA system to inform everyone to buckle up and stay in their seats until the plane flew through the bumpy air. The sound of those words left Madden petrified. Cuniberti was sitting in one of the first few rows of the coach section, maybe six rows behind Madden, working on her game story. There was no curtain that separated first class from coach, and as she typed away, she looked up and noticed a commotion in first class.

Madden was having a panic attack. A flight attendant was kneeling in the aisle, toweling him off and unsuccessfully trying to calm him down.

"I'm back in coach, and I'm typing away, and I look and see this," Cuniberti recalls. "And all I'm thinking is, *Geez, this doesn't look good*. It made me very nervous. It got so bad, the way he was reacting to the turbulence, that I was really afraid they were going to have to emergency land the plane. I hate to say it, but I was really sure I was going to have to cover his death from some stress-induced heart attack."

Whatever anxiety he was feeling in the air, on the ground, things were going better than ever. The Raiders clinched their ninth AFC

West title in 10 years by the 11th week of the season with a 26–7 victory in Philadelphia. At 11–1, they also wrapped up home-field advantage for the length of the postseason. Clinching the title so early created yet another distraction two weeks later when the Raiders met the Cincinnati Bengals at home. It was supposed to be a meaningless game for the Raiders, except there were countless stories in the local and national media that raised a rather curious issue.

If the Raiders beat the Bengals, who were tied with Pittsburgh for the AFC Central lead, it would give the Steelers a playoff bid. Losing to the Bengals would allow them to win the division and eliminate the hated Steelers—Oakland's playoff nemesis—from the playoffs. Madden kept reading these stories and answering questions about the benefits of losing to Cincinnati, and it struck a deep emotional chord.

"That's the worst thing you can say to someone, that they lost on purpose," Madden said. "Now, for the sake of the organization, for the sake of football, for the sake of what's right, you gotta go win."

The game was on *Monday Night Football*, and the Raiders bested Cincinnati 35–20. Madden laid it out in no uncertain terms to his players that he wanted them to annihilate the Bengals. The Raiders might be the nasty renegades who loved breaking all the conventional rules, but they would uphold the integrity of the game by any means necessary.

"There were some speeches given about the integrity of the game," Madden recalls. "If ever you were going to win or lose because you did or didn't want to, we don't even have a sport. So we beat them, and we beat them bad…. We knocked Cincinnati out of the playoffs and put Pittsburgh in, and that game was the most proud moment of my coaching life. I don't know any other way to play, and thank goodness my players didn't either."

The circumstances of that Cincinnati game would resonate throughout Madden's football life. Thirty-one years later, when he was a retired coach and famous TV broadcaster, Madden was reminded of the Bengals game when the New York Giants faced the unbeaten New

England Patriots in the final contest of the regular season. The game took on huge significance because the Patriots were 15–0 and needed just one more win to become the first team in NFL history to go 16–0 in the regular season. A New York victory would have no effect on the Giants' playoff status. Stories ran both locally and nationally suggesting that Giants coach Tom Coughlin rest his starters, some of whom were playing injured. Coughlin ignored those suggestions and played all his starters.

The only thing the Giants were playing for was pride. And while they would ultimately lose the game in a 38–35 thriller, the Giants put a scare into the Patriots and gained the necessary confidence to ruin the Pats' unbeaten streak several weeks later in Super Bowl XLII. The day after the game, Coughlin found a message on his office voicemail. It was from John Madden, praising the Giants for standing up for the integrity of the game.

In their Tuesday morning team meeting, Coughlin played the Madden phone message for the entire squad to hear.

"It was something else, just great," recalled St. Louis Rams head coach Steve Spagnuolo, who was the Giants defensive coordinator at the time. "He thanked Tom for playing the game to win it, talked about how happy he was that we did the right thing, upholding the integrity of the game. It was a legitimately inspirational phone call."

Defensive tackle Fred Robbins, who was a starter on the 2007 Giants squad, said the sound of Madden's voice left a lasting impression on the players. "To hear John Madden praise us like that, wow," Robbins said. "He told us that is what football was all about. I honestly think that really helped us push to the Super Bowl. It let us know that he was looking at us and respected what we did. It definitely was something that gave us a great deal of confidence."

The rest of the regular season and even the first-round playoff game against New England were nothing more than the warm-up act for the biggest game on the 1976 football calendar, the game everyone had been anticipating since hostilities erupted between the Raiders and Steelers way back in Week 1. Judgment Week had arrived, and neither side wasted time creating the much-needed nasty drumbeat. As the days slowly moved by before the AFC championship showdown in Oakland—the third consecutive year the Raiders and Steelers would meet for a trip to the Super Bowl—the animosity was building. Joe Greene started the hype by saying if George Atkinson took any more swipes at Lynn Swann on the field, he promised to "come off the bench to get [Atkinson's] butt if I have to…. That stuff [the Raiders] did to Lynn when we played them ticked off a lot of guys on this team. Then I watched Atkinson do the same kind of thing against New England. That's the vengeful part of football. It shouldn't exist at all, but it seems to be the way Oakland is taught. I saw movies of what Atkinson did to Swann. It was illegal and dirty. It was flagrant, but nothing Oakland does surprises me. Well, we have guys who can play that kind of football, too. We can play it any way they want it."

Steelers defensive lineman Dwight White said, "Hey, we can play rough and nasty, just like Oakland. Maybe that's what it will take."

For his part, Atkinson refused to back down. "We never go out on the field with the intention of hurting someone," he said. "But we do go out on the field with the intention of getting the job done. If he don't want to get hit, his best bet is to not show up on Sunday, because he will get hit."

"It's being treated like World War III," Madden said of all the hyperbole.

For all the hype and buildup leading up to the game, it was not your typical Raiders-Steelers duel in the dirt. For one thing, Pittsburgh's offense was playing without injured running backs Franco Harris and Rocky Bleier. The Raiders won easily, pounding the shorthanded Steelers 24–7. Said *Sports Illustrated* of the anticlimatic results: "There was not a single 15-yard penalty called in the game, a conflict that probably could have been fought in a drawing room with no harm done to the wainscoting. The closest thing to an outburst came late in the second half when the frustrated Swann had a shoving match with Oakland free safety Jack Tatum after taking what he considered a late hit from behind. Some war."

The players were celebrating inside the same Oakland locker room that was once full of so many depressed faces. In the midst of that celebration, Willie Brown took the time to give credit to Madden for guiding the team through so many controversies during the season. "Things were tough at the beginning of the year," Brown said, "but John helped keep us together."

Brown and Gene Upshaw and big Art Shell—three future Hall of Fame players—cornered Madden on the narrow path between the lockers and dragged him into the shower fully clothed to toast this long-awaited AFC championship. It was another one of those moments that crystallized how genuinely fond of their head coach the players were. This was not a gesture afforded a coach the players grumbled about behind his back. This was not a gesture afforded a coach the players hated. This was a gesture that symbolized true affection, admiration, and respect, and Madden accepted the honor with fake resistance and a cheesy grin.

A few minutes later, the media came into the locker room and were greeted by a soaked and soggy head coach who couldn't stop smiling. He had this goofy, giddy expression on his face. His long red hair was matted down on his head like some wet shaggy dog.

"We're going to the Super Bowl," a giddy Madden chuckled when surrounded by the same media horde that stood around him 12 months earlier under much darker circumstances. "I feel happiness and jubilation now. We've been so close so many times, I'm just happy."

But as quickly as he got caught up in all the celebrations, joining his players in all manner of silliness, Madden reminded himself and his team of how carried away they got in 1974 after beating Miami and forgetting that they still had the AFC Championship Game to deal with.

"Hey," he told that joyful locker room, "we haven't won anything yet. If we get this far and don't win in Pasadena, we haven't done anything."

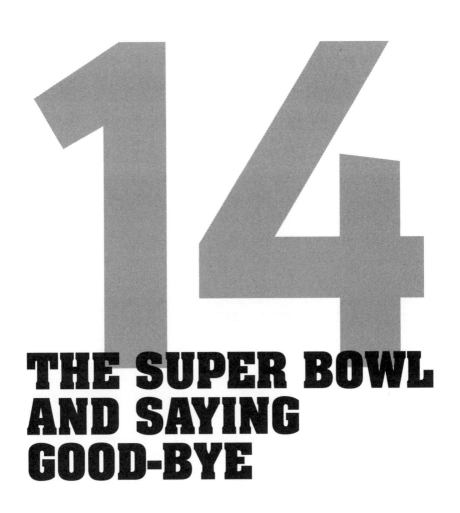

14

THE SUPER BOWL AND SAYING GOOD-BYE

*"This will be the single biggest event in your whole life...
as long as you win."*

John Madden

IT TOOK JOHN MADDEN AND THE RAIDERS NINE YEARS TO GET back to the Super Bowl, but they were on their way to Pasadena for the Super Bowl XI matchup against the NFC champion Minnesota Vikings. To his credit, Al Davis practically vanished during Super Bowl week, preferring the light shine on his players—and his young head coach. This allowed Madden to bask in the frenzy of Super Bowl week. He shined in his daily press conferences, offering up funny one-liners to the assembled media mobs every morning and thanking them for all their kindnesses.

Reporters who had covered the NFL for years were shocked when they discovered Madden not only had a personality but a brain to go along with it. "He stood in front of us, huge, leaning forward, patting his beefy palms, bellowing at us, shrieking, getting louder and louder in a hypertense voice that grated our eardrums," longtime *Detroit News* columnist Jerry Green wrote. "But as I sat there, I realized there was a special intelligence in the words he was speaking."

Madden stood there and gave a memorable performance, articulately taking a room full of writers, columnists, and TV types through an oral history of the 1976 season. Whatever images they had of him before, Madden destroyed them during Super Bowl week.

"This man speaking was not an oaf," Green wrote. "Somebody new had joined us at the Super Bowl, and we had a football coach who wouldn't drone on as we fought our urges to snooze during the daily briefings that had become so much a part of the Super Bowl routine."

As Madden left the room one day, Green looked at one of his colleagues with a surprised and delighted expression. "Man," he said. "An articulate football coach."

But on Super Bowl Sunday, Madden was once again unable to escape the giant shadow of Al Davis. On the front sports page of the *Los Angeles Times* and hometown *Oakland Tribune*, Jim Murray, the legendary columnist for the *Times*, piled on Madden with yet another article that suggested Davis, not the outstanding head coach, was the man behind the Raiders machine.

"Al Davis is football's Svengali," Murray wrote. "Coach John Madden? Al Davis puts him in a trunk at night. When John Madden talks, Al Davis has to make sure people don't see his lips move."

Davis attempted to debunk Murray's theory. "Listen, John Madden is a freaking genius," Davis told Murray. "He's just a brilliant football coach. To suggest that he's just a switchboard is to miss the whole point of John Madden. I mean, he doesn't convey your field marshal image on the sidelines, but he knows what you're doing to him out there and vice-versa."

So what in the world would Madden have to do to get people like Murray to stop calling him a marionette? Even winning the Super Bowl, it seemed, wouldn't be enough to satisfy some critics.

Inside the Raiders' locker room, just before the team left to go out onto the field, Madden gathered them all together one last time and said something that resonated with every one of his renegades. "This will be the single biggest event in your whole life," Madden told them, pausing for dramatic emphasis. *"As long as you win."*

And win the Super Bowl is exactly what Madden's Raiders did. They came into the Rose Bowl and dominated the poor Vikings in every manner possible. Even when the Vikes got a major break in the early moments of the game by doing what was considered a near impossibility—blocking a Ray Guy punt—they botched a chance to capitalize on it by fumbling near the goal line and giving the ball right back to the Raiders.

The Raiders broke a club record with 429 yards of total offense. Clarence Davis rushed for 137 yards, Gene Upshaw and Art Shell mauled the Purple People Eaters, Stabler picked the Minnesota secondary apart, and old man Willie Brown put the final touches on the victory with a 75-yard interception for another score, a play that would become immortalized in slow motion by NFL Films.

This was a victory that should have emphasized the sort of coach Madden was. The Raiders went through the season with only one loss in 17 games. In the history of the NFL, only three other teams have ended their seasons with a better record than the 16–1 Raiders of 1976—the perfect 17–0 Miami Dolphins (1972) and 1984 San Francisco 49ers (18–1), who both won the Super Bowl, and the 2007 New England Patriots whose 18–1 record ended in defeat in the Super Bowl.

The next morning, on page A-1 of the *Tribune*, there was a photo of Madden in all his everyman glory, tumbling to the ground after riding on the shoulders of his players in a victory celebration. "We've waited so darned long for this moment," Madden would say. "I'm happy for our players, who had to live with the criticism that we couldn't win the big one. I'm happy for our fans, too, who have been behind us all these seasons through the frustration and controversy."

He could have easily said how happy he was for himself because he was the one who had to endure the most abuse for "losing the big one." While Madden stood in the middle of the locker room after the wild celebration finally died down, still dripping wet from the fully clothed shower that his players gave him, he quietly gazed out at all the happy faces in the room. That's when he spotted his bride of 17 years, Virginia. She came bounding across the room, looked up at her 6'4" husband, and planted a loving kiss on his lips. She had come into the room clutching John Robinson's arm. As the couple embraced, Robinson stepped out of the way. But now Madden focused his attention on his best friend. A week earlier, Robinson stood in this same locker room, having led Southern California to an 11–1 record, the No. 2 ranking in the nation, and a Rose Bowl victory in his first year as the Trojans head coach.

As they stood about six feet apart, these lifelong friends who started playing football together on Madden's Lot in Daly City nearly 30 years before and spent their childhoods dreaming impossible athletic dreams could now share the fulfillment of the delirious circumstances that brought them to this moment.

And what did they do? They just started laughing out loud at the improbability of it all.

"I mean, just think about what kind of odds it would take to say that two best friends from childhood could end up winning the Rose Bowl and the Super Bowl in the space of a week," Robinson would say.

How could this have happened to both of them? How could they both manage to reach the top of their professional mountains within the space of eight days, do it on the same field, and end up in the same locker room?

"Not too bad for a couple of doofuses from Daly City, huh?" Madden said, a broad smile beaming across his face. It was the sort of look that only the best of friends could share and understand.

THERE WOULD BE A GREAT PARADE BACK IN OAKLAND, of course, but not everyone could attend. Several key members of the team had Pro Bowl obligations and headed to Seattle after the Super Bowl. The full team would not assemble again for another six months, when it headed to Santa Rosa in July. In the interim, Madden found himself watching film of the Super Bowl, and a particular play struck him as significant and even inspirational. So he stopped whatever he was doing, picked up the phone, and called a certain player.

Monte Johnson remembers receiving that unexpected call in the middle of the winter. "After we beat Minnesota…I went back home to Nebraska," Johnson recalls. "I lived in Lincoln during the off-season and…it was early in the morning and the phone rang, and it was John. This had to be about 6:00 in the morning out in California, and the first thing that came to my mind was that I was traded. I said, 'John, what in the world are you doing?' He said, 'Well, I'm just sitting here watching the Super Bowl over again, and I just wanted to call you and tell you how much I recognize what was your major contribution in that game. In fact, there was a play that I think was the turning point of the game. Can you remember what that play might be?'

"There was a play that stuck out in my head. It was just after the half, and it was a running play, and they had pulled their guard, and I shot the gap and tackled the running back for a loss, which put them into a passing situation. The next play, we intercepted the ball. I said, 'John, I'm thinking about that play.' He said, 'That's the play that I was thinking about. That was a great read and a great play. I think it was the turning point of the game and just want to tell you I really appreciate it.'"

These were the moments when the best of John Madden, the player's coach, came out, when you could understand why players wanted to win for him. These were the sorts of moments that made Madden feel like he could coach forever. This is what he loved the most about being the head coach of the Raiders, those unpretentious moments away from the spotlight when relationships between men develop into something deeper than player and coach. It's why he would come into the locker room with a cup of coffee in one hand, a newspaper in the other, and pull up a stool and engage a player in a conversation about something he had just read. It's why he could comfortably stroll through the motel at training camp, walk into any player's room, sit on the bed, and talk with a 12-year veteran or an undrafted rookie free agent about life for an hour.

It's why, while breaking down game film in the middle of the off-season, he had the decency to call one of his players and thank him for helping to win a Super Bowl game. These were the sorts of moments Madden had shared with his players since the day he got into coaching 17 years earlier.

But now he was beginning to recognize that there were not nearly enough of these moments to keep a smile on his face, not nearly enough moments like these to keep his stomach from churning with all sorts of uncomfortable gastric fireworks. These comforting moments of solitude were being outpaced by too many less restful ones: the panic fits caused by his overwhelming fear of flying, the aggravation of grinding all-nighters, and too many disturbing issues off the field.

This would force Madden to contemplate whether all the aggravation was worth it. He knew after winning the Super Bowl and going into his ninth year as a head coach, he was living on borrowed time. "I think 10 years is pretty much the time to leave as a head coach," Madden says. "Ten years is a long time. Players stop listening to you after 10 years. The message doesn't change; you don't stop being smart or anything. It's just sometimes players need a different voice." The only thing that was left to achieve was reaching 100 coaching victories in 10 years' time. That would be a legacy-building accomplishment, something that would put him in some fairly select company in his profession. If he could get that done, it would be so much easier to walk away.

THE RAIDERS REPORTED TO TRAINING CAMP OF 1977 as Super Bowl champions, and one of the first things Madden did when the players walked into the first team meeting in early July was to dim the lights and turn on the highlight film of the Raiders' championship season. It was the first time since they had all left the Rose Bowl locker room in January that the entire team had gathered together, and the excitement filled the room.

When the NFL Films camera went to a slow-motion shot of Jack Tatum whacking a near-knockout blow on Vikings receiver Sammy White, sending that purple helmet flying in the air and leaving White dazed on the ground, players hooted. When the film showed Tatum standing over his victim, flicking his hands in a dismissive gesture—a quintessentially Raidersesque move—it was celebrated with a rousing chant of, "Tate! Tate! Tate!" as Tatum was mobbed by rowdy teammates.

The noise grew as the highlights whirled by, and when a shot of Madden leaping along the sideline like some Sansabelt-wearing dancing bear popped up on the screen, the room exploded in laughter and good-natured insults of their beloved coach. Madden sat in the front of the room with a giant grin spread across his flushed face.

Training camp had barely begun when the first distraction cropped up. George Atkinson's case against Chuck Noll and the Pittsburgh Steelers got underway across the bay in the San Francisco federal courtroom of the Honorable Samuel Conti on July 11. The trial lasted only 11 days, but Atkinson and several teammates were called as witnesses, and the trial gained national headlines as federal subpoenas revealed confidential letters and memos directly from Rozelle's desk.

Noll himself took the stand in a confrontational cross-examination, during which Atkinson's attorney, Daniel S. Mason, ultimately forced the Pittsburgh coach to lump his own players into the same "criminal element" with Atkinson and the Raiders. Mel Blount, the Steelers cornerback, was so angry that he was labeled a criminal that he also filed a $5 million suit and vowed to never play for Noll again.

The trial created one big awkward and divisive mess. When it was over after 11 days and the jury ruled against Atkinson, it just added to the unnecessary circus atmosphere that Madden would have to deal with. He had replaced the Pepto-Bismol with something chalky in a brown bottle. He walked around training camp with the bottle and antacid pills in his pocket, and he would constantly chew on towels as he watched practice.

Amateur psychologists would have a field day observing Madden during his final two seasons in Oakland. They could have picked up on all the mounting evidence that he was on the brink of a breakdown of some sort, be it physical or emotional. Guzzling bottles of Maalox or Pepto-Bismol, chewing on antacid tablets like they were Pez candies, biting down on a towel as if it were a pacifier, the grueling late nights, the constant pileup of internal and external influences—these were all symptoms that indicated he was shouldering an overly stressful burden.

Madden and all of his players could add on the stress of believing that Pete Rozelle would take out his retribution on Davis through the players. They were all convinced that the NFL referees were out to get them. They saw demons everywhere, and Madden—who already had a healthy distrust of game officials—would empty his lungs with even more profanity-laced insults shouted from the sideline.

Interestingly enough, 1977 and 1978 were two of the Raiders' least-penalized seasons. But if you were a true believer in the Al Davis camp, you were convinced that Rozelle's minions were always at work, looking not for volume but timeliness in their plot against the Raiders. And so it was that after an 11–3 regular season and another trip to the AFC Championship Game—just as they were on the verge of back-to-back trips to the Super Bowl—their worst fears were realized.

If timing is everything and you believed in the Davis conspiracies, then this was a master stroke for Rozelle's sinister forces. The Raiders were trailing the Denver Broncos 7–3 at Mile High Stadium in the third quarter. They had fumbled away the ball on their own 17-yard line, and the Broncos marched the ball down to the 2-yard line and threatened to take a 14–3 lead. On the next play, Broncos fullback Rob Lytle took the handoff, leaped over the pile of humanity at the goal line, and was hit in midair by Jack Tatum, knocking the ball out of Lytle's hands. Raiders defensive tackle Mike McCoy picked up the fumble and began running the other way for what looked like an easy Raiders touchdown. But the play was stopped cold by a referee's whistle. The play was ruled dead. No fumble.

Upstairs in the press box and on TV sets around the country, replays showed that the refs had blown it. It was clearly a fumble, but there was nothing Oakland could do to change the call. One play later, Denver scored to take that 14–3 lead.

History would look back on this game and say the nonfumble did in the Raiders. But the game was not over after the fumble, and several Raiders would look back on that game and recall that it wasn't only the fumble that did them in. Before the game, as the Raiders defensive linemen were warming up, it was obvious that John Matuszak was all screwed up. While getting into his three-point stance, he tipped over like a sleeping cow. Tooz was wasted. The night before the game, when teammates returned to the hotel around 11:00 PM, they found Tooz, stripped to his waist and in a drunken and drug-induced stupor, sitting in the middle of a room he had just trashed.

"Evidently, he'd kept it up for the rest of the night, drinking, popping Quaaludes," recalls teammate Pat Toomay.

In the locker room before the game, team trainers worked feverishly to get Tooz ready for the game. Madden was surely seething, because unlike all the other wild men he had coached over the years, Tooz was ignoring Madden's three simple rules. None of the team leaders could get to him and make him understand how out of control he was.

Matuszak shouldn't have played, but when the game started, there he was in the starting lineup.

It didn't take the Broncos long to figure out that Tooz was useless. In the fourth quarter, Stabler completed two touchdown passes to Dave Casper to draw within 20–17 with three minutes to go. The Raiders could sense they were taking over the contest. All they had to do was get another defensive hold and turn the ball back over to the Snake and let him do his thing. The only problem was, the Broncos played keep-away, piling up yardage and killing the clock by running the ball right at the sluggish Tooz.

During one timeout, an angry Raiders player begged defensive coordinator Don Shinnick to get Matuszak out of the game. "It ain't gonna happen," the coach said, nodding his head toward the owner's box upstairs.

After the game, the visitors' locker room was filled with angry Raiders players willing to spew out vulgar insults toward the refs. Madden tried to give the Broncos credit for playing a good game, but when someone brought up the controversial nonfumble, he did not bite his tongue. "Hell yes, it was a fumble," he said. "How can it not be a fumble when one of my guys comes out of there with the ball like that?"

A nearby television showed the replay one more time, and Madden recoiled. "I'm not saying anything else about it…. But look at that. Twenty million people saw it. Let them make their own judgments."

But there were just as many players in that locker room who also knew that if Madden had his way, Tooz would not have stayed in the game. No one would say it publicly, but the players knew that there were other unseen powers at play that had nothing to do with Rozelle and his minions.

Add this to the pile of emotional debris that would push Madden one step closer to burnout.

AS THE RAIDERS WENT INTO THE OFF-SEASON, more changes were on the way. The stable core of veterans Madden relied on to keep things moving internally took a major blow with the departures of Willie Brown, Fred Biletnikoff, George Buehler, and Clarence Davis. During the preseason, John Vella and Villapiano were lost for the season due to injuries. Shinnick, who privately chafed at what he was sure was Davis' interference in the Matuszak situation, complained too much and made foolish demonstrations of his disgust through his antics on the sideline. It cost him his job when Davis fired him after Shinnick refused to resign. To replace Shinnick, Myrel Moore came in from Denver and brought with him the 3-4 defense, which the Raiders had used in the past only situationally.

This created another question in people's minds about Madden. Was this his hire, or was the Machiavellian Davis behind this dramatic change? Had Madden been forced to get rid of his own coordinator and not only deal with a new one but one who was going to change the entire philosophy of the Raiders defense?

Another log on the pile.

Off the field, more impactful changes were under way. Kenny Stabler, now 32 years old chronologically but much older because of his hard living off the field, was being publicly scrutinized by Al Davis more than ever before, and in the process the owner also took a shot at Madden. "You've got to point to someone, so blame Stabler," Davis said. "He makes the most money…. If you can't get the ball to your wide receivers, you can't win. It all starts with the left-hander…. He gets paid to take the pressure. I'm certainly not going to make excuses for him, but he doesn't do any work in the off-season. I'm dissatisfied with the condition of the team and with the coaching staff for allowing the players to get out of shape."

That last sentence could not have gone unnoticed.

What sort of impact did all of this have on Madden? It was all circumstantial, but clearly the wear and tear of 10 years under the microscope as the Raiders head coach was breaking him down. The evidence that could not be ignored occurred during a May minicamp when Madden was hospitalized with a bleeding ulcer. Privately, the mental wear and tear was already making him consider getting out of the game. Now he had to consider the physical wear and tear, too. Plus, there were other outside forces. He was missing out on the lives of his teenage sons. He was embarrassed that because of his tunnel-vision approach to coaching, he had lost complete awareness of what was going on outside his coaching life.

Before the start of the season, he and Virginia talked about it. It started out almost as a casual conversation, but when he mentioned that he thought 10 years seemed like enough time to spend coaching, that he might be coming to the end of the road real soon, Virginia surprised him with a firmness in her response. "Okay, it's 10 years," she told him. "That should be it."

He didn't mention it to anyone else, but as the year progressed, Madden became more committed than ever to keeping his promise to get out of the game.

As they arrived in Santa Rosa for training camp, the players started to notice that the loud and excitable coach they called "Pinky" wasn't the same guy. The tension that he only showed in private moments on those late-night car rides home was now coming out publicly. He seemed to always be agitated. They saw him have uncontrollable vomiting spasms on the practice field and in the locker room. They saw the panic attacks on the airplane. On one preseason trip, Pat Toomay found Madden standing in the waiting area, pacing nervously, sweating profusely, clinging to a towel. Toomay could see that something was wrong. He could see the anxiety in Madden's face.

"I can't get on until the last second," Madden told him.

It was the same unnatural, unhealthy panic that Betty Cuniberti had witnessed during that turbulent charter flight in the skies over Denver a year earlier.

"Before heading down the ramp, I stood there for a moment, taking it all in," Toomay recalled. "Madden's fear was deeper and darker than anything I'd imagined."

If the final moments before every road-trip flight were beginning to make Madden resemble a man walking the plank, the entire summer was taking on a symbolic vision of a man taking the final steps of another journey. Madden was drawing closer and closer to the end of his life as a football coach, and with each passing day something happened that made those close to him know that the end was near. Toomay, George Atkinson, and many of the other players had noticed the panic attacks on those flights. But something more disturbing happened during a home preseason game on August 12 against the New England Patriots that convinced Madden he no longer had the stomach for being an NFL head coach.

The play was called 94-Slant, and the Patriots were boldly sending their receivers right into the teeth of Madden's head-hunting, nasty secondary. It was a meaningless exhibition game, and as he stood on the sideline watching, Madden complained aloud that Patriots head coach Chuck Fairbanks was putting his players at risk by calling these plays.

"Someone's gonna get hurt," Madden said.

It didn't take long for the coach's words to come true. On a third down and eight at the Raiders' 24-yard line, Patriots quarterback Steve Grogan sent 26-year-old wide receiver Darryl Stingley on his primary route, an eight-yard slant-in pattern. Stingley lined up flanked to the right, just outside tight end Russ Francis. His job was to find that slight gap between the linebacker and cornerback. He found it, but it was a fool's mission, because Oakland safety Jack Tatum, a heat-seeking missile, came bearing down on him with his elbow cocked. Tatum's blow was merciless, and it dropped Stingley to the ground. Immediately, everyone in the stadium knew something tragic had happened.

Trainers from both teams rushed out on the field. Stingley lay on the ground, motionless. The trainers tended to Stingley for a long time. Everyone knew something was wrong, particularly when an ambulance was summoned and the medical staff took great care to strap Stingley onto a stretcher without moving his head or neck or put any additional pressure on his spine.

The game continued but with an emotional numbness that was palpable.

Almost immediately after the game, Madden raced to Eden Hospital in nearby Castro Valley. When he arrived, John learned the worst news he could imagine. Stingley had a fractured vertebra in his neck and was being fitted with a halo brace to stabilize the injury. With the help of the Raiders team physicians—and with Al Davis and Madden caring for Stingley like one of their own—everything was in place to give the Patriots wide receiver the best possible care.

Madden was furious that there was no one there from Stingley's own team. The owner hadn't stayed behind. Neither had a coach. Not even a trainer or some bottom-of-the-food-chain assistant to an assistant. Madden was the only one there for Stingley, and he was incensed. Darryl couldn't wake up thousands of miles away from home, suffering from a catastrophic injury, and find no one at his bedside.

Madden stormed down the hallway like an enraged bull moose, looking for a telephone. He grabbed the receiver, his thick fingers punching out the telephone number to the charter terminal at the Oakland airport. He was immediately patched through to the cockpit of the New England charter that was already on the tarmac and heading for the runway. When he finally got someone from the team on the phone, Madden unleashed a tirade of profanity. Whatever he said must have worked, because the plane returned to the gate, the door opened, and the team's business manager got off the plane and made his way to the hospital.

Madden slept at the hospital on Saturday night. He wanted to be there when Stingley woke up. He didn't want him to be alone when the worst news of his life would be delivered to him by some stranger in a lab coat. When he woke up on the morning of August 13, Stingley had no idea that he was in a hospital room, that more than 12 hours had passed since the tragic collision, or why none of the people who were milling around looked familiar. Every time he dozed off then woke in a groggy haze, he thought he was stuck in a bad dream. He was disoriented. He couldn't figure out why he was flat on his back, staring at a white acoustical ceiling. The last thing he could recall was looking up from the ground of the Oakland Coliseum, staring at the sky. Now there was some lady in a white coat standing at the edge of his bed speaking to him.

"Good morning, Mr. Stingley."

There was this frightful flush of confusion that swept over his body.

He couldn't move his head. He couldn't move his right arm. He couldn't move his left arm. He couldn't move his feet.

What the hell was going on?

It was an incomprehensible terror. A great athlete, a man whose entire being was defined by his physical gifts, was imprisoned in a limp and lifeless body. This wasn't a bad dream. It was a horrific nightmare. "I started to cry and couldn't even wipe the tears that were forming in puddles on my face," Stingley recalled.

He tried to call out to his mother, but the words wouldn't come out. He tried to call out to his wife, Tina. Again, the words would not travel from his brain out through his mouth. And then that lady in the white coat told him not to try and talk. She explained that he had plastic tubes in his mouth that were attached to a machine that would help prevent him from choking to death on his own phlegm. There were tubes in his nose attached to a respirator. Then it hit him. Through a stream of tears, Stingley remembered everything. He remembered the call in the huddle. He remembered running the eight-yard slant-in. He remembered the split second before the collision, seeing Jack Tatum's cold eyes and trying to no avail to duck the blow.

All Stingley could do now was close his eyes and cry.

Eventually he fell asleep for an hour or so, and when he woke up, Stingley felt the presence of a familiar figure in the room. A football guy, not one of these mysterious hospital people. It was John Madden, tears streaming from his bloodshot eyes. The big, disheveled Raiders coach was at Stingley's bedside, holding his hand and stroking his face with a gentle, loving touch. Stingley thought it was the tender caress of a father trying to comfort his own child. Recounting the moment to *Sports Illustrated* years later, Stingley remembered the soothing, soft, and distinctive voice of Madden as he awoke.

"Darryl...Darryl...Darryl...it'll be all right."

Then just as Stingley remembered hearing Madden's unforgettable soft voice, he remembered Madden's soothing bedside manner making a sudden shift to frantic urgency. Madden noticed one of the machines that was hooked up to the tubes in Stingley's mouth stopped making that suction sound. The sound of Madden's voice went from soft to demanding. He started screaming for a nurse to come into the room, and in moments a nurse did run into the room.

"That's stopped," Madden shouted, his hands waving excitedly toward the contraption next to Stingley's bed. "It was working when I came in here to see Darryl, but then it stopped. Just a minute ago. Fix the goddamned thing!"

The nurse looked down and replaced a plug that had come dislodged. It was the machine that was supposed to suction the phlegm. She had to shove a new tube down his throat and remove the buildup that had collected in his throat. It was not a painless exercise, and it caused Stingley to cry as she executed the procedure. Madden stayed right at Stingley's bedside, holding his hand, rubbing his face and doing anything he could to comfort him, even as tears flowed down his flushed face. When Madden left that morning and drove back to Santa Rosa to training camp, the nurse told Stingley that Madden had just saved his life by noticing that the machine had shut down.

Stingley remained at Eden Hospital for two months, and John and Virginia made the trip from Santa Rosa to Castro Valley every day to be with Stingley. They also extended their home in Pleasanton to Stingley's wife, Tina, and brought clothes to the hospital for her until she was able to have clothes sent to her from back home.

Even after road trips, Madden kept Stingley as a priority. No matter what time the team plane landed in Oakland at night, Madden would get in a car and drive directly from the airport to the hospital to visit Stingley.

Years later, when writing about Madden in his autobiography, Stingley would simply say, "I love that man."

A FEW MONTHS LATER, THE SEASON WAS OVER. The Raiders finished 9–7 and out of the playoffs. Madden walked into Al Davis' office and told him he was done. Davis figured he could talk Madden out of quitting, but John wouldn't back down. He had seen enough, done enough. Nothing could change his mind. So exactly 10 years to the day after he was promoted to be the Raiders head coach, John Madden walked away.

At his press conference, with tears in his eyes, Madden said, "I'm not resigning, quitting for doing anything else. I'm retiring. I'll never coach another game of football. I gave it everything I had for 10 years, and I don't have any more."

That was the God's honest truth. He was done, and he would never stand on the sideline again.

Everyone has theories about what made Madden quit coaching while he was such a young man and in his professional prime. "It was probably the stress," said Atkinson. "That and the fear of flying. Plus, 10 years is a long time, and you could tell he got tired, and he could see that the players who were coming into the league were changing. Plus I think the Stingley thing really had an effect on him."

"You know, I thought he would have gotten out of coaching for a while and gotten back in," said Robinson, "but he never wavered. When he said he didn't want to come back, he really meant it."

Was it too much Davis? Was it too many drug-addled players, like Matuszak? Was it the ulcer that was eating away at his stomach? Madden barely changes expressions when asked about his motivations. "It was a lot of things," he says. "The biggest thing of all was I just coached for 10 years, and that was enough. Besides, we didn't exactly make a lot of money back then. I started out making about $30,000, and by the end I was only making about $100,000. Why did I walk away? Shit, I could make more money *not* coaching.

"Besides, my kids were getting older, and as a coach I was such a tunnel-vision kind of guy I had lost touch with my family. I'm not terribly proud of this, but shit, I didn't even know how old my kids were. It's sad but true. I didn't have any idea how old my kids were."

So Madden walked away and never looked back. He went home to Pleasanton and thought he would catch up on the family life. But the family wasn't at home. The boys had their own lives. They were in high school, playing sports and doing their own thing. And Virginia, always the independent one, had started her own business, operating a local saloon she had opened two years earlier.

So Madden spent his free time in retirement watching daytime TV and going to city hall to stand in line for permits for his new business interests.

There was one business interest beckoning Madden that he hadn't given much thought: television. CBS asked him to audition as a game analyst, and at first he wasn't interested.

"But they thought I was negotiating," Madden recalls. "It went back and forth, and finally my agent, Barry Frank, said, 'You ought to do it. We'll get a four-or-five-game guarantee. If you like it, you can continue. If you don't, you don't have to. But if you say no now and change your mind several years later, they may not be interested in you anymore.'"

15

DISCOVERING TELEVISION

IF JOHN MADDEN WAS GOING TO DO THIS TELEVISION THING, it would be a fascinating experiment. When he departed the pro football sideline, he truly didn't know a thing about the business of broadcasting his sport. His exposure to what was already out there and the approach various color commentators were taking to explain the game to viewers on CBS, NBC, and ABC was extremely limited. Actually, it was nonexistent. Madden's exposure had been reduced to the occasional conversations he had with the network broadcast crews that would visit briefly at walk-through practices the day before games.

"I wasn't going to be able to pattern myself after anyone because, as a coach, I didn't have time to watch any games on TV," he says now. "I didn't watch any college games on Saturdays because we were either practicing, traveling, or in meetings." On Sundays, the Raiders were normally one of the late games on NBC, going off at 4:00 PM on the East Coast, 1:00 out West. Out of professional necessity, Madden refused to watch those earlier games, and if someone absentmindedly left on a TV around him, the coach would either leave the room or turn the TV off.

"I thought it could confuse my mind and distract me from what I wanted to do in my game," he says. "I was afraid it would take me away from getting my mind right for my game plans, for my strategies. I was worried that I might see a coach do something different in one of those games and it would make me have second thoughts about what I was about to do. So I refused to watch."

Madden's sole influence when it came to televised professional football came from halftime of the *Monday Night Football* broadcasts, when a certain bombastic and multisyllabic announcer would narrate a highlight package of the best games and top plays from selected Sunday afternoon games.

In the early and mid-1970s, long before the existence of ESPN, NFL Network, and NBC's Sunday prime-time *Football Night in America*, pro football highlights on television were strictly local. The sports segments on local news programs would show extensive clips of the home team but rarely—if ever—bothered with much action from around the rest of the league.

Unless you could wait until Thursday nights for HBO's *Inside the NFL* or Saturday mornings for NFL Films' syndicated *This Week in Pro Football*, the best and quickest turnaround you could get for national highlights came in that capsulized seven-minute package of NFL Films clips provided for *Monday Night Football*. Unless you are over 50, it's hard to understand what a big deal those halftime highlights were. Kids wouldn't go to bed until they saw whether or not their team was featured in those highlights. Even if the game had already turned into a blowout in the second quarter, ABC never lost its audience at halftime because of the highlights. Teams measured their status by their appearances on *MNF* halftimes. Fans spewed their rage in the form of hate mail and vulgar phone calls to the ABC switchboards if their teams were excluded on a particular Monday night.

A large part of that massive viewing audience was the coaching staffs from around the NFL, like John Madden's in Oakland. "We would work late on Mondays, and the game started at 6:00 PM out here," Madden says. "So I would always make sure that food was brought in right around halftime. I would tell the coaches, 'Dinner at 7:30' because I knew that was the halftime highlights time. Then we would all sit around eating dinner and watching Howard Cosell do halftime highlights."

How ironic was it that the single most influential television voice Madden the coach was exposed to back then would be the notorious Cosell?

In the course of American sports broadcasting, have there ever been two larger cultural phenomena—and more dramatically polar opposite characters—roaming the booth than the grandiose and aloof Cosell and the frumpy everyman Madden?

It would take a few years to see Madden in full as the broadcaster. By the late 1970s, America had already taken in a snootful of Cosell. Author Michael MacCambridge wrote vividly of the essential Cosell in his definitive book on the National Football League, *America's Game: The Epic Story of How Pro Football Captured a Nation*:

"Cosell's brand of pointed, often trenchant, pontification—'just telling it like it is' he insisted—earned dramatic responses, both positive and negative. Many critics felt he played it both ways, stirring up a froth of hyperbole with each Monday night while at the same time bemoaning the lack of journalistic credibility in the sports media field ('What a horizontal ladder of mediocrity,' mused Cosell of his competition in a 1967 interview). Many fans hated him for his erudition, his arrogance, and for the approbation he offered the boxer Muhammad Ali after he'd changed his name from Cassius Clay. Some undoubtedly disliked him for the simple fact that he was Jewish. But his presence changed the environment surrounding the games.... Cosell was forever the cultural critic, investing the game and the surroundings with portent, an effort to bring context and gravity to the occasion."

At his best, Cosell was a fearless journalist. At his worst, he was a pompous caricature. But he did bring an element of the Big Event to every game he broadcast, particularly because of the unforgettable dynamic tension he helped generate with his broadcast mate, Dandy Don Meredith.

Madden had no inkling when he embarked on this latest adventure that he could one day be as significant or entertaining as Cosell when he decided to give television a try. All he knew was that he couldn't bear to spend the rest of his retirement days sitting at home in the den watching daytime television shows like *General Hospital* and chatting it up with the dog.

So here he was, in 1979, with a new TV contract as a part-time analyst, and he had absolutely no idea how to be a television analyst. This troubled him to no end because as a player, a coach, and a teacher, he had always been prepared. He was meticulous in his preparation in all three phases of his life, studying game films, arriving early and staying late to practice, and carefully mapping out classroom plans.

If he was going to do this TV thing, he wanted to give it an honest effort. But most of all, he wanted to sit down with someone in the business—a producer, a director, a play-by-play man—who could walk a neophyte broadcaster through the learning process. He spent weeks worrying about this during the summer, but all he heard repeatedly from the executives at CBS was this vague bit of advice: "Just be yourself."

The more he heard that, the more it drove Madden crazy. "The single worst piece of advice you can get in TV when you're making that transition is that ridiculous phrase, 'Well, just be yourself,'" says Madden. "Well, what the hell does that mean? I think we all like to think of ourselves as a little complex. You're just not one thing. So what 'myself' do you want? No one's ever explained that to me, and I don't think any of them understand what they're saying when they keep telling people that."

The second-worst piece of advice Madden heard after taking the job at CBS was, "Don't worry, we'll explain everything when you come to the seminar."

The CBS seminar was an annual early summer gathering in New York of all the production and broadcast staffs at the network who did pro football games, including producers, directors, cameramen, technical staff from the mobile trucks, sideline reporters, play-by-play men, game and studio analysts, and all the other multitudes of support staff.

So by the time Madden arrived at CBS headquarters in midtown Manhattan in June 1979, he walked into the large boardroom in Black Rock assuming that all the mysteries of broadcast journalism would be revealed to him over the course of the few days he was in the city. "So I told everybody, 'Hey I'm going to New York to learn how to broadcast a TV game,'" Madden says. "Well, it was the most disappointing thing I'd ever seen. All they talked about were expenses. How to fill out an expense report and what you could do and couldn't do. We talked expenses and we had a cocktail party, and that was it. I left New York not knowing anything more about television than before I came there."

They sent him back to California with no notebooks, no thick instruction manual, no tapes to study, no advice to follow. They did promise to bring him along slowly, putting him on low-priority games that would be seen in small percentages of the national viewing audience.

But Madden still was clinging to his roots as a coach and player. When they gave him his first new assignment, a game in San Francisco between the 49ers and New Orleans Saints in the fourth week of the season, Madden grew increasingly uncomfortable with the idea of doing a game with no prior preparation.

"So I told them, 'I can't go on the air without ever doing it,'" Madden says. "I said I needed a practice game. They looked at me all odd because they had never done that before. But I wasn't going to go out there and make a fool of myself."

Because the network wanted to bring him along slowly, Madden did not get a full-season schedule of games in 1979. Instead, the plan was to work him in with various partners on a limited schedule that would begin with that 49ers-Saints game. So he was inactive for the first two weeks of that first season. He did try to get a feel for what it would be like to watch a football game for the first time as a nonparticipant, attending a Raiders preseason game in the Oakland Coliseum, but when he got to the stadium, Madden suddenly felt lost and out of place. It was no longer his team. He no longer belonged on the sideline, but he didn't know where he should go to watch the game.

Madden felt so out of place that he ended up leaving the stadium in the middle of the game and driving home, where his wife was shocked to see him.

"How come you left early?" Virginia asked.

"I just left," he said. "I didn't know what to do."

The network did keep its promise to give him a rehearsal that would simulate a real game broadcast, and on September 16, 1979, in the Los Angeles Coliseum, with the hometown Rams hosting the 49ers, CBS flew Madden in for his "practice" game. With Vin Scully and George Allen in the real booth doing the network broadcast, Madden was assigned an auxiliary booth with his own producer, director, and a young play-by-play guy to take him through the process.

Madden's partner was an incredibly youthful-looking 27-year-old named Bob Costas, whose promising broadcasting career was just getting started. Outside of St. Louis, Costas was not a household face or voice. But he was enthusiastic and more than willing to serve as Madden's original sidekick.

The meeting of the two future sports-broadcasting legends was memorable for two reasons: 1) neither of them had any clue how big the other man would become in the sports TV business and 2) they both were well aware how young Costas looked.

Madden: "He looked like he was 15, and I couldn't believe it. We meet in the hotel, and as we're taking a cab together over to the LA Coliseum, all I'm thinking [is], *Geez, they put me in here with this kid.*"

Costas: "Even though I was a kid at 27, I looked more like a kid, like I was 13. Yet he was very nice to me. He actually deferred to me constantly and looked to me for guidance."

They spent their first few awkward minutes together trying to hash out how the day would go. Costas wanted to provide all the structure he could for Madden, then get out of the coach's way and let him gain as much experience as he could. He wanted to make Madden comfortable. He wanted to make sure that the coach felt like there would be no surprises as the game drew closer.

Finally, someone was telling Madden something useful. He wasn't entirely comfortable as they headed to the stadium, but he was no longer terrified that he would make an idiot of himself. If he looked and sounded bad now, it wouldn't be from lack of preparation.

As they arrived at the Coliseum, found a parking spot, and headed into the media entrance, Costas took the elevator up to the booth, while Madden, the old football coach, lingered on the field talking to players and coaches from both teams to prep for the practice broadcast.

While on the field, he did a taped stand-up that would be played later in the mock pregame broadcast. But Madden then lingered a bit too long down on the sideline and was forced to scramble to get up to the booth several levels above the field.

"Well, it was the first time I would be watching a game from upstairs," says Madden. "I'd never in all my coaching life been upstairs. So I'm talking to the players and coaches, and I don't go upstairs until only 10 minutes before the game."

As he rode up the slow elevator to the press box, Madden was in for the surprise of his young broadcasting life. He walked into the cramped auxiliary booth where Costas was already standing in the front row with the glass window raised up so they could see and hear everything. Madden stepped down to the broadcast position and suddenly he saw football in an entirely different—and decidedly unfamiliar—way.

"When I got there, I was like, 'Holy shit!'" he says. Everything looked different to the old coach turned broadcaster. He felt like he was a mile away from the game. His eyes and instincts for football had been honed on a lifetime of being right there on the sideline. He was never one of those coordinators who called plays from upstairs, never an assistant who sat next to that guy. He was a hands-on coach who loved the interaction with his players. But now he was being asked to explain the game from a point of view that was as foreign to him as if they had asked him to talk about cooking from the living room.

It was at this moment that Madden finally realized how far away from the game, both metaphorically and emotionally, he had moved. Standing up there in that booth high above the playing field, the old coach felt miles away from the game that he had been deeply connected to all his life.

BECAUSE HE HAD WAITED SO LONG TO GET UP TO THE BOOTH, Madden had little time to dwell on the poignancy of the moment. He had to scramble to get up there. The press-box elevator in the Coliseum was like every other press-box elevator in America: slow and unreliable. He was cutting it close as he arrived in the booth, quickly slipped on his headset, gathered his thoughts, took a deep breath, and waited for his cue from his partner with the Beatles haircut and the face of a schoolboy.

Whatever apprehension Madden had brought with him into the booth quickly flew out the window the moment Costas opened his mouth. "He has this big, booming voice," Madden recalls with a robust laugh. "And I was like, 'Holy shit, is this the same guy I was talking to in the cab? Wow, this guy is good.'"

Costas, too, was taking mental notes about the guy next to him. "He did not come in there with the cocky supposition that, 'I'm going to come in there and be terrific and revolutionize this,'" says Costas. "I was trying to take care of as many of the nuts and bolts of the broadcast as I could. I wanted to get out of the way so he could do his thing. And he showed some of the personality that subsequently he showed on the air, but only a little bit. It wasn't the arms flailing and the big personality. But there was something different about him."

The late 1970s were still a time when most of the football color commentators were either very straightforward ex-jocks or coaches who delivered their commentary like the antiseptic narration of Jack Webb on *Dragnet* or good ol' boy jesters who were heavy on style but mostly lacking in substance.

Madden didn't revolutionize broadcasting in that first practice game—and he didn't noticeably alter the color-commentary landscape immediately—but he did show a glint of something different from the start.

He was destined to be a lot more like Don Meredith than Al DeRogatis—witty and informative, more interested in finding a way to educate and entertain.

"I'd be lying if I said I walked out of that booth thinking, *This guy is going to be the next Big Thing*," says Costas. "I'd like to say I saw that, but I wasn't that prescient. But did I think he had a chance to be good? I definitely did. There was something about him that was genuine. He wasn't trying to sound like an announcer. There was something potentially spontaneous about him."

Oddly enough, that spontaneity didn't come out as much when the cameras were rolling on that first day in the booth. Instead, the Madden persona that America would eventually come to know and love only emerged during commercial breaks. "I remember there was all of this nervous energy when we went to commercials, and it came out in the form of him heaping praise on me during the commercials," Costas says. "That's when you saw that famous John Madden personality."

As Costas recalls the day, he does what most people do when recreating a Madden moment. He falls easily into his own version of the recognizable Madden patois: "*HEYhow'boutthisKID??!!! How'dHE KNOW ALLLTHATSTUFF!!!??? WOW, we'retalking about THIS and then—BAM!—hesaysTHAT!!!! WOW...howaboutTHAT,HUH???!!*"

There was one other indelible impression that Madden left on young Bob Costas, something that resonated with him far more than his potential for future broadcast excellence.

"I always tell people this. He was extremely nice to me," says Costas. "And when I do say that, a lot of people might hear this and will say, 'Well, what's the big deal about that?' You have to remember in 1979, he was a year removed from winning a Super Bowl, and at that time outside of St. Louis no one knew who the heck I was. There was no way he could have known that I would be subsequently successful in the business. Yet he was extremely nice to me…. He wasn't patronizing. He was really respectful. I always remember that. I am a firm believer in this: one of the measures of a person is how do they treat someone they have no reason to believe can do them that much good. I will always remember John Madden for that."

After the game, Madden and Costas parted company and the producers handed Madden a copy of the rehearsal tapes. They were on big 16" reels, so Madden couldn't just pop them into his home VCR. The next day, he called ahead to a local TV station, and he and Virginia drove up to Oakland and watched the game tape together. As the tape whirled away, Madden made a quick determination about his maiden voyage into broadcasting. "I thought, *Man, I'm terrible*," he remembers.

16

THE MAKING OF
A TV STAR

"Once a journey is designed, equipped, and put in process, a new factor enters and takes over. A trip, a safari, an exploration, is an entity, different from all other journeys.... We find after years of struggle that we do not take a trip; a trip takes us."

John Steinbeck, *Travels With Charley: In Search of America*

IN THE WINTER OF 1979, JOHN MADDEN WAS ON HIS WAY DOWN A new career path. He was 43 years old, an age by which the destinies of most men have already been determined, their fates irreversibly locked on cruise control. Even in the sports world, where men of a certain age retire from their athletic lives and begin anew, this change of course was considered rather unusual. Athletes usually experience their midlife crisis in their mid-thirties when time, age, and injuries finally catch up with them. But for a professional head coach, particularly one as successful as Madden, it was unheard of to retreat into the coaching shadows at such a relatively young age.

Madden was leaving one career out of pure self-preservation. He was embarking on another one for several reasons: out of boredom with the monotony of retirement and also out of equal parts ambivalence and trepidation with his new career choice. What Madden didn't know, what he couldn't know at the time, was where this trip would take him. All he knew was it beat the hell out of those damned lines at the license bureau. Ultimately, it turns out his internal GPS had set a course that would ultimately lead him to even more fame—and decidedly more fortune—than he had already achieved as a Super Bowl–winning head coach.

He was a burned-out football coach looking for the next great challenge in his life, and television was placed in front of him like a plate of exotic-looking hors d'oeuvres in the face of a starving man. He grabbed it out of reflex. He wasn't convinced that this was necessarily the best thing or most appetizing thing for him, but he was hungry to fill this gaping void in his life. So television it was, even if he cringed when he looked at that first rehearsal tape.

His first TV contract with CBS was indeed an appetizer—only four games and $12,000. Most of the nation had no idea what sort of broadcaster Madden could be because he spent those first two years lost in regional telecasts. He had four games in 1979 and about a half-dozen more in 1980, working with a wide variety of play-by-play partners, from Frank Gleiber to Dick Stockton, Stockton to Gary Bender, Bender to Vin Scully.

His final assignment of his rookie season was November 25, 1979. There was John Madden, high above Tampa Stadium, doing his pregame stand-up with Pat Summerall. It was a Week 13 matchup between the hometown Buccaneers and the visiting Minnesota Vikings. With little fanfare, one of the most celebrated chapters in sports-broadcasting history began like this: "Good afternoon to you, I'm Pat Summerall and this is the former great coach of the Oakland Raiders, John Madden, and John, I haven't had an opportunity to see the Buccaneers this year, but you have. Tell us a little about them."

Madden: "They're very impressive, Pat. Last year they had a good defense, and they still have a very good and strong defense. But their biggest improvement this year has been in their offense. Their offensive line has jelled and is doing a fine job of blocking. Ricky Bell is doing a fine job of running. He's gained 909 yards, and Doug Williams is maturing as a top quarterback."

Summerall: "A lot of people have said that the Buccaneers do not play a representative schedule. That it's not tough enough. What's your feeling on that?"

Madden: "I feel that the schedule is overrated. The Buccaneers play 16 games like everyone else, and a lot of those losses that their opponents have, have been caused by the Buccaneers and their success this year."

No one in charge at CBS at the time noticed that Madden and Summerall had a particular chemistry. In fact, they would not team up again for another two years. And if first impressions meant anything, Summerall was convinced this was a pairing that could not possibly endure. As they stood side by side on this rickety tower hundreds of feet above the football field with the wind whipping up, to hear Summerall tell it, Madden looked positively terrified. Rivulets of perspiration were running down his face. Under the big beige sports coat, the old coach's white dress shirt was soaking with sweat. "I knew him from his days as a coach," says Summerall. "But I looked at him the first time we were together and thought, *My gosh, he knows what he's talking about and he has the ability that very few people have to articulate his thoughts and knowledge,* but he was soaking wet with sweat. I thought he was nervous about being on the air. I remember thinking, *This guy is in the wrong business if he's this nervous about being on television.*"

As it turned out, Madden wasn't jittery about television. He was terrified of heights. The old Tampa Stadium press box was not exactly state-of-the-art, so CBS constructed a temporary platform outside the press box several stories above the upper rim of the big bowl stadium for the two men to do their pregame stand-ups. It exposed them to the wind, and it also put Madden in the most uncomfortable place he could be other than inside a pressurized airplane cabin. He was exposed on a precarious perch high in the air. "When we had to come out on this platform out over the second deck, it was almost frightening to me to be up there," says Summerall. "For John, oh, he was scared to death."

After the game, Summerall went back to his longtime partner Tom Brookshier, while Madden went back to another year of part-time work and rotating partners. But sports broadcasting as we knew it—particularly the art of broadcasting professional football—was on its way to undergoing a dramatic change in style and substance.

It would not be a sudden, seismic shift. Rather, it would be a more subtle process as executives and production people at CBS first had to realize what they had in John Madden.

MADDEN HAD ARRIVED AT CBS SPORTS AT AN INTERESTING TIME. Van Gordon Sauter took over as president of CBS Sports in 1980, and he quickly began making strategic changes that would lead to a radical overhaul of the way the network did business. Sauter also figured out what, inexplicably, no one before him seemed to notice: Madden was being underutilized at CBS. When he hired Terry O'Neil away from ABC in January 1981 to become the executive producer of CBS Sports, it was already on Sauter's agenda to break up the lead NFL broadcast team of Summerall and Brookshier, and he was mulling over the possibility that Madden would be the most likely candidate to step into the lead-analyst chair.

Sauter had brought O'Neil in to assist in the daunting assignment of bringing the lifeless sports division into a modern era of broadcasting. Within months, the all-encompassing shakeup was underway, revamping several shows, dumping the NBA property and replacing it with college basketball and the lucrative NCAA tournament (stolen from NBC) and redesigning the entire on-air look of the network, from graphics to music, from studio sets to the CBS Sports logo.

Next up on the to-do list was fixing the NFL coverage, which had grown stale and predictable. The first priority was to put together a new No. 1 broadcast team. Before making the decision of who it would be, he asked O'Neil for his thoughts on Madden. "I don't know," O'Neil said. "I've only ever seen him for 30 seconds at a time."

The old regime at CBS had not given Madden much exposure at all, so O'Neil could only base his opinion on the image that Madden portrayed in those memorable Miller Lite beer commercials. That was America's first hint that there was something altogether different about the coach. A self-deprecating star quality, if you will, was emerging every time he was on screen pitching beer.

In those commercials, Madden was a bit goofy, loud, excitable, but, most of all, extremely likeable. He was the big, rumpled everyman you wanted to sit around and have a beer with. And if that personality was coming across in 30-second bursts when he was surrounded by all those other larger-than-life sports personalities in the Miller ads, both Sauter and O'Neil wondered why he wasn't being allowed to show that same charm in the broadcast booth.

O'Neil was a student of the Roone Arledge school at ABC, where he believed that a "star system" was necessary to create a strong sports network. For the monstrous *Monday Night Football* prime-time package, Arledge had masterfully developed that star quality with Howard Cosell, Don Meredith, and Frank Gifford. Down the street at NBC, they had stars in their booth as well, with Al McGuire, Dick Enberg, Billy Packer, Bryant Gumbel, and a young Bob Costas.

From O'Neil's perspective, CBS was void of stars on its NFL coverage. They had no one who could be considered young and promising or a seasoned veteran with gravitas.

But as he spent hours poring over videotapes of Madden, O'Neil saw that some of the same magnetism that fairly exploded off the screen in those beer commercials could be replicated in an NFL broadcast. O'Neil remembered the way Al Davis had described his first encounter with Madden back in 1966 when Madden was a young assistant coach at San Diego State. And now, as he looked and listened to Madden the football analyst talk, O'Neil was getting the same vibe that Davis had sensed.

"That's what those videotapes revealed," O'Neil recalled. "It was an emotional love of football and something about him that was a little different…it was no more explicable than that. But Sauter and I would take it. Madden was on board."

Google John Madden's name and click on the video icon. It may take some time, but eventually you will find early footage of Madden in the booth. What you will see is that he was not immediately the guy we all came to know and love for his hyperkinetic manner.

Actually, he was a little stiff and prone to stating the obvious. But the longer he worked at it, the better he got. Yet in 1980, he was still not anchored with a permanent partner. He was passed up and down the play-by-play food chain. But even in his first encounter with Summerall, the always-perceptive Madden picked up on the faint signs of good chemistry. It wasn't instant magic, but chemistry was incubating in Tampa Stadium. When Summerall sat down with Madden before the broadcast to discuss what they were doing and what would be said, he established a pattern that would lead to creating the lasting bonds of the best broadcast duo ever.

Very simply, he asked Madden beforehand what points he wanted to make in his pregame stand-up. "I don't know if anyone learned from Pat Summerall what the secret to his success was, but I'll tell you what it was," Madden says. "A lot of play-by-play guys think they have to lead the analyst where they want him to go, which is really a huge mistake. Too many of them often lead [the analyst] to a place where he doesn't want to go or, even worse, where he's not prepared to go. But Pat's genius was that instead of leading you, [he would] would always tag you. In other words, he would let you start and talk about something that you felt was significant, then let you go, and then put his commentary on the end of whatever you were saying."

What Madden noticed almost right away, it would take CBS executives a bit longer to discover. Sauter was not a fan of Summerall's. Over the years, Summerall and Brookshier had developed a bad reputation as party boys on the road. In his book *The Game Behind The Game: High Stakes, High Pressure in Television Sports*, O'Neil described their partying ways in these unflattering terms: "Alcohol was the lifeblood of the old CBS Sports. Summerall and Brookshier regularly drank their way through the 4:00 PM football telecasts. After all, it was cocktail hour."

Sauter had his eye on Vin Scully for the job. Scully was an elegant voice who had become a legend as the radio voice of the Los Angeles Dodgers and a network play-by-play man for pro football and pro golf. Scully was from the old school of baseball radio broadcasting, an on-air poet who painted lovely pictures of baseball and golf, games with similarly languid paces. He crafted moods, scenery, and the intricate strategies of those games as if they were scenes from a Norman Rockwell painting. Since Sauter and Scully shared the same agent, Ed

Hookstratten, it fueled speculation around the network that the deal was already done.

O'Neil thought Scully was a masterful broadcaster but felt he was too verbose to be paired with the extremely talkative Madden. With Madden's need to paint his own football pictures, there wouldn't be enough time between plays for both of them to make breathless strokes on the canvas. O'Neil thought Summerall's minimalist style was a better match for Madden.

After much hand-wringing, a compromise was reached. The first eight weeks of the '81 season would turn into an audition between Scully and Summerall. Madden would do the first four games of the season with Scully while Summerall was in New York doing the U.S. Open tennis tournament. When Summerall finished his tennis duties and Scully peeled off in October for the baseball playoffs, Summerall moved into the booth with Madden for his four-game stint. A decision would be made on Monday, October 26.

The winner would get a permanent gig with Madden, plus Super Bowl XVI at the end of the season. "It turned out to be something like a sweepstakes to see who would be the play-by-play man," Sandy Grossman recalled. The technical crew stayed intact for all of the games with Grossman directing, O'Neil producing, and both taking mental notes of comparison. Even while the Madden sweepstakes was going on, there was a belief among the production crew similar to that in the CBS executive suites: this "sweepstakes" was all for show, and Scully had already been promised the job by Sauter.

The competition turned out to create just as many problems as it was supposed to solve. Summerall, for one, wasn't buying the notion that it was an even playing field. He had heard the gossip in the production truck, too. In early October, he told O'Neil as much in a private conversation where he announced that he would be taking his talents to NBC at the end of the year since he was not going to get Scully's job. Summerall told O'Neil this "competition" was an elaborate ruse, the sole purpose of which was to let him down easy.

When O'Neil disputed that, Summerall retaliated. If O'Neil hadn't hatched the idea of this conspiracy, then it was much worse. He was Sauter's stooge, forced to go along with the charade.

But as the auditions went on and both men had their crack at the microphone, O'Neil saw all that he needed to see. He now thought he had all the evidence he needed to convince Sauter that Summerall was the right man for the job, even if he couldn't convince the old place kicker that he was his No. 1 promoter.

A week after this uncomfortable confrontation, Grossman remembers O'Neil asking him what he thought of the sweepstakes. "I thought it was fairly obvious. 'Summerall, for sure,' I told him," says Grossman. Grossman remembers that O'Neil smiled and nodded his head in agreement. They both could see from the truck that there was just something that made sense about the pairing of the baritone-voiced Summerall and his minimalist style with the frenetic Madden. And the coach agreed. "No matter where I would go, no matter how far off the range I would roam, he had the amazing ability to bring it all back in a concise manner and make sense of whatever craziness I had just blabbered," Madden says.

What Madden didn't say publicly but did express privately was that he always regarded Summerall as a football guy and Scully as a baseball guy, and to anyone who knew John Madden well, that was a relevant distinction. "Scully was great," says Grossman, "but there were things about him that John wasn't happy about." The Dodgers were a priority in his professional life. "That meant he wasn't really a full-time football guy," Grossman remembers. "And if you're going to be working with John, there's only one sport, and it's football. He might give lip service to other sports, but the bottom line is football with him, and when you work with John, you have to know that."

Still, Summerall's suspicions about the competition weren't exactly off base. After the eight-week auditions, O'Neil could sense that Sauter was still strongly in the Scully camp. He remembered how on every Monday in September he could count on Sauter peeking his head into

O'Neil's office to recite every stylish bit of purple prose Scully had uttered the day before. If Summerall was going to have any shot at this—and if O'Neil had any hope of preventing a long-term disaster that he envisioned with the Scully-Madden marriage—he would have to rally additional support within the sports-division hierarchy. O'Neil wanted Sauter to make this decision based on a consensus of all his top aides. He wanted all five vice presidents and the senior producer for the NFL to weigh in, too. It was now turning into a calculated bit of high-stakes office politics.

O'Neil had already gotten a sense from everyone else in the room which way they were leaning, and he walked into that meeting knowing that at least four other men were going to support Summerall. By the time Sauter asked for votes, it turned out to be unanimous. His six trusted advisers had seen that Summerall and Madden were a better match than Scully and Madden.

The mood in the room suddenly got very uncomfortable. The only sound in the room was the jarring bang of Sauter's fist onto the conference table, the rattling of coffee cups and silverware, and the distinctive anger in the boss' voice. *"All right!"* he shouted. "I've heard enough. If you people want him, you can have him."

O'Neil could feel his heart plummeting down his throat.

"But mark my words," Sauter warned. "You'll have to manage him. I hope you know what you're letting yourselves in for. I'm not going to be responsible for his alcoholic binges."

The boss was demanding an accountability check, and his angry words were painting a humongous bull's-eye on O'Neil's butt if this decision didn't work out.

The decision was made, or, rather, "O'Neil's decision" was made. And that is exactly how this would play out if it failed. While Sauter would be in the front of the room when the decision was announced, O'Neil was being positioned to take the fall if Summerall crashed and burned. Madden and Summerall would be CBS' No. 1 team and would spend the rest of the season together, including getting the plum assignment of the season, Super Bowl XVI on January 24, 1982, in Pontiac, Michigan. Scully was paired with Hank Stram, and they would do the NFC Championship Game as a consolation prize.

Scully did not take the news well. He was ticked off with O'Neil, who had awkwardly handled the task of informing Scully that he had lost the sweepstakes. It didn't take long before Scully was walking into Sauter's office to reject a new contract offer, instead heading down the street from CBS' Black Rock to 30 Rock at NBC.

17

"TO YOU IT'S A SHOW, BUT TO ME IT'S A GODDAMNED GAME..."

"Good company in a journey makes the way seem shorter."

Izaak Walton, *The Compleat Angler*

NOW THAT HE HAD ASSEMBLED HIS DREAM TEAM IN THE BOOTH, Terry O'Neil would embark on another equally difficult bit of housecleaning that was sure to cause just as many headaches for the ambitious young executive producer. This wasn't about personnel issues. One of the more troubling issues that O'Neil would have to confront was the task of changing attitudes within a production team that, by all appearances, was vigorously resistant to change. John Madden had picked up on something almost immediately when he began doing games, and it greatly troubled him. It was one of the reasons why Madden the coach was always suspicious of network TV guys and spent little time talking to them. Now his suspicions were being confirmed to him as a broadcaster. He felt the people who were assigned to doing the games on television with him didn't know a damned thing about the games they were covering.

As early as May 1981, Madden expressed this concern during a conversation with O'Neil over lunch. Madden was upset that everyone on the production team was thinking of his precious game of football rather cavalierly as "a show." It was that same description that had angered him the first time he heard it seven years earlier when Howard Cosell had approached him after a *Monday Night Football* game that the Raiders had just lost 21–20 to the Buffalo Bills.

"John," Cosell gushed. "You gave us a great show!"

"*Show?* A great *show?*" Madden exploded. "To you it's a show, but to me it's a goddamned *game* we just lost! And there's nothing great about it!"

During his lunch meeting with O'Neil, Madden conjured up that same contempt. "Our people are always saying, 'The show this and the show that.' Hell, this isn't a show. *Kukla, Fran and Ollie* is a show! *Laverne and Shirley* is a show! This is a *game!*"

O'Neil promised to change that attitude with the troops.

"What else?" he asked.

"Well, they don't know anything about the game. Don't know and don't care," Madden said.

"What do you mean?"

"You know, football. They don't know whether you blow it up or stuff it…take defense. Simple things, like showing what a zone coverage is. Or showing a pass rusher coming onto the field on third down."

"Yeah, so?" O'Neil asked.

"So the producer and director tell me they can't show it. Say they don't know it's going to happen until it's over."

"Well, don't they pick these things up when they watch game film?"

"*Game film? Game film?* Hell, some of these guys don't even show up until the morning of the game," Madden retorted.

The industry critics agreed with Madden's brutal assessment. They too were convinced that "old" CBS Sports had a problem, but unlike the coach, who was coming at it from a football sense, the newspaper critics shaped their evaluations from a technical point of view. They saw uninspired people who were just showing up and putting out a product that was "produced in a stodgy, schizophrenic manner almost, it sometimes seemed, half-heartedly," according to *Television Age* magazine.

When Madden and O'Neil arrived at CBS, they were walking into a culture that desperately needed to be changed. To put it mildly, O'Neil (and his new boss Van Gordon Sauter) believed it was an enterprise built on laziness and excessive partying. Pregame preparation was nonexistent. "Before Madden, the way we prepared for a game was showing up on Saturday," Sandy Grossman says. "With [Pat] Summerall and [Tom] Brookshier, we'd sit down with the PR directors on Saturday, and they'd hand us their press guides, a few newspaper clippings, and that was it."

The height of this cavalier attitude came during preparation for Super Bowl XIV (Los Angeles Rams vs. Pittsburgh Steelers) when the CBS crew was informed that a meeting had been arranged with Steelers coach Chuck Noll, and Brookshier's initial response was, "Do we have to go?"

If Brookshier was the class cut-up, then Madden was the teacher who gave homework on the weekends. He brought a coach's work ethic to television. He wanted the entire production team to study game film and attend practices. He wanted them to interview players and coaches, gain better insight into the broadcast, and better prepare for essential camera shots that would capture important elements of the coming game. The deeper he got into the television business, the more his personality came out. Madden wasn't upset that they liked to party. Hell, he used to coach the Raiders. But his wild and rambunctious players worked hard, prepared meticulously, and cared deeply about the jobs they were expected to do. Most of all, they knew the game.

So Madden had to become a control freak. He had to take charge because if their broadcasts looked bad, that was a reflection on him. So he once again was a coach and teacher, and he was going to have to coach up an entirely new group of students, many of whom weren't all that interested in learning.

Noted sports television critic Bob Raissman, who has covered the industry at *Advertising Age* and the *New York Daily News* for the last 27 years, remembers sitting in on some of those production meetings in the early years. "He would teach these guys football," says Raissman. "He had longtime producers and director [Bob] Stenner and Grossman, and he was telling them what he was looking for. He was instructing them on what to look for in an important football game. I know some people thought he was overbearing, but I was in the room. He wasn't necessarily ordering them around, but he was putting out a game plan for these guys. His attitude was like this was his team. They were his players, his coaching staff. They were his team."

Grossman and the rest of the crew began to feel that "team" vibe almost immediately, even if they weren't all that thrilled to be sitting there with glazed eyes, entranced by the *whirl-click, whirl-click* of Madden at the control of the game films. "Yes, it was like we were becoming a part of his new coaching staff," Grossman chuckled. "We would watch [game film], and we'd go back and forth, back and forth on certain plays and, to be honest with you, it was boring to us. But we kept doing it and listening to him. And as we went along, we did start to see things, and we would then ask questions."

All of the technical staff would be there for hours. Summerall didn't always stick around very long. But then again, he didn't have to because Madden already knew Summerall had built-in credibility. "Pat had been everywhere," says Madden. "He had been a player, a coach, an analyst, and a play-by-play man. So that [gave me] a lot of confidence that the guy sitting next to [me] knew more about what was going on than [I] did."

We look back historically and think of Madden and Summerall as the quintessential broadcast partners. They lasted 22 years together, becoming synonymous with every big game in the NFC, from Thanksgiving Day in Dallas to championship duels in San Francisco, from Gatorade baths in the Meadowlands to unbridled celebrations of the Hogs in D.C., to marveling at the Greatest Show on Turf in St. Louis. However, Summerall wasn't completely sold on his new partner right off the bat.

In early September, right before a preseason game they would be broadcasting between the Dallas Cowboys and the Houston Oilers, Summerall gave the *Dallas Morning News* a rather clear picture of how different it was working with Brookshier and surprisingly how apprehensive he felt about Madden's more serious approach:

"It puts me in a tough position. Deep down, it's really true that I'd rather be with Brookshier.... It was not like going to work when

Brookie and I did games. It was like I couldn't wait to get there. As he is fond of saying, when we arrived we were laughing and when we left on Sunday night we were still laughing. If it were Brookshier and me, we would have had the production meeting, then we would have been out drinking margaritas. Now I'm not sure what's going to happen."

But on that September 4 morning, before that exhibition game in Dallas, as Terry O'Neil laid in his bed in a Dallas hotel before the official debut of this new partnership, there was tangible tension in the air. Before the partnership even got started, O'Neil was scared that it might all blow up if Madden was reading the same *Dallas Morning News* article he was reading over his room-service breakfast. When O'Neil read Summerall's words in the *Morning News*, it killed his appetite. He didn't bother to eat a thing. Instead, he hurriedly got dressed and raced downstairs to the lobby, where he found Madden slouched in an overstuffed lounge chair with the morning paper covering his face.

The split second after he had read Summerall's words, O'Neil wondered if Madden would see it, and if so, how he would react to it. As he saw Madden's face slowly emerge as he put down the newspaper, O'Neil got his answer.

The coach was pissed off, and his anger was written all over his big, round face. He was not the pleasant fellow America came to love in the Miller Lite commercials. He was the angry old coach, confronted with the same sort of needless tension in his gut that had driven him out of the coaching profession.

Before O'Neil could get a complete assessment of the damage that had been done, within seconds, Summerall appeared in the lobby, too. O'Neil didn't know what to expect. Would the slender young man with the Ivy League education find himself in the middle of two much larger former football players who might act out their feelings in the middle of the crowded hotel lobby? Would he be forced to defuse a potentially embarrassing public scene?

Nothing.

Summerall said, "Good morning, John" pleasantly enough and kept walking toward the front door as if nothing was wrong. Madden mumbled something under his breath, barely looked at Summerall, and slowly ambled toward the door as well. And that was that. Over and done with. No public displays, no harsh words. But in that split second, everyone had to be wondering whether this union would last.

SOMETHING ELSE HAPPENED on that warm September evening in Dallas that would prove to be vital to the Summerall-Madden longevity. It was a brief but blunt conversation O'Neil had with Summerall outside the production truck about an hour before the preseason broadcast began. O'Neil laid down the law, something that no one at CBS Sports had bothered to consider before then. He told Summerall the days of cocktail parties in the booth during telecasts were over.

It was a smart play by O'Neil, informing Summerall that the stage manager's job was on the line if alcohol ended up in the booth and if he found out that anyone—commentators, production staff, or technicians—was caught drinking before they had gone off the air. Summerall knew that he would be taking down others if he committed any indiscretions.

As O'Neil remembers, Summerall glared at him for a few uncomfortable seconds, then said, "Whatever you say." As quickly as the awkward moment in the lobby ended, so had this one. And while they had to wait more than a month to get Madden and Summerall back together again (as the sweepstakes began with Scully's four-game stint), by October, O'Neil could see that whatever apprehension had been in the air between Madden and Summerall in August had disappeared.

"Pat was just the perfect guy for me," says Madden. "Pat was everything I wasn't. He was concise. I wasn't. In a game, you're often dictated to by time. You have commercials, change of possession, penalties. So many times you have to get in and get out, and you don't make sense. I would worry about that, worry about not making sense with what I am saying because of [a lack of] time. But with Pat I had the confidence that I could do anything and say anything I wanted to because Pat could get me out of it and make sense of it in three or four words."

For his part, Summerall quickly began to appreciate the advantages of the extra film work and commitment to pregame preparation with his new partner. At one point, he even acknowledged that he wished he could have played under Madden. Much later, he acknowledged that he had learned a very important tidbit from a radio and television star of the 1950s and '60s that would serve him well in forming his chemistry with Madden. "I think [it] comes with something Art Linkletter told me when I first came into the broadcast business," Summerall says. "It was a very simple piece of advice. You have to listen to your partner. You have to listen to what he says and the point he is trying to make. I don't want to come across as a critic of other play-by-play broadcasters, but I think a lot of people don't listen to what their partner is trying to say and the point he's trying to make. They're too busy trying to get their point across."

Summerall's strength was that he never got in Madden's way, on or off the air. If Madden wanted everyone to be better prepared, then that's what Summerall did. He began watching game tapes of both teams that were sent to his home in Dallas on Tuesdays. He would sit in his office watching those tapes until he was completely familiar with every player on both teams. "It got to the point by Friday that I knew the players regardless of numbers," says Summerall. "I knew them by mannerisms. I knew them by their height, their body shapes, the way they moved."

He credited that to Madden's insistence that everyone be as prepared for the game as the teams they were covering. "[Madden's] preparation and presentation made everyone better," Summerall says. "He wanted [everyone] looking at film carefully. We got tapes from the network of previous games of both teams and we got [coaches tapes] from the league.

"We all became better at what we were doing than before John came on the scene. We prepared like coaches. We knew why so-and-so missed a block. We knew why this happened or that happened. I remember before one Super Bowl we interviewed everyone on both teams. Seriously, every single player. We were never surprised. We were ready for any situation that arose…. And I think his knowledge of football [as a player and coach] and my knowledge [as a player and coach] mattered. Us knowing what constituted a good block for example, and to me that helped the broadcast. There's nothing like preparation, nothing like being ready."

O'Neil kept his promise to Madden and made sure that this insistence on being prepared became a network-wide practice. Every crew had a similar schedule during the week, arriving on Friday for mandatory 8:00 PM dinner meetings between the producer, director, and commentators to discuss the plans for the weekend. With the Madden team, that usually meant the entire production crew was invited. They would usually meet in Madden's room and dine on either room-service food or delivery from a local restaurant that had landed on Madden's list of favorite eating places around the league.

For Madden's crew, large boxes full of brown paper bags filled with dinner became a familiar sight—and an indication that it was going to be a long night of football talk. They would play a little poker, goof around a bit, but no matter where the conversation started, it always ended up on football.

The guys on the production crew referred to the time they spent sitting in a hotel lobby or meeting room with Madden as "hang time." There was no such thing as going out to a fancy restaurant with Madden. He didn't like going out in the first place. To him there was nothing better than hanging out watching game film or hanging out talking football or hanging out playing poker *then* talking football. Or just talking football into the wee hours of the morning.

"It wasn't until the last five years we were together that we started going out to dinner," Grossman recalls. "And then one time a few years ago, I don't even remember where we were, but John's bus was late, and we all figured this was our chance to get out and go to a good place to eat before he showed up, and we could have the meeting afterward. Well, a bunch of us were downstairs standing in front of the hotel, and one guy was running late. We're all standing there looking at our watches, getting a little nervous because we knew that John's bus could be showing up any minute, and if he came before we were able to get out, that was it. We were stuck. We weren't going anywhere."

The poker games were a blast, but every once in a while, a man needs a good steak dinner with fancy table linens, a fine bottle of wine, waiters and maître d's, and maybe a fine-looking waitress or barmaid, too. And this was one of those nights. Yet as Grossman, Stenner, and the rest of the crew stood there waiting for that one straggler to come meet them, they heard the familiar sounds of a large bus engine coming into the hotel parking lot.

"It was the funniest thing you ever saw," says Grossman. "We were like, 'Oh shit! There's the fuckin' bus! If he sees us, we're screwed.'"

Now there were a half-dozen grown men diving in the bushes, ducking behind the shrubbery to avoid John Madden.

They did go out that night, but it was one of the few times in those first 15 years that they were able to slip away before Madden arrived.

18
THE HALL
FINALLY CALLS

"They can't take this away, can they?"

John Madden

IT WAS FEBRUARY 4, 2006, AND JUST LIKE HE HAD DONE ON every Super Bowl Saturday since the day he'd retired from coaching nearly 30 years ago, John Madden waited for a particular phone call that so far had not came. On the Saturday before every Super Bowl, the Pro Football Hall of Fame selection committee meets in a boardroom of the media hotel to determine the annual class members for Canton. For decades, despite a coaching record that seemed to scream "Hall of Fame," Madden's phone never rang.

The continued snubs bothered him more than he let on. As much as Madden publicly tried to downplay how much it meant to him to get in, John Robinson says behind the scenes it was an entirely different story. "John really wanted it, he made no secret of it to [his friends]," Robinson said. "It bothered him that he hadn't gotten in. He wondered if he would ever get in."

He privately rationalized why the selection committee never deemed him worthy. He wondered whether or not an anti-Raiders bias was keeping him out ("He thought the voters believed there already were too many Raiders in," one friend says.). He wondered if his 1–6 record in AFL/AFC Championship Games had hurt him. Only once before 2006 had he made it to the finalist round, but a few years ago his name was taken off the regular ballot. This year, however, due to a vote by the veterans' committee, Madden and former Dallas Cowboys offensive lineman Rayfield Wright were the two senior nominees who advanced to Saturday's final round along with 13 other regular-ballot finalists.

By any standard, Madden had done more than enough to get in on his coaching credentials. He coached the Raiders for 10 seasons, posting a regular-season record of 103–32–7. Madden's Raiders won seven Western Division titles, including five in a row from 1972 to 1976. Under Madden's guidance, Oakland never experienced a losing season, made eight playoff appearances, and never finished with fewer than eight wins in the then-14-game season (8–4–2 in 1970 and 1971). Six times in 10 seasons, Oakland recorded 10 or more victories. In 1976 the coach guided his team to a near-perfect 13–1 record to win the AFC Western division. In the postseason he had victories over New England in the divisional playoff game and beat the Steel Curtain dynasty Pittsburgh Steelers 24–7 in an AFC Championship Game, finishing that 1976 season with a 32–14 win over the Minnesota Vikings in Super Bowl XI. Between the 1976 and 1977 seasons, the Raiders won 17 consecutive games, one short of the NFL record for consecutive wins, and his .759 regular-season winning percentage ranks as the highest ever among coaches with 100 career victories. Only Hall of Fame coaches George Halas and Curly Lambeau reached 100 career wins at an earlier age.

On the eve of Super Bowl XL in downtown Detroit, Madden's stalled Hall of Fame candidacy was finally about to change. The 39 members of the Hall of Fame selection committee who gathered at the Renaissance Center Marriott Hotel, a 73-story glass-enclosed pentagon soaring above the city and overlooking the Detroit River and the Canadian city of Windsor on the other side of the river, were a decidedly different lot from the previous committees that continually rejected Madden over the past two decades.

Many of the old-guard voters were being replaced by younger men who had grown up developing their love of the National Football League just about the time Madden was in his coaching heyday. This new breed of selection committee members did not appear to bring any old biases with them. The old-guard voters/reporters who covered the bitter AFL-NFL wars were often forced to choose sides back then and clung passionately to those alliances, particularly the men who had aligned themselves with the old-school National Football League. This younger breed of voters might not have been old enough to have covered Madden the coach, but they certainly were old enough to remember how talented his teams were and didn't regard his playoff losses to the Dolphins, Steelers, and Chiefs with disrespect.

Instead, they seemed far more willing to acknowledge the quality of the opponents that defeated some of Madden's teams. "When you realized who this guy was going to battle against every week and every year," remembers Bernie Miklasz, a columnist from the *St. Louis Post-Dispatch*, "it was baffling to me how he could have slipped through the cracks for so long. This guy was having head-on showdowns not just with good teams, but with some of the greatest teams in NFL history. So he lost to some of them? So what? That's like saying Joe Frazier wasn't great because he lost to Ali and George Foreman. It made no sense to me."

So amidst the Danishes and croissants, the sliced fruit and tall carafes of juice and water and the endless pots of hot coffee, these 39 writers and broadcasters—men who had all been watching and reporting on the NFL for most of their adult lives—began to debate which of these extraordinary former stars of the game would become the latest to join the most select fraternity in pro football.

Each one of the 15 finalists would have one representative on the selection committee state his case. In some instances when an obvious NFL immortal was up for nomination, the pitch could cut straight to the point, such as, "Gentlemen, I give you John Elway." In most cases, it was a heated debate where someone would speak on behalf of each nominee, and then each athlete or coach would be discussed in an open forum. At the end of the debates, there would be several rounds of voting to narrow down the field. It would be a simple yes or no vote, and it would take only eight "no" votes to kill a nomination.

On this particular morning, during the grinding five-hour meeting, Rick Gosslin of the *Dallas Morning News* was the busiest man in the room, speaking on behalf of three former Dallas Cowboys finalists: Troy Aikman, Rayfield Wright, and Michael Irvin. Ira Miller of the *San Francisco Chronicle* was chosen to represent Madden's interests. Miller was a curious choice to be Madden's champion since he would admit much later that in previous votes when Madden was eligible on the regular ballot, he did not seriously consider the coach Hall worthy.

"I'll be honest, when John was eligible those first few years, I didn't vote for him either," says Miller. "In the early years, I wasn't the guy standing in the front of the room making his case. I wasn't on the committee then, and by the time I did [get] on the committee, I sort of kept my mouth shut and listened a lot. In those early years, it was Frank Cooney [of the *San Francisco Examiner*] who spoke up for Madden."

Before Miller rose to present Madden's case, another discussion arose in the room that centered around the voting procedures and at least on the surface would cause even more harm to Madden's Hall of Fame chances. According to the Hall's bylaws, voters are to consider only what a player or coach did on the field. Character flaws, arrests, or other off-field incidents—both positive and negative—are to be ignored. So, for example, if O.J. Simpson had not already been elected to the Hall before his sensational murder trial, his legal woes should technically have no impact on his Hall worthiness.

Historically, though, that particular bylaw was often ignored. Despite admonishments to the contrary, off-the-field matters often greatly impacted the Hall process. There was at the very least a perception that John Mackey's groundbreaking union activism kept him out of Canton for decades. Michael Irvin had to pay penance for his legal entanglements for a few years. Joe Namath's playboy image and gruff relationship with some writers allegedly kept him outside the Hall gates needlessly for a few years, too. And you can bet that Art Modell, the longtime NFL owner who moved the Browns from Cleveland to Baltimore, has had his path blocked by some voters who hold a grudge against him.

Now Madden was back in the room, and by 2006 he had become much more than a retired coaching legend. He had become the preeminent voice of NFL broadcasts, arguably the best color commentator of all time. He had become an icon with the younger generation as a result of his eponymous video game. In essence, he had influenced generations of football lovers. Yet because he had gotten back into the selection committee room as a coach, not a contributor, the bylaws specified that voters could only consider his accomplishments on the field.

"The Hall of Fame tells us we're not supposed to consider anything but John as a coach, and that is silly," recalls *Sports Illustrated* football writer Peter King, one of the more vocal members of the selection committee. "How was I not supposed to consider all the other things he's done in his career? I'm not supposed to have memories of his contributions as a great broadcaster in my head? I'm supposed to ignore that? Well, it's impossible. It is something that we all considered no matter what the rules say we're supposed to do."

Another selection committee member, *USA Today* football columnist Jarrett Bell, remembered that conversation well. "Once that question went around the room, the conversation about how Madden was able to expose so many generations to football and how we were now supposed to ignore that he had done all that, it actually laid the foundation for what was to come next," he said.

What came next was a huge surprise from the most unlikely source.

FRANK COONEY HAD GROWN ALMOST AS FRUSTRATED AS MADDEN that after years of campaigning vigorously for his close friend and occasional business partner, he was unable to sway the room in Madden's favor. When Cooney passed the responsibility over to Miller, he couldn't have known that he had handed the torch to someone who was not Madden's staunchest advocate. Yet even though he had never voted for the old Raiders coach before, Miller took on the new responsibility like a true professional. He researched Madden's résumé thoroughly, trying to find some weapon he could introduce into the room as if it were a mighty cudgel, a superior weapon that would pound some sense into the good voters in the room and, even more importantly, remove the lingering doubts Miller had carried with him all these years.

One day, in the weeks leading up to the meeting in Detroit, Miller found the weapon he was seeking. The Hall bylaws said it had to be all about Madden's coaching record and nothing else. So Miller unearthed a particular statistic of Madden's that had gone largely unnoticed in the past and presented it as Exhibit A in his opening argument.

"John had coached in an incredible era for great Hall of Fame coaches," says Miller. "Don Shula, Chuck Noll, George Allen, Hank Stram.... I know I'm missing someone. But the point is, his record against them was spectacular."

As he pored over all of Madden's victories and defeats, Miller discovered a stunning pattern. In 42 games against eight other coaching contemporaries who were already in the Hall of Fame, Madden had compiled an impressive .642 winning percentage (27–13–2). None of those coaches individually had a winning record against Madden. Here's how it broke down:

Madden vs. Chuck Noll: 6–5

Madden vs. Don Shula: 5–3

Madden vs. Hank Stram: 7–4–2

Madden vs. George Allen: 1–0

Madden vs. Tom Landry: 1–0

Madden vs. Weeb Ewbank: 3–0

Madden vs. Sid Gillman: 2–0

Madden vs. Bud Grant: 2–1

"I think when I heard the stats about his record against the Hall of Fame coaches, that swayed me big time," King says. "And I'm sure that's what did it for all the other voters in that room."

"This got everyone excited," remembers Bell. "Ira was the guy who made the point that put [Madden] over the top in that part of the argument.... I don't think there were ever any dissenting voices after that. It was like, 'Hey guys, we kind of missed the boat on this one all along.'"

To be sure, a vast majority of the voters not-so-secretly exercised some civil disobedience when it came to Madden's candidacy. It was great that they were armed with the statistical pearl that Miller had given them to strengthen the argument that Madden's coaching record alone was good enough to provide him with a ticket to Canton. But the reality was, this new class of selection committee members was sophisticated enough to realize that Madden was the rare exception to the rule. His all-around greatness as a contributor to the game was unlike anything they'd ever seen in pro football history. The Hall may have officially wanted to ignore that fact, but these voters wished to embrace and celebrate it.

"We were told 'no,'" says Miklasz, "but saying 'no' to everything but his coaching would be like someone saying, 'Well, Frank Sinatra's one of the greatest entertainers of all time, but because he was such an amazing singer, we're not allowed to bring up the fact that he won an Oscar for his role in *From Here to Eternity*.' How silly would that be? In the end, I think a lot of people left that room with smiles on their faces knowing what we had done. I was very delighted to vote for John Madden and a little embarrassed that he slipped through the cracks for so long."

As the voters finished their five-hour deliberations and the votes were being tabulated and recorded by Joe Horrigan and his Hall of Fame staffers, Madden was eight blocks up the street from the Marriott inside Ford Field along with broadcast partner Al Michaels and other members of the ABC crew as they went through their normal Super Bowl eve broadcast preparations. They were all trying to concentrate on their work, but they were keeping an eye on the clock, too. "Somebody in the room said, 'If it's good news, they're going to call,'" recalls Mike Madden, one of John's two sons.

John recalls thinking, *"They would call you an hour before and let you know you'd been elected.* But it was 1:00, and no call; 1:15, no call; 1:30, no call; 1:45, no call. I figured I didn't get in. Now it gets to be 2:00, we're in a little room in the stadium, and someone turns on the TV." Like every other television in the stadium, this one was tuned to the NFL Network, and there was Rich Eisen, the lead network anchor, in front of the podium with the Hall of Fame backdrop draped behind him.

There was a brief moment of awkward silence by everyone in the room as they heard Eisen begin to speak.

"And now for the much anticipated Pro Football Hall of Fame Class of 2006 announcement press conference…"

Then just as quickly, everyone glanced at Madden to sense what sort of mood he was in. "We [thought we] were about ready to watch a train wreck," his son Mike recalled.

Thinking quickly, someone asked Madden if he wanted them to turn the TV off or turn it down. "I said, 'Nah,'" Madden recalls. "'I didn't make it, but let's watch and see who did make it.'"

As Madden relives the moment, he said he glanced up at the television casually when Ron Dougherty, interim executive director of the Hall of Fame, began to read the names of the new enshrinees:

"Troy Aikman…"

Madden nodded his head. "Yeah, kind of figured."

"Harry Carson…"

Again, Madden nodded his approval.

"John Madden…"

His mouth was agape. He stood in stunned silence for what seemed like an hour but was only a few glorious seconds of shock, joy, relief, and long-overdue confirmation. "I didn't come down or remember anything for 24 hours," Madden recalls. "You go from believing you had a shot to going in, all the way down to no, you didn't make it, to now you're in the Hall of Fame."

At the very moment he stopped staring at the TV, everyone in the room exploded with screams and cries of joy, and several men raced to hug this big, frumpy bear of a man, who was wearing a blue denim shirt, a black Raiders cap, and his familiar untied sneakers. Mike Madden was smart enough to take a picture at that very moment. Everyone who was moving was slightly blurred, but it was clear how much everyone was laughing, throwing their hands in the air, jumping off the ground, and racing toward big John Madden, the happiest and most delirious of them all. "I know my son took a picture of that moment," Madden recalled. "But I don't remember what happened. I just had tingles all over me. I'd never been so emotional for so long. I mean the feeling never went away."

Pretty soon, the phone did finally ring. First it was a series of calls from his family. He heard from his son Joe, who had remained back in Pleasanton, and from his tearful wife, Virginia. And finally, it was the Hall of Fame people calling, requesting his presence at a press conference later in the afternoon. Madden quickly changed clothes, ditching the cap, sneakers, and denim for a more dignified look with a brown-and-black-striped shirt and black suit coat as he walked into the crowded ballroom back at the downtown Marriott and greeted a room full of reporters and delighted supporters.

His jowly face was turning red as a furnace, and even though he had done a good job of combing his white hair before he walked into the room, it was starting to get messy as he started waving his arms around excitedly as if he were in one of those old Miller Lite commercials. "I'm in shock," he said. "I was coming over here, and I said, 'They can't take this away, can they?' They can't say, 'We're kidding, we want it back?' I mean…ummmm…yeaaaaaaa…HEYYYYYYYY!"

At that point, his words just seemed to blend into an unsuppressed jumble of nonsensical happiness as he slammed both of his big, hammy fists on the podium then shook them in the air in that unmistakable gesture for "At last! At long, freakin' last!"

He kept talking and talking, his thoughts darting wildly and joyfully all over creation. He looked at his old buddy Robinson, who was sitting two rows back, gave him a knowing glance, then brought up that same phrase he said the night the two of them embraced in the bowels of the Rose Bowl after Super Bowl XI, trying to figure out how the boys from Madden's Lot had managed to win a college national championship and a pro football world title in the same stadium only a week apart.

"Not bad for two doofuses from Daly City, huh?"

Finally, he looked out at all the reporters who were enjoying his unrestrained emotion almost as much as he was and told them, "I'm not going to make a lot of sense, but I don't care. Believe me, it comes from my heart. I'm humbled and I'm grateful. I gotta sit down."

ON AUGUST 1, 2006, JUST PAST 11:30 AM, the NFL Films production crews were running around the Red Bear, Inc. building in Pleasanton, California, rolling their expensive cameras as Madden began preparing for his three-day cross-country journey to Canton, Ohio, for the Hall of Fame induction weekend. They were documenting the journey as part of an NFL Network special they were doing called *John Madden: My Road to Canton.*

The camera crews had arrived several hours earlier to set up for the shoot, and by 11:30, just as Madden was standing in front of his desk in his spacious office stuffing old photographs, notebooks, and memorabilia from his Hall of Fame career into a black Raiders duffel bag, the Madden Cruiser, now sponsored by Outback Steakhouse, pulled into the parking lot just outside his office window.

As the bus pulled away from his office building on that Monday morning, the Hall induction was still five days away. Madden would arrive in Canton a few days later, and he would go to parties and press conferences, dinners and parades. He would see old teammates and players as well as family and friends—including more than 300 people who he was flying from Oakland to Canton on a charter flight that he had arranged with Jet Blue. He would meet new Hall teammates, too.

As the bus made its way through nine states, Madden would use the time to put the finishing touches on his Hall of Fame speech and help put together the key production elements of his own life's story for television.

The weekend culminated on a Saturday afternoon under the blazing-hot summer sun on the big stage outside the front doors of the Hall. Al Davis, the aging owner of the Raiders and a 1992 inductee, was accorded the honor of presenting Madden into the Hall.

Davis, dressed in all black with a silver tie, and with his silver reading glasses dangling on a chain around his neck, walked to the podium. He was no longer the dark-haired, dashing figure he was 37 years earlier when he named Madden the youngest head coach in the NFL. He was a gray-haired man in his seventies with bags under his eyes and a slight tremor in his hands. But the voice was still the same voice of that tough-as-nails hard-ass from Brooklyn. Davis spoke eloquently about the most successful coach in the history of the great Raiders franchise:

"It's always great to come back to the Hall of Fame. Today it's a very emotional and inspirational experience for me to present the great John Madden into the enshrinement in the Pro Football Hall of Fame. John Madden, a brilliant coach, a loyal and trusted friend, a Raider. His record is self-explanatory. One hundred and three victories in 10 years is unparalleled in National Football League history. The Raiders always wanted to have the best organization in professional sports, wanted to have the best players, the best coaches playing in the best games, have the best plays, have the best record in professional football.

"Some 40 years ago, I hired a 32-year-old coach to carry the torch for the Raiders and do all the things that I just talked about that we wanted to do. John Madden, over the 10 seasons of his coaching career, led the Raiders to the playoffs eight of those years, including seven division championships, bringing the Raiders their first world championship. John's .759 regular-season percentage ranks as the highest ever with coaches in the National Football League.

"John coached in the golden era of great coaches. In his 10 years, John coached against many who are enshrined in this Hall of Fame. Don Shula of Miami. Chuck Noll of Pittsburgh. Tom Landry of Dallas. Weeb Ewbank, Sid Gillman, Hank Stram, Gil Brandt, Bud Grant, and others who are enshrined in this Hall of Fame.

"John's first professional head job, he was 32 years old. John did what you would call the impossible. In his 10 years of coaching against these great legends, he won more games than he lost against every

Hall of Fame coach in this great shrine here in the National Football League. His record was the Raiders record of 36–16–2 against those great coaches. Dominating the stage that was *Monday Night Football*, Madden's teams had a record of 11–1–1. And, boy, did the Raiders dominate *Monday Night Football*. I told you we wanted to play in the greatest games, we wanted the greatest plays.

"You all remember the 'Immaculate Reception.' You all remember the *'Heidi'* game. You all remember 'Sea of Hands,' the 'Holy Roller,' 'Ghost to the Post,' the Lytle fumble, the miracles of George Blanda. The man on the sideline during all those events that have become synonymous with Raider football was John Madden. He loved the game. He loved his team. He loved the Raiders. He loved this league. You can see it today in everything he does with his games and his TV work. He loved the AFL and the NFL, and especially his players.

"At a time when our country needed it, John Madden saw no color. The Raiders, more than any other organization—politically, football, sports—led the fight for diversity. John Madden was in the middle of that fight. It was pretty tough in those days, in the '70s and early '80s, to lead that fight. But the Raiders had one thing in mind: we wanted to win, and to win you had to have the best players. So, as I said, you saw no color.

"Nine Raiders legends, nine are in this Hall. The indestructible Jim Otto, he's here today. Great clutch player George Blanda. The undefeated Willie Brown, who was only beaten by father time as a cornerback. The magical hands of Fred Biletnikoff. The famed Highway 63 and 78. Gene Upshaw, president of the Players Association. Art Shell, head coach of the Raiders. Ted Hendricks is here today, the great linebacker. And, of course, the 'Ghost to the Post,' Dave Casper, along with myself, have waited patiently for some 25 years for John to join us as enshrined in this Hall of Fame.

"We recognize you, Virginia Madden. That's John's wife. His sons Mike and Joey. They were a football family. So that John could pursue his dreams. When you worked for Al Davis, you worked for the Raiders, there was no time for golf, there was no time for the kids, there was one thing: Raider football, silver and black football. Virginia, you were there when it was important; we'll be there for you. Today is a day when our heroes of the past become the legends of the future. I've said this before: time never really stops for the great ones. We wrap them in a cloak of immortality and remember what great people they were. It's a great inspiration for me to come to this Field of Dreams every year. I've had the honor to present nine other people, eight who played for the Raiders, one who played for the San Diego Chargers, the great Lance Alworth. But I love to come here because I wanted to pay tribute to this great class. I wanted to say hello once again to the great players behind me in whose glory we all shared those legends.

"It has always, as Harry Carson said, brought a realization to the Raiders that we owe a debt to these great people behind us. And, as I've said before, the Raiders will never forget that day. But let's go back to Oakland for a moment. Let's go back to the 1970s. Let's fill that stadium one more time with the staff and the administrative people who poured their heart and soul into the Raiders. Let's go back to the great Raider warriors who are here today, and to those who are no longer with us, but whose memories we cherish, and those great warriors who are watching up there today who will lead us in the future.

"I say let's line you up under the goalposts one more time, one more time, and have you introduced all individually once again to the roar of that Oakland crowd. We can never forget those great moments. The roar would be deafening to see you trot out in those black jerseys, silver helmets.

"John Madden, the chill goes through my body as I hear that roar and think of all those special people, but seeing you, John, down on the sidelines prowling those sidelines, yelling at officials, that flaming red hair, those arms moving left and right, screaming at Raider players, and most of all, winning football games. But that is fantasy. Fantasy isn't the answer here today. But what is not fantasy is you coming up to this podium to be enshrined into the Pro Football Hall of Fame. Ladies and gentlemen, the great John Madden."

IT WAS MADDEN'S TURN AT THE MICROPHONE. With his hair a bit tousled, wearing the canary-yellow Hall of Fame blazer with the embroidered NFL patch over the left breast pocket and a white rose boutonniere pinned to the right lapel of his custom-made jacket, he behaved just as anyone who had watched him over the past 40 or 50 years of public life would have expected. He was a bundle of unfettered energy. He was a man who, with every fiber in his body, was not just happy to be standing there, but deeply and completely grateful, humbled, honored, and slightly baffled by it all.

And in typical Madden fashion, he went on a delightful stream-of-consciousness road trip through time:

"Wow, wow, wow. You know, you always think of what it would be like if you are ever enshrined into the Hall of Fame. People say, 'What are you going to say when you get up to the podium?' I tell them, 'I don't know. I'll tell you when I get up there.' And right now, I don't have…I got like numb, you know, a tingle from the bottom of my toes to the top of my head.

"I mean, this is so special. All the guys talk about who is going to break up. I started to break up when Al Davis was talking. If they have a contest or any bet, I knew I was going to lose that one anyway. I just wanted to take this first moment just to make a memory and say how special this feeling is. To be in here, you know, in Canton with these great people of Canton, Ohio. You can't believe the job that they do. It's not only today. I mean, the game, the parade. They have 100,000 people at the parade at 8:00 in the morning. This is a special place.

"This is a celebration of football. When you celebrate pro football, it has to be here in Canton, Ohio, because this is where the NFL started. I want to thank you people, all the pro football fans, the pro football writers that voted me into the Hall of Fame, led by Frank Cooney and Ira Miller; a special thanks to them.

"But everyone that made that possible, it was a long wait, but it was a wait, you know, when you finally get in, it's made it all worthwhile, because the feeling is so special and you appreciate it so much more. The class that I go in with—Harry Carson, Rayfield Wright, Warren

Moon, Reggie White, [Reggie's wife] Sara, Troy Aikman—is such a great thing. I'm proud to be in this class, because we're always going to be connected with each other. We'll always be the Class of 2006. That will be forever. I'll tell you, these are all good people, good guys. I am proud as hell to go into this 2006 Hall of Fame class with these guys.

"Then the Hall of Famers behind me, that's what it's all about. I was reading the NFL stats and history book. That's what you do when you ride a bus. When you don't fly, you read big old thick books like that. But they had a chapter on history. The first page in the chapter of history was a list of the Hall of Famers. I said, 'That's right, they got it. That is our history.'

"The players that played before us, the players that played when they didn't have face masks, when they had leather helmets, when we got this thing started, the players that played in smaller stadiums, didn't have the medical thing, didn't have anything. They laid the foundation for this great game, and we should never forget it. I say [to] the NFL teams, you ought to honor your history more. Sometimes we tend to get caught up in the players, the games now. Honor your history. Bring back the Hall of Famers. Bring back their teammates. Let the fans show their appreciation to the history.

"I know going in with these guys is so special. We always talk about immortality. Some of us think maybe we will be immortal, that we'll live forever. When you really think about it, we're not going to be. But I say this, and this is overwhelming, mind-blowing, that through this bust, with these guys, in that Hall, we will be forever. You know, when you think of that, it just blows your mind. It's forever and ever and ever.

"You have to stay with me a moment on this one. This is a little goofy here. You're going to say, 'There is old Madden being goofy again.' But I started thinking about this after I got voted into the Hall of Fame. The more I think about it, the more I think it's true. Now I know it's true, and I believe it.

"Here is the deal: I think over in the Hall of Fame, that during the day, the people go through, they look at everything. At night, there's a time when they all leave. All the fans and all the visitors leave the Hall of Fame. Then there's just the workers. Then the workers start to leave. It gets down to there's just one person. That person turns out the light, locks the door.

"[That's the time] I believe that the busts talk to each other. I can't wait for that conversation, I really can't. Vince Lombardi, Knute Rockne, Reggie, Walter Payton, all my ex-players, we'll be there forever and ever and ever talking about whatever. That's what I believe. That's what I think is going to happen, and no one's ever going to talk me out of that."

By now, the crowd was laughing along with him. The Hall members on the stage doubled over in laughter too, some of them shaking their heads. All of them understood that one of the most folksy poet laureates pro football had ever known was now in their midst forever.

Madden motioned to the scene behind him.

"These guys are going, 'Oh, no, hope I don't have to put up with his BS for an eternity.'"

Actually, none of them were complaining, only rejoicing.

"This is a celebration," Madden went on. "It has to be fun. To have Al Davis here is something special. I mean, if it weren't for Al, I wouldn't be here. He was a guy that gave me an opportunity. He was a guy that hired me 40 years ago, brought me into pro football. He was a guy that made me a head coach when I was 32 years old. I had two years of pro coaching experience.

"Who the heck names a guy 32 years old as a head coach? Al Davis did. But he not only named me head coach, he stood behind me and he helped me and he provided me with players, with great players. As he was saying, nine of the players are in the Hall of Fame. I mean, those are the types of players that he provided me with. He stood behind me not only the 10 years I was the head coach, but he stood behind me for the last 40 years. Al Davis is a friend, always has been a friend. I remember I had the opportunity to induct him into the Hall of Fame. At the time I said, you know, talking about loyalty, what a guy Al Davis was. I said that he's the guy, you know, if you had anything happen, you had one phone call, who would you make that phone call to? I said it would be Al Davis.

"All these years later, I got an opportunity, I got voted into the Hall of Fame, I had a phone call to make for a presenter, and I called Al Davis.

"I just talked to my mom. She's watching. Hi, Mom, I love you. I was talking about how excited I am, how I haven't slept in three days. My mind is mush. She just said, 'Me too!' She has the same feelings. She's not right here, but she's here in spirit. She's a special person that's been with me for the 70 years of my life. I know that my dad, who died in 1960, is up there looking down and laughing.

"My mom's probably laughing right now, too, because when I was like a sophomore in high school, I was playing in summer baseball. I was playing on three or four different teams. I told my dad, 'I'm going to drop a couple of these because I want to get a job to make some money.' My dad said, 'I'll give you a couple bucks, go caddie, make a few loops, you'll be okay.' He said, 'Don't work. Once you start work, you're going to have to work the rest of your life.'

"My dad worked hard. He was a mechanic. He worked hard. The reason I say that he's up there laughing right now is because I listened to him and I continued to play, and I have never worked a day in my life. I went from player to coach to a broadcaster, and I am the luckiest guy in the world.

"My sisters, Dolores and Judy, they were there with me. They supported everything that I did, because life with me as a kid was just a locker room. Every day was recess. They knew that. They went along with it, supported everything. I love them and I appreciate that. If there was a Hall of Fame for families, my family would be in the Hall of Fame. My wife, Virginia. My two sons, Joe and Mike. They talk about how hard coaches work. They work 18, 20 hours a day. They sleep on a couch. They don't come home. You know, that's not the hard job. The hard job is a coach's wife, believe me. The job of the coach's wife, she has to be mother, father, driver, doctor, nurse, coach, everything, because the coach is out there working.

"When anyone is appreciated, they have to appreciate their wife. I have the greatest in Virginia. Thank you. Stand up, you deserve it. After all those years putting up with me, you deserve to stand up and take a bow on this day. And my two sons, Mike and Joe, I'm so proud of them. They're not only my two sons, but they're my two best friends. Just everything that they do. When they were kids, I used to take them to practice on Saturdays. I'd take them to the Pro Bowl. I coached the Pro Bowl way too many damn times. I used to take them to the Pro Bowl, Super Bowl, every time I could. Those were special times.

"As I look back now on my coaching career, I think of my family, I think of the days that we spent together. I say this to coaches everywhere: if you ever have a chance to take your kids with you, take them. Don't miss that opportunity. Because when it's all over and done with, when you look back, those are going to be your fondest memories. When you go in the Hall of Fame at my age, then you have kids who have wives, then they have kids. Mike's wife is Noelle. Joe's wife is Wendy. Between them, they've given me five grandkids that I love to death. They're the love of my life. They're five, four, three, two, one. Sam, Jack, Jesse, Aidan, and McKenna. That's what it's all about. It's about family and having them and having them here, with your team.

"I go into the Hall of Fame as a coach. I know that I go into the Hall of Fame because of my players and what they did. I'm so proud. Al already introduced the players that are in the Hall of Fame behind me. If they'd just stand up. All my players that are out there, there's between 30 and 40 ex-Raider players.

"My family, stand up. Just take your day. I mean, you remember. You remember all these guys that did all these things. No, no, stay up. This is our day in the sun. Doggone it, take it. If we're here, stay up and take it. You guys stand up and take it, too. Fred Biletnikoff, Big Ben Davidson. This is what it's all about. These are the guys. I go in here…no, no, stand up, Ben. All of a sudden…I mean, 30 or 40 years ago, they were ready to hit anything: 'Let's go to the party, let's do all this.' Now they want to sit down.

"Stand up, enjoy the moment. This is ours. They can't take it away from us. They can't ever take this away from us. Thanks to all of you. The whole bunch of you, I love you. Thank you very, very much. You remember all those great Raider names in the '70s? We had such special fans, the whole thing. It was just something, you know, that I'll never forget. We'll have a party after, too. Don't worry about it. We'll go through and...

"It's been a great road from Madden's Lot in Daly City, John Robinson. John, who would believe this, huh? This is amazing. Jefferson High School with my first real coach, Joe McGrath. Then Roy Hughes at Cal Poly. My roommate Pat is here, my college roommate. Philadelphia Eagles, Norm Van Brocklin had a great influence on me. Hancock College with Al Balder. Then to San Diego State with a great coach that someday will be in here, Don Coryell. He had a real influence on my coaching. Joe Gibbs was on that staff, too. Then we went to the Oakland Raiders, John Rauch was the head coach, Ollie Spencer, Tom Dons, Charlie Sumner, John Polonchek, Joe Scanelli, Tom Flores came later, all those great coaches, John Robinson, I thank you all.

"Again, you go in as a coach, but you take your players and your assistant coaches with you. It's been so long that I had a pretty good road afterward also. I ride a bus. I don't fly. The road has been with Dave Hahn, my first bus driver who passed away, Willie Yarborough. Joe Mitchell. I spend so much time with them that they're part of my team now and my family. Then Sandy Montag is my agent. He's been with me for over 20 years. You know, I mean, agent smagent. He's a friend, a very good friend. I thank him for everything that he's done for me.

"My years at CBS and FOX were pretty good with Pat Summerall, you know, that team, Bob Stenner, Sandy Grossman. I say I'm the luckiest guy in the world. I go to ABC, now NBC with Al Michaels, Fred Gaudelli, Drew Esocoff. By the way, we have a game right over here tomorrow night.

"You talk about a full weekend. I mean, man, they have dinners, parades, induction ceremonies, then a game tomorrow night, which will be broadcast, the first one I do with NBC. I just want to say in closing that it's been a great ride. I want to thank everyone who has been along for any part of it. Speaking of great rides, I was lucky enough to be carried off the field after we won Super Bowl XI. I was told it took like five or six guys to lift me up, then they dropped me. But that's okay, because that was me and that was them. They aren't going to carry me off. You carry him off for a while, boom, you dump him on the ground. But it was the happiest moment of my life.

"Today feels like the second time in my life that I'm being carried [on] the shoulders of others. Yet instead of off the field, it's into the Hall of Fame. Instead of five or six guys today, I ride on the shoulders of hundreds of friends, coaches, players, colleagues, family. I just say this: I thank you all very much. This has been the sweetest ride of 'em all. Thank you."

MADDEN IS ON THE HALL OF FAME TEAM FOR A LIFETIME, and he deeply understands the impact of this privilege. Every year since his '06 induction, Madden makes sure that he returns to Canton to roam the hallways talking to the bronze busts, to shake hands and sign autographs for the fans, and to thoroughly enjoy all the benefits afforded members of this elite professional fraternity. The best part of the deal, though, isn't something that Madden receives. It's something he continues to give: his time and energy.

"I've been in that [lunch room] in Canton where the old Hall of Famers speak to the new guys about how much this means, how it will change your life, how meaningful it is," said Miklasz. "The last time I did it was [2007] when Madden spoke to [that] class. It was one of the most amazing speeches I've ever heard. It was so full of the emotion of a man who completely understood the significance of what the Hall induction means, and he was able to express it better than I've ever heard anyone else do. It was all about, 'Hey, this is your team for life. No one can cut you. No one can waive you. These are your teammates forever.' It was just beautiful."

According to most of the old Hall of Famers, it used to be mandatory during the weekend you were inducted into the Hall that every new enshrinee meet and listen to one specific living legend explain the meaning of the Hall of Fame. Until 2006, that one man was Deacon Jones, a 1980 class member.

Now there are two: Jones and John Madden.

19

THE END IS NEAR

"I was on the road with him in 2008 every week, and for the first time I think I saw him wear down. But the thing is, it wasn't the travel that was bothering him. He enjoyed being on the road. That wasn't wearing him out. It was being away from his family."

John Robinson

ON FRIDAY, JANUARY 30, 2009, JUST TWO DAYS BEFORE SUPER Bowl XLIII, the *Wall Street Journal* published an article that greatly angered NBC Sports boss Dick Ebersol and offended plenty of others close to John Madden who still considered him a rare television gem. The article was an occasionally unflattering portrait of the 72-year-old legend who, according to the opinionated observations of writer Matthew Futterman, had lost a little off his fastball. The headline was the first clue that this was not going to be a kind look at Madden: "John Madden's Missed Tackles: Still Working at 72, NBC's Beloved NFL Analyst Is Often Brilliant, Even If He's Not Always Right."

For the last 30 years, Madden had been considered the unquestioned king of the sports-television jungle, arguably the best color commentator ever, regardless of the sport. He was beloved by everyone, and until Futterman's article, the only person who came close to finding fault with anything Madden did or said on the air was the comedian Frank Caliendo, whose spot-on impersonations on the FOX NFL pregame shows were wickedly funny homages (even if Madden probably didn't see the humor in being mocked). Even the acerbic New York sports TV critics and *USA Today*'s Rudy Martzke tended to treat him with iconic respect. Yet here was Futterman, who dared to suggest that Madden might be an old lion who may have overstayed his welcome as America's most famous guest.

"Earlier this month from his home in Northern California, Mr. Madden said keeping up with the new faces and strategies in the NFL takes more work than ever," the article read. "When he signed a six-year contract with NBC in 2005 for roughly $25 million, the network decided to hire his oldest friend, former coach John Robinson, to sit next to him in the booth to help him handle the onslaught of player substitutions.

"As for statistical errors, Mr. Madden says he views each game as a 'separate entity' and that long-term statistics for teams and players are not as important to him as what happens during a particular game. On the night the Giants faced that third-and-long situation, he notes, the team had failed in that situation two times previously. 'Statistically they may be the best, but they weren't that day,' he says...."

"It's a live three-hour broadcast," said Madden's agent, Sandy Montag. "You can't be right 100 percent of the time."

Ebersol was less diplomatic. "That article was bullshit," he snapped. "I was in the [production] truck for every game but one that he's done in three years [at NBC]. I heard his attention to detail in off-air exchanges. Anyone who heard him and Al in the pressurized fourth quarter of the Super Bowl knows that he deserved the rave reviews they got for the game. And he was the same way every week, even in a game that turned out to be a slaughter in October."

While he weaved in and out of paragraphs intended to flatter Madden, Futterman seemed to use them only as brief transitions to fortify his true agenda, which clearly was the audacious suggestion that it was time for Madden to retire. These points were the crux of Futterman's argument:

- "As a broadcaster, Mr. Madden remains the standard-bearer of the old guard—the gruff, barstool voice that harkens back to a time when a famous group of linemen were known as 'the Hogs' and clumps of mud got stuck in players' face masks. Nostalgia may be a large part of his enduring appeal: according to Scarborough Sports Marketing, 69 percent of all NFL fans are over the age of 35."

- "How long can Mr. Madden continue to entertain and educate football fans—especially at a time when the NFL is growing exponentially more complex? Ed Goren, the president of FOX Sports and Mr. Madden's former boss from 1994 to 2002, compares Mr. Madden to an old, comfortable pair of shoes. 'I know I've had them for a long time and they don't work the way they once did, but boy, are they comfortable,' he says...."
- "Mr. Madden is clearly a talented analyst. He still spends hours each day watching game video, working phones, and attending practices. There are moments during every broadcast when his instinct for the game is impressive. At the start of a recent playoff game between San Diego and Indianapolis, Mr. Madden said San Diego's backup running back, Darren Sproles, would get 20 to 25 carries. He got 23. In another game, he noted that Panthers wide receiver Muhsin Muhammad, who'd just made a great catch, was an excellent receiver but an even better blocker. Like clockwork, Mr. Muhammad leveled a defender, opening up a big gain. 'It's basically all I do, and I do it every day, all day,' Mr. Madden says...."
- "In other moments, his grasp of the game isn't so strong. During these playoffs, Mr. Madden said San Diego used to be a running team but is now a passing team. In fact, San Diego called running plays this season about 5 percent more often than the average NFL team. In a December game, Mr. Madden saw the Giants execute several running plays out of the shotgun—a formation that has long signified a pass play—and said NFL teams in general now run the ball from the shotgun as often as they throw it. In fact, NFL teams ran from the shotgun this season just 17 percent of the time. During the same game, Mr. Madden said the Giants had planned to run the ball at an undersized Carolina defensive lineman, Tyler Brayton, and also that in recent games, Giants quarterback Eli Manning had automatically audibled, or switched, from run plays to pass plays whenever he counted eight defenders on the line of scrimmage. After the game, Giants players said neither statement was true...."

In the online edition of the *Wall Street Journal* that day, there were 43 reader comments after the article. Only one reader agreed with the writer's observations about Madden. Everyone else either insulted the writer or praised Madden. One of those commenters wrote, "First time commenting on WSJ. The economic crisis couldn't bring me out. But I have to defend an American Icon. I look forward to the Super Bowls he covers. It's an extra treat." Another correspondent was more succinct: "A 72-year-old John Madden is still better than a 40-year-old anyone else."

It was a jarring piece of criticism that was the first on-record public suggestion that Madden's reign as the preeminent sports-television commentator was being questioned. It was clearly not the universal opinion of the day, but it was a significant one considering what would happen a little more than two months later. On April 16, 2009, seemingly out of the blue, Madden decided to call it quits, retiring from television after 30 years in the booth. Madden insists the two events were not connected, but others certainly wondered whether or not the *Wall Street Journal* article at the very least put him in the frame of mind to consider whether or not it was time to contemplate retirement.

He had been doing his third career for three decades—10 years longer than he had coached in college and the pros combined—and Madden had become richer and more famous than he could have ever imagined when this TV thing began as a second thought back in 1979. His first contract paid him $3,000 per game for four games, but now his combined income checked in at nearly $10 million per year. He had worked on all four networks, broadcast 11 Super Bowls, won 16 Emmys, and created a financial empire as a result of his video game, commercial endorsement deals, and real-estate holdings. Yet as great a success as he'd become on TV, Madden had watched what happened to Pat Summerall nine years earlier and vividly recalled how his old partner had been treated once he reached his seventies. Summerall, who had once been considered the best play-by-play man in the business, was forced into TV oblivion after living on the mountaintop for 20 years. Summerall had been criticized in print and treated rudely by the network. None of this went unnoticed by Madden, who told Bob Raissman of the *New York Daily News* in a January 2000 interview how he felt about seeing his good friend defrocked. "Hell, yes, it bothers me…I think it bothers everyone," he said. "Everyone has a need to be loved."

John Madden had been loved almost from the moment he first entered the American sports consciousness. It began with those Miller Lite commercials after he retired from coaching, when he first showed America his loveable-lug personality. It only grew when he got that Telestrator in his hands and started squiggling maniacally on our collective TV screens. It peaked as he moved from network to network, telling us stories that humanized the players as he took everyone from the most knowledgeable football insider to the most casual fan inside the complicated Xs and Os.

But months before the *Wall Street Journal* article was printed, Madden was contemplating retirement. As soon as the 2008 NBC *Sunday Night Football* schedule came out, the old coach knew there might be problems. The first six games on NBC's Sunday night schedule were either on the East Coast or in the Midwest. Game 1 was in New York, Game 2 was Indianapolis, followed by games in Cleveland, Green Bay, Chicago, and Jacksonville.

The Madden Cruiser didn't return to the West Coast until the seventh game of the season, with a trip to San Diego. Then the bus went right back east to Tampa Bay, Indy, Philly, and Washington and back to San Diego before finishing up in Minnesota, Seattle, Dallas, and Tampa Bay. There was one more regular-season game left on the schedule, and it looked like it would be the Dolphins versus the Jets in New York, followed by a potential first-round playoff game in New York as well.

Two weeks in New York meant John and Virginia could spend two full weeks together in their Big Apple apartment and celebrate their 49th wedding anniversary in fine fashion. So Virginia flew out to New York to meet her husband, and just as she was landing, the network enforced its flex-schedule privilege and opted instead for Denver at San Diego for the regular-season finale. The planned extended celebration lasted all of one day before John had to hop on the bus and begin the lengthy cross-country journey to San Diego.

"I basically left home in the bus in August and didn't come home until January," Madden remembers.

John Robinson spent that 2008 season as Madden's travel companion and in-game eyes and ears. As someone who had known Madden since elementary school, he noticed a change in John's love of cross-country travel. "I was on the road with him in 2008 every week," says Robinson, "and for the first time I think I saw him wear down. But the thing is, it wasn't the travel that was bothering him. He enjoyed being on the road. That wasn't wearing him out. It was being away from his family. His grandkids were old enough now, and they were starting to notice that their grandfather wasn't around. I know that was bothering him."

Robinson doesn't remember the specific week that he first suspected that Madden was ready to get off the road. But at some point during those first six weeks, as they sat on the bus watching America roll by through the tinted windows, Madden looked at his best friend and said something Robinson thought he'd never hear uttered from John Madden's lips.

"You know, I'm just tired of this," Madden said.

Robinson was stunned. It wasn't a long, angry soliloquy, and he didn't elaborate in great detail. "But it was the first time I ever heard him say anything like that," says Robinson. "I should have known right then that he was getting ready to retire."

There was exhaustion in his voice and maybe even a hint of sadness. His grandkids were growing up fast, and John had already missed out on seeing his sons grow up. He viewed that as a necessary evil of his coaching career. Even though he was able to justify the time away from Joe and Mike, he did not want to repeat the same experiences with the grandkids.

In the fall of 2011, as he sat in the lobby of his boutique hotel in downtown Pleasanton, California, Madden explained himself. He had earlier talked about how far away he had grown from his family in the final years of his coaching days. He started to feel that same uncomfortable feeling again as his TV career wound down. He didn't want to repeat the same mistakes with his grandsons that he'd made with Mike and Joe. "But now I get to go to my grandsons' flag football games on Saturdays and I get to take everybody out to eat after the games. I am around to see them grow up. I love being a part of their lives," he says.

He pauses for a second and says all that needs to be said. "It was just time. It was time for me to walk away."

On April 14, 2009, Madden called Dick Ebersol, the NBC Sports chairman, and told him rather simply, "I'm going to retire."

Ebersol thought he was joking. In 1982, two hours before Madden was to host *Saturday Night Live*, the wisecracking coach yelled at Ebersol, then the SNL producer: "Come here! I have not enjoyed a single bit of this…. As soon as we're done with this dress rehearsal, I'm outta here, and you better figure out how you're going to do a show at 11:30 because your host is leaving."

Ebersol was dumbstruck.

Madden waited for several agonizing seconds before grinning and letting Ebersol know he'd just been punked.

So now Ebersol was waiting for the punch line. "But I realized very quickly he was very serious," he says now.

Ebersol wasn't willing to accept Madden's resignation over the phone. He got on a plane, flew across the country, and spent all day Wednesday attempting to talk him out of his decision. He offered Madden a variety of options that would decrease his workload and time on the road, including the opportunity to split the season with Cris Collinsworth. "I tried every way I could to make sure he was sure about his decision," Ebersol said. "And in true John Madden fashion, he was sure."

Once he had not only made up his mind but convinced Ebersol too, Madden spent the rest of the day calling friends and family. When Pat Summerall answered his phone in Dallas that morning, he remembers Madden telling him that exact story. "He talked about his grandkids knowing when he was there and when he wasn't," Summerall recalls. "I think he realized he missed those years of seeing how old his son was and he didn't want to do that again with the grandkids."

When the news was officially announced one day later, voices throughout football and broadcasting offered tributes and insight into Madden's contributions. "John is an original," said FOX Sports president Ed Goren. "He's been the face of the NFL for three decades and by far and away the No. 1 sports analyst on television. Amazingly, he's been so dominant that he's never been challenged. John's impact on the way television covers the NFL is a legacy that will last well into the future. During the time I worked with him at CBS and FOX, he wasn't just a lead analyst, John was always our 'head coach.'"

Former Bronco Tom Jackson, who hated Madden when he was the competition on the field, paid tribute to him as a broadcaster without hesitation. "Let me say this right: he made the game understandable," says Jackson. "He made it more understandable for a pro like me, and I knew the game. He made it more understandable for me while at the same time making it more understandable for the housewife who's never watched football. That gift had a universal appeal.

"As good a coach as he was, and he was a Hall of Fame coach, he was as good or better at analyzing football on TV. We're never going to see the likes of John Madden again. I think everyone became so comfortable having him in their house. In the TV business, longevity is determined by how many people want you in their house. For you to be successful in this business, people have to want you in their home, want to listen to you, want to hear your voice, want to see what it is that you're doing. I don't think anybody has had the appeal that Coach Madden had."

And now—whether still at the top of his game, or perhaps sliding even slightly—John Madden was walking away.

EPILOGUE: THIS IS MY GAME

SO WHO IS THE *REAL* JOHN MADDEN?

The old coach is not the retiring type. He does not want to slow down. It was an ideal football Saturday afternoon in the autumn of 2010, and the old coach had already been to one game in the morning to watch his grandsons play. Sunday morning would be filled with football, too. John Madden gets up early every NFL Sunday, heads to his massive studio near his Pleasanton, California, home, and watches all the early games on the giant screens with a select group of friends. Then they pile into the Madden Cruiser and head up the highway to the Coliseum to watch the Raiders in the afternoon.

He sits in the owner's suite, right next to the man who used to cause him ulcers. But it is so much different now. When Madden and Al Davis watch the Raiders, the coach no longer needs to throw back bottles of Pepto-Bismol like tequila shots. The indomitable force and gastric nightmare that was once Al Davis is now trapped inside the frail shell of a wheelchair-bound old man, serving as yet another lingering reminder of the mortality all around Madden. Everyone is growing old. In the summer and fall of 2010, he spoke at the funerals of Jack Tatum, Don Coryell, and George Blanda. Maybe that has something to do with why he won't slow down. Tangible evidence of mortality's creeping shadow keeps drawing near. The 74-year-old Madden is as fit as any man his age. He still stands tall, still walks with an athletic strut, not the shriveling affectations of most 74-year-olds. When he rises from the overstuffed armchair, he does not gather himself in creaking, arthritic stages. He pops up quickly, bounds across the room with an easy glide, and plops back down in the chair like a gathering storm.

So who is the *real* John Madden?

Well, now we know that he is so many things. He was a youthful slacker who, out of necessity, grew into an earnest man of limitless passions. "He is like a voluptuary," says his good friend Lesley Visser. "If something was playful, it was most playful. If it was passion, he had the most passion. If it was annoying, it was the most annoying. His emotions, his whole being, was to the max. If he wanted barbeque, he wanted the best barbeque. He got an ulcer coaching. He won the Super Bowl and had to back away because he had no middle speed."

His success came not simply because he had the talent, but because he worked so damned hard to maximize his talent and the gifts of everyone who worked around him, and he was many things to many people.

He was the goofball student who grew into the dedicated teacher with a master's degree, the workaholic coach who could get the miscreants to follow him to the ends of the earth, the perfectionist broadcaster who found a new team to lead to excellence. He was a chauvinist young coach who initially begrudged women sportswriters who wanted to cover his favorite game, yet he became an enlightened television broadcaster who went out of his way to practice inclusion, making pro football appealing, understandable, and accessible to women of all ages.

"You turn on the television in any living room in America on a football Sunday, and there's a grandmother, a grandfather, there's a 50-year-old father, a 35-year-old wife, an 18-year-old son, or a 10-year-old boy or girl, and they all know John Madden and for entirely different reasons," says John Robinson. "He spans four or five generations, and man, woman, and child relate to him. That's his gift. I am out in the streets sometimes, and old ladies find out I know John Madden, and they just scream, 'I love him! Tell him I love him. He has that common touch, the same touch that Ronald Reagan had, where he can talk to anybody about anything.'"

SO WHO IS THE *REAL* JOHN MADDEN?

The scene: it is a Tuesday during Super Week at Super Bowl XLIV, and there is plenty of evidence on display that tells you who John Madden is today.

There is a press conference inside a giant ballroom in the Broward County Convention Center for the inaugural Madden Most Valuable Protectors Award (presented by Prilosec OTC). The ballroom is packed. There are rows and rows of chairs lined up perfectly like church pews, and almost all of them are filled with men of every generation who have become locked into the religion of football because of the larger-than-life character whose image is being beamed out on the gargantuan projection screen in the front of the room.

It is typical of one of those year-end sports awards that corporate sponsors love to attach their names to, like a Coach of the Year or Player of the Year award. But since this one has Madden's name on it, there is a twist. Of course it involves the offensive linemen, because John has always been one of them. But this award goes not to the individual best offensive lineman, but to the top offensive line.

The award is a giant chunk of bronze, a thick block of forged metal.

And, of course, Madden is omnipresent, a giant talking head beamed via satellite to present the award.

"John made linemen important on television," says one of the greatest ever, Hall of Famer Anthony Munoz. "Every offensive lineman out there loved seeing him come to do our games because we knew he would talk about us more than to say we were called for holding or giving up a sack. He helped glamorize offensive linemen. We all love him for that."

WHO IS THE *REAL* JOHN MADDEN?

He is the new Wizard of Oz, the omnipresent force behind the video screen.

Later in the week, in a courtyard in front of an ultra-swank Miami Beach hotel, there's another made-for-media event with Madden's name attached to it: an electric circus at the Clevelander Hotel for his *Madden Bowl XVI* video game. The folks from EA Sports have set up an outdoor parlor of Xbox 360 games for a fleet of famous NFL players, and the evening has become an al fresco competition complete with the essential South Beach eye candy strolling around as scenery.

You cannot tell the story of John Madden's life without an explanation of how a 74-year-old man has managed to remain relevant to the generation of the video-obsessed who are all nearly a quarter-century younger than he is. This is the final piece to Madden's remarkable three-pronged football legacy, the way he has influenced a generation that has no idea that he was a great football coach, or even a legendary television broadcaster.

Since 1989, when EA Sports created the *John Madden Football* game for Apple II, Commodore 64, and DOS-based computer systems, the company has sold more than 85 million copies of the video game and created a $3 billion-plus enterprise. It is the single-most-popular video game in America, and Madden earns somewhere between $2 million to $2.5 million annually from the video game.

He wants you to know that he did not simply sign his name on a contract, collect a paycheck, and get out of the way so a crew of anonymous video-game designers could create whatever they pleased. "Oh no," he says firmly. "This is my game. This isn't like one of those deals where it's a game someone else invented and I lent my name to it. I invented this game. I was part of the team that invented the game. We started this before there were video games. It was supposed to be a computer game that would be used to help high school coaches teach and learn football. I wanted to create a computer program that would allow you to put in a play, run it against a defense on a computer to see if it would have success or not. That would be a way to teach and test plays."

He teamed up with a computer genius with a Harvard education named Trip Hawkins in 1986, and they experimented with countless designs until they got it right. Madden had no idea one day that people would have game systems and smart phone applications and iPads and iPhones. "We just knew that everyone was going to have computers one day soon, and this would give them a chance to do something more than business on it," he says.

He had certain demands that had to be met. At the time, the only football computer games did not simulate the real game. Linemen didn't exist. The game did not have a real football game quality to it. So Madden made it clear at the onset that the primary goal of the design had to be to continue to reach perfection. Twenty-two players on the field. Everyone had an assignment. Defensive commands as well as offensive ones. Every year, they added something new. Real NFL team names. Real player names. Real player faces. Players could get injured. Penalties could be called. Video-camera angles that replicated the look and feel of network television broadcasts.

"I always tell the story about how I used to tell the designers that we had to keep working to make sure our game looked like the TV game," Madden says. "And I think we have accomplished that fairly well. But a few years ago, I'm sitting in one of those FOX Sports seminars and David Hill, the head of the division, tells everyone that his goal is to make the FOX broadcasts look more like the Madden video games. That's why they developed that camera on a wire so you could have a camera angle that went almost right into the huddle. That's why we miked the referees and put cameras on the refs, too.

"And so now I'm sitting there listening to David Hill say he wants to make TV look more like my game, and I start cracking up. Wow, well there we go. We have now officially made it. All I was trying to do was have our video game get close to simulating the real game and to hear Hill say that, obviously we got more than close. But we have to keep improving. If you try and stay the same, if you ever say, 'Okay, we got it, this is it,' that's when we lose [popularity]. We can never stay the same. It's like everything else in life for me, you either go up or you go down. What makes me most proud is every year we go up."

At least once a year, Madden invites a team of EA Sports designers out to Pleasanton, California, where the nine-man crew can sit with the coach in his Goal Line Production, a 7,000-square-foot studio and sound stage. They spend an entire NFL Sunday with Madden in the darkened studio watching games, talking shop, and brainstorming how they can improve the next version of the video game.

They have a full buffet for breakfast and lunch, and they watch the games on 10 HDTVs, including a 120' projection screen surrounded by nine additional 63" flat-panel displays. Every game has a different network broadcast feed. With a touch of a button, sound from any game will come blasting through the speakers. With the EA Sports designers surrounding him, Madden feeds them information for six straight hours. They have their laptops out, they have the video game going. And Madden is showing them what is going on in the real games and asking—no, *demanding*—that they find a way to incorporate what is happening on TV and get it into *Madden NFL 12*.

And just in case you still believe that Madden is a silent partner in this video enterprise, just ask him what he thinks about the players who complain about the individual player ratings for the *Madden* game. "Guys really get riled up," he says. "They try to tell me how their speed rating should be higher. And I always say, 'Okay, I'll look into it.' But there's a reason why some of them are rated the way they are. It's like if you give a guy who is an okay player with great speed a higher rating on speed, it might end up sending his overall rating above a truly great player. I will never do that. I take this stuff very serious. I really do."

So do the players. True story: after a game in 2010, St. Louis Rams linebacker James Laurinaitis explained to reporters why he was making more exaggerated celebrations after sacks and other big defensive plays. "My teammates have been making fun of my 'swagger ratings' in the *Madden* game," Laurinaitis said. "Gotta get my swagger ratings up."

Madden gives a nod of approval when he hears that story.

"This is my game," he says. "I take it very seriously."

SO WHO IS THE *REAL* JOHN MADDEN?

Well, a part of him is that caricature you see waving his hands like a wild man, bursting through a paper wall on the TV screen. He is the guy Frank Caliendo mimics to a T, right down to the goofy, nonsensical ramble where the words get slurred into an excitable jumble.

"Wellyaknowitsahhhhhhgaaaaoooooooohh…OHHHHHHKAY!!!"

He said that very thing on the day he was named to the Hall of Fame. Go ahead, dig up the video on YouTube. What the hell did he say there at the end?

He knows that you think he's in love with Brett Favre, and maybe he is, because the old quarterback sort of epitomized everything the old coach loves about football: grit and color and personality and attack, attack, attack.

"But you know what the greatest secret about John Madden was?" says Visser. "He's always in on the joke. And he's okay with it. He didn't care."

He laughed all the way to the bank.

There is a serious side to Madden now. Now that he has retired, he has decided to create a resource center for pro football history. "This all came to me a while ago when I was listening to someone on one of those football TV shows, and they were talking about all the great coaches who came through Cincinnati," Madden says. "They named Sam Wyche, Dick LeBeau, Bill Walsh. But they forget Paul Brown."

His face turns bright red and he tosses his hands in the air in an exasperated windmill motion. "How the hell can you forget Paul Brown?" he says. "So I realized that it must be a generational thing, and I need to do something to correct that so that as history goes on, he doesn't gets lost. But I'm afraid that as things go on, it will only get worse unless we get our history down in one place. So I am going to try and create a research center where people who want to be football scholars can go and look up what they were doing in 1940, 1950, 1960, 1970, and on and on. I will collect all the playbooks from the past to make sure we don't lose that history. I was in Al [Davis'] office the other day, just looking at Sid Gillman's old playbooks. Sid had collected some of the books other guys had."

MADDEN SAYS HIS STYLE OF COACHING COULD HAVE WORKED TODAY, and I guess technically it could have. At least the on-field version. But off the field, I am not so sure. In Roger Goodell's modern NFL, the renegade Raiders could not have possibly flown under the radar with some of their "mischief." The Raiders organization would not have enough efficient "cleaners" to sweep up some of the mess because TMZ or Deadspin or some citizen journalist with a cell-phone camera would have surely recorded all their outrageous antics away from the field or paid someone to kiss and tell. With the drug testing that exists today, it would have been impossible to keep all of this cleaned up or kept under wraps with winks and nods and "boys will be boys" acceptance that worked so well in the late '60s and early '70s.

Goodell would have invited half of Madden's roster of rascals and reprobates—probably all of them at some point—into his office for one of those "Come to Jesus" meetings. These are the sort of meetings that usually end with the announcement of a substantial fine, a lengthy suspension, a salacious public trial, and a humbling, televised mea culpa a la Ben Roethlisberger or Michael Vick.

Or maybe under the circumstances of the modern NFL, Madden and his strong-willed team leaders would have simply adapted to the climate of the times. They would have made the necessary superficial attitude adjustments, and we'd be talking about Madden and his Bad

Boy Raiders in much the same way we talk about Rex Ryan and his colorful New York Jets today.

"I don't know," says Madden. "I love *Hard Knocks*, and I watch every one of those episodes, but they would have never been able to put a microphone on me. I wouldn't have allowed those TV cameras or microphones in."

Most likely, Madden would have found a way to make it all work, because he relied on the most preposterous secret to success. He treated his players like men. Actually, he assumed that they would act like grown men even when there was plenty of evidence to the contrary. But as long as they showed up at work, practiced hard, played hard, and acted intelligently on the field, they could play as hard as they wanted to off the field. It was an antithetical way of thinking, revolutionary really. Vince Lombardi, George Halas, and Paul Brown would never give up that authoritarian power.

During training camp in 1976, Madden was informed by an assistant coach that Ted Hendricks had missed bed check, which believe it or not actually carried an automatic $500 fine. When Madden called him into his office the next morning, he asked Hendricks what happened. The big linebacker said he had been out late with fullback Marv Hubbard, who had just been cut. After seven years with the Raiders, Hendricks felt that Hubbard needed a proper sendoff. So he gave him one last glorious night out on the town.

Madden thought a moment, then smiled.

"I would have done the same thing," he said. "No fine."

Even today, Madden rejects the idea of the iron-willed authoritarian. When Mike Singletary was making headlines in 2010 for his brusque manner of coaching the San Francisco 49ers, Madden did a rare thing: he publicly criticized a coach. "That's really not part of coaching," he told listeners on his KCBS radio show in the Bay Area. "I worry about that. I see youth football and I see high school football coaches yelling at players, and I cringe when I see it. I think people get the picture that's what coaching is, and believe me, that's not what coaching is."

HIS FRIENDS AND HIS CRITICS ALL HAVE A MILLION STORIES TO TELL, everyone carefully helping to piece together the string of fortunate events that tell the story of John Madden in full. Every last tale becomes a precious thread that weaves the complete life story together, describing in short snippets and voluminous detail precisely who John Madden is.

Yet now as we come to the end, John Robinson tells one more story that leaves us with a burning question.

He wonders who John Madden *could have been.*

"You know what's a real shame?" says Robinson. "It's a shame John never was able to conquer his fear of flying. When I was with the Raiders, I saw it happening to him, and he was a real basket case. He tried to keep quiet about it, but we all knew. And a few years ago we were talking about it, and he admitted how much he regretted not going to therapy and overcoming it. Instead of solving the issue, he avoided it by getting on a bus. And now at a time in his life when this man who is one of the greatest observers of the world around him ought to be able to jump on a private jet for all his travels, and could be traveling all over the world in retirement, [he] is bound to the earth and one continent. I've told John this a hundred times. Can you imagine how wonderful it would be if John could travel to Europe just so he could be able to sit in an English courtyard or some Italian piazza, just watching the world go by? I wish we could go to Italy and sit in front of the Vatican for a week, just looking at everything. Or London or Spain. Can you imagine how much different John's life would be if you could put the man on a plane and let him jet-set around the world?"

Travels with John: In Search of the World?

"But since he can't do that," says Robinson, "I already know what he ought to do next. He ought to go to CBS and tell them he wants Andy Rooney's job when he's done. Can you imagine what *60 Minutes* would be like if John had something to say every week? There's no telling what we'd learn."

ACKNOWLEDGMENTS

When I first discussed taking on the task of writing John Madden's story, no matter who I talked to and what sport they favored, I got the same repeated reaction: "I'd buy that." Everyone I knew in every sport I covered wanted to know more about one of the most fascinating and uniquely gifted men in the history of American sports. So with that motivation, I set out to trace the life's journey of the coach everyone loves. I could not have begun to do justice to the subject without the cooperation and graciousness of John Madden himself. Many thanks also go out to his agent, Sandy Montag of IMG, who facilitated my access to the coach, and Raiders public-relations director Mike Taylor, who helped me track down many of the old Raiders. In an undertaking of this sort, there are many people who provided insights and information who preferred to remain in the background. Your insights were greatly appreciated. Thanks to the smart folks at Triumph Books—Scott Rowan, Don Gulbrandsen, and Adam Motin—for their faith and patience. Of the countless interviews that were required to put together the oral history of John Madden, I am particularly thankful to the following people for their friendship, ideas, support, and conversations: Tom Jackson, Pat Summerall, Mark Kriegel, Jane Leavy, Howie Long, Peter King, Bernie Miklasz, Mike O'Hara, Ira

Miller, Frank Cooney, Betty Cuniberti, Jay Randolph, John Robinson, Shelley Smith, Bob Costas, Lesley Visser, George Atkinson, Fred Biletnikoff, Jerry Green, Steve Sabol, Bobby Beathard, Willie Brown, Sandy Grossman, Bob Raissman, Michael Ornstein, Ron Wolf, Michael Silver, Michael Wilbon, and Jarrett Bell. Thankfully, there was much great literature to cull from on that wonderful era in pro football and Madden's notorious Oakland Raiders during the height of their popularity. A huge debt of gratitude to my boss at the *St. Louis Post-Dispatch*, executive sports editor Reid Laymance, for his encouragement and support throughout this project.

SELECTED SOURCES

BOOKS

The Games That Changed The Game, Ron Jaworski, Random House, Inc., 2010

Slick, The Silver & Black Life of Al Davis, Mark Ribowsky, Macmillan Books, 1991

Badasses: The Legend of Snake, Foo, Dr Death and John Madden's Oakland Raiders, Peter Richmond, Harper Books, 2010

Raiders Forever, John Lombardo, McGraw-Hill, 2001

Namath, a Biography, Mark Kriegel, Viking Books, 2004

America's Game, The Epic Story of How Pro Football Captured a Nation, Michael MacCambridge, Random House, 2004

When Pride Still Mattered, A Life of Vince Lombardi, David Maraniss, Simon & Schuster, 1999

Hey Wait a Minute (I Wrote a Book), John Madden with Dave Anderson, Ballantine Books, 1984

One Size Doesn't Fit All (And Other Thoughts From the Road), John Madden with Dave Anderson, Villard Books, 1988

Snake, The Candid Autobiography of Football's Most Outrageous Renegade, Ken Stabler with Berry Stainback, Doubleday & Company, 1986

All Madden, Hey I'm Talking Pro Football!, John Madden with Dave Anderson, Harper Collins, 1996

The League: The Rise and Decline of the NFL, David Harris, Bantam Books, 1986

One Knee Equals Two Feet, John Madden with Dave Anderson, Villard Books, 1986

The Ones Who Hit the Hardest, the Steelers, the Cowboys, the 70s and the fight for America's Soul, Chad Millman and Shawn Coyne, Gotham Books, 2010

The Game Behind the Game, High Stakes, High Pressure in Television Sports, Terry O'Neil, Harper and Row, 1989

Looking Deep, Terry Bradshaw with Buddy Martin, Contemporary Books,1989

The Need to Win, Otis Taylor with Mark Stallard, Sports Publishing, LLC, 2003

Super Bowl Chronicles, Jerry Green, Masters Press, 1991

Iowa: The Middle Land, Dorothy Schwieder, Iowa State University Press, 1996

Mean Joe Greene and The Steelers Front Four, Larry Fox, Dodd, Mead & Company, 1975

Double Yoi! Myron Cope, Sports Publishing, LLC, 2002

NEWSPAPERS & PERIODICALS

"Busman's Holiday," Peter King, *Sports Illustrated*, November 26, 1990

"Hey Wait A Minute! I Want To Talk!" Sarah Pileggi, *Sports Illustrated*, September 1, 1983

"Double Dip For Daly City: Like boyhood pal John Madden, the Rams' John Robinson has made it big in the NFL," Kenny Moore, October 26, 1987

"The Healer: No Sting of Bitterness," Ron Borges, *The Boston Globe*, August 12, 2003

"THEN AND NOW: Raiders saw no quit in Blanda," Jim McConnell, *San Gabriel Valley Tribune*, October 4, 2010

"This Defense Never Rested," Ron Reid, *Sports Illustrated*, January 6, 1975.

"Where Am I? It Has To Be A Bad Dream," Darryl Stingley and Mark Mulvoy, *Sports Illustrated*, August 29, 1983

"Behind The Scenes of the Stingley Game," Pat Toomay, ESPN.com, April 5, 2007

"A Madden in Full," Pat Toomay, ESPN.com, http://sports.espn.go.com/espn/page2/story?page=toomay/021114

"Understanding Madden, Part I," Pat Toomay, ESPN.com, http://espn.go.com/page2/s/toomay/021105.html

"Darryl Stingley, paralyzed by Tatum hit, dies at 55," Associated Press, April 5, 2007

"Spend a Day With the Team Crafting 'Madden NFL'," Mike Snider, *USA Today*, December 10, 2010

"Madden, Tollner recall deadly plane crash of '60," Associated Press, December 24, 2008

Oakland Tribune

INTERNET AND OTHER SOURCES

Ancestry.com

Huskerpedia.com, Interview with Monte Johnson, 2004

University of Northern Iowa, "Explorations in Iowa History Project." Malcolm Price Laboratory School, University of Northern Iowa, 2003 Cedar Falls, IA.

National Park Service, Hardin County history.

U.S. Census reports

Mary R. Howes, Iowa Department of Natural Resources, Iowa Geological Survey, Intergovernmental Benchmarking Workshop on Underground Mine Mapping, Louisville, Kentucky, October 15-16, 2003.

Lees, James H. and Beyer, S. W. (1908) "History of Coal Mining In Iowa & Coal Statistics," Iowa Geological Survey Annual Report: Vol. 19: p. 580-581.

John Madden's enshrinement speech transcript, Pro Football Hall of Fame, http://www.profootballhof.com/hof/release.aspx?release_id=2178

VIDEOS
This is the NFL, Show 14. NFL Films 1989

America's Game: The 1976 Oakland Raiders. NFL Films 2010

Al Davis, Legend-Maverick: The Courage of His Convictions. NFL Films 1999

John Madden: Road to Canton. NFL Films 2006

The Super Bowl Champions: Pittsburgh Steelers Collection. NFL Films 2007

ABOUT THE AUTHOR

Bryan Burwell is an award-winning sports columnist with the *St. Louis Post-Dispatch*. The author of two books, including *At The Buzzer! The Greatest Moments in NBA History*, Burwell's work has also appeared in several sports anthologies, *USA Today*, the *New York Daily News*, *The Sporting News*, and *Sports Illustrated*. On television, Burwell is a regular contributor to ESPN's *The Sports Reporters* and spent 14 years with HBO Sports. In 2007, he was the host and writer of a nationally syndicated TV documentary on the Negro baseball leagues called *The Color of Change*, which won two 2008 Telly Awards.